CUT AND FOLD TECHNIQUES FOR PROMOTIONAL MATERIALS

Paul Jackson

Laurence King Publishing

Contents

Before watching TV became the main leisure activity of most Western households in the 1950s and '60s, many books were published that contained a comprehensive variety of activities for the enterprising family to do in the home; anything from building your own billiards table or shortwave radio receiver, to learning esoteric card games or staging an amateur dramatics production. If the illustrations were to be believed, all you needed to succeed were a neatly knotted tie or a pearl necklace and a cheery smile.

These books often contained many wonderful puzzles, models, games and tricks, all made by folding and cutting paper. Some of these paper ideas have survived into modern times, but many – sadly – have been forgotten.

This book brings together classics from that bygone time, with little-known cut-and-fold classics from the worlds of puzzling, magic, topology, origami and graphic design, all chosen for their special ability to amaze and amuse. A few designs were adapted or created especially for the book.

The addition of texts, photographs and illustrations transforms these superb paper constructions into ideal promotional giveaways. They provide a great way to describe a new product or service, market yourself, promote a sale or simply say 'Happy New Year' to present and future clients and customers. Some constructions in the book need no additional surface graphics to carry your message, but can be played with or have some useful function. Whatever your needs, there is certain to be something in this book that you can use to promote you or yours.

Everything can be mass-produced using conventional die-cutting and printing technologies, or can be made in small numbers in the studio or at home, using graphic design software and a printer. Many of them will fold flat for easy mailing and transform into three-dimensions when opened.

Today we are bombarded with visual information and it can be difficult to make our message stand out. By using these smart, witty and above all memorable cut-and-fold paper constructions, you give yourself a better chance to be heard and for your message to be remembered.

Paul Jackson

01:

BEFORE YOU START

1.1 How to Use the Book

Almost everything in the book is interactive. That is: almost everything will open, close, collapse, turn inside out, change shape or need assembling. These interactions and movements are very difficult to show on the printed page, so if something takes your fancy, but you are uncertain from the drawings and photos how it will move or perform, you are strongly recommended to make it and then to play with it. Don't dismiss something too hastily because you didn't understand every subtlety and nuance from the static, two-dimensional instructions on the page. Trust that the designs have been chosen for their elegance and ingenuity (they have, they have!) and enjoy discovering them as much when they are in your hands, as when they were on the page. Many of the designs are a total delight – mini masterpieces of paper engineering – but they need to be *made* to be enjoyed.

Due to lack of space, some of the more esoteric manipulations buried deep within some of the designs are not explained. So, when you have made something, experiment with it by folding it this way and that, by doing the opposite (however you interpret that) to what you are instructed, add extra material here and there and generally play with it as though you have never seen it before and don't know what it is supposed to do. Your experiments will be well rewarded.

1.2 How to Cut and Fold

1.2.1 Cutting

If you are cutting card by hand, it is important to use a quality craft knife or, better still, a scalpel. Avoid using inexpensive 'snap-off' craft knives, as they can be unstable and dangerous. The stronger, chunkier, 'snap-off' knives are more stable and much safer; however, for the same price you can buy a scalpel with a slim metal handle and a packet of replaceable blades. Scalpels are generally more manoeuvrable through the card than craft knives and are more helpful in creating an accurately cut line. Whichever knife you use, it is imperative to change the blade regularly.

A metal ruler or straight edge will ensure a strong, straight cut, though transparent plastic rulers are acceptable and have the added advantage that you can see the drawing beneath the ruler. Use a handy 15cm ruler to cut short lines. Generally, when cutting, place the ruler on the drawing, so that if your blade slips away it will cut harmlessly into the waste card around the outside of the drawing.

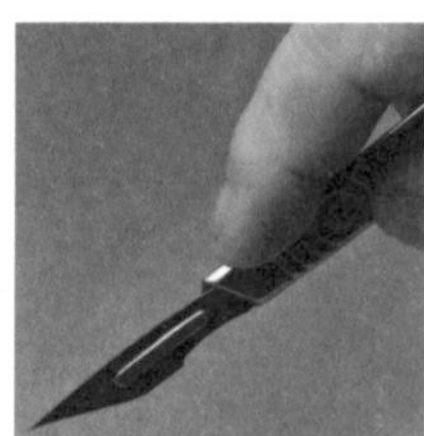

A scalpel is shown here held in the standard position for cutting. For safety reasons, be sure to always keep your non-cutting hand above your cutting hand.

1.2.2. Folding

While cutting paper is relatively straightforward, folding is less so. Whatever method you use, the crucial element is never to cut through the card along the fold line but, by using pressure, to compress the fold line. This is done using a tool. Whether the tool is purpose-made or improvised is a matter of personal choice and habit.

Bookbinders use a range of specialist creasing tools called bone folders. They compress the card very well, though the fold line is usually 1–2mm or so away from the edge of the ruler, so if your tolerances are small, a bone folder may be considered inaccurate.

A good improvised tool is a dry ball-point pen. The ball makes an excellent crease line, though like the bone folder, it may be a little distance away from the edge of the ruler. I have also seen people use a scissor point, a food knife, a tool usually used for smoothing down wet clay, a fingernail (!) and a nail file.

But my own preference is a dull scalpel blade (or a dull craft knife blade). The trick is to turn the blade upside down (see left). It compresses the card along a reliably consistent line, immediately adjacent to the edge of the ruler.

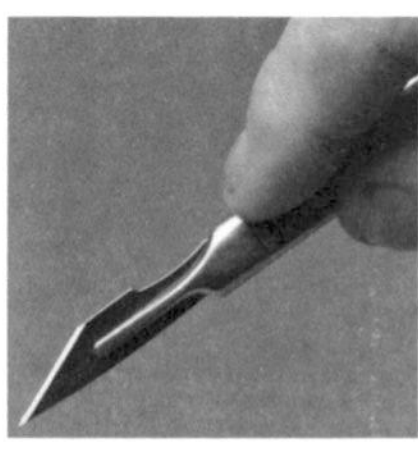

A scalpel or craft knife makes an excellent tool with which to create a fold. Held upside down against the edge of a ruler, it does not cut the card along the length of the fold line, but compresses it.

1.3 Equipment

Most of the designs in the book are made from simple polygons such as squares, rectangles and triangles, and from simple angles such as 90 degrees, 45 degrees and 60 degrees. Even with little prior practice, these polygons and angles can be constructed easily using basic geometry equipment. Making the designs this way may seem old fashioned, but it is often quicker than designing by software and avoids the need for a printer to print out the result.

Here is a list of the basic equipment you will need:

- Hard pencil (2H is good)
- Good eraser (not the one on the end of a pencil)
- Good pencil sharpener if your pencil is not mechanical
- 15cm plastic ruler
- 30cm metal or plastic ruler
- Large 360-degree protractor
- Quality craft knife or scalpel, with replacement blades
- Pair of sharp scissors
- Pair of compasses
- 45-degree set square
- Invisible tape and/or masking tape
- Self-healing cutting mat, as large as possible

The above equipment – with one exception – can be purchased at little cost. As with most things, it pays to buy items of quality, though it is more important to use equipment which is inexpensive but clean, rather than equipment that is expensive but dirty. Age-old grime on a ruler or protractor will quickly transfer to your paper or card and make everything you create look grubby and trivial. Work cleanly and you will work better.

The one relatively expensive item is a self-healing cutting mat. It is pure vandalism to cut through paper or card on a tabletop and the alternatives of wood or thick card quickly become rutted and problematic. A specialist cutting mat will ensure that every cut line runs straight and smooth. Buy the biggest you can afford. If it is looked after carefully, it will remain in good condition for a decade or more. A nice bonus with a cutting mat is that it will have a grid of centimetres and/or inches printed on it, meaning that for some constructions you will rarely, if ever, need to use a ruler.

1.4 Choosing Paper and Card

Many of the designs in the book specify an approximate weight of paper or card to use. This advice should be followed, though you may find that other weights work just as well or better, particularly if you are making something unusually small or unusually large.

The interactivity of many the designs means that they must be held in the hand. For this reason, you might consider using a textured paper or card, rather than one that is more conventionally smooth ('coated'). Textured surfaces are very tactile, increasing the sensuality and thus also the enjoyment of handling a design. It follows that the more tactile the material is, the less it needs to be hidden behind busy surface graphics.

For some of the designs, consider using handmade paper, even handmade paper with a very colourful, decorative surface. The black and white aesthetic of the book may suggest that you should use the same aesthetic, but there is no reason why you shouldn't use handmade papers, coloured papers, textured papers, mirrored card, corrugated card, recycled paper, junk mail and even thin plastic or stiff fabric, providing – of course – that your choice of materials meets the needs of the design brief.

If you are printing a surface design through a computer printer or copying machine, your choice of papers and cards will be more limited than if they are handmade. If you are die-cutting a design (see 'How to Use What You Make', page 124), the choice may be even more limited, as dictated by the technical constraints of the manufacturing process. Nevertheless, although the weight parameters may be limited, the choice of the paper or card's texture and colour should still be wide. A three-way discussion with the die-cutting and offset printing companies will help you make a correct and interesting choice.

The best way to make an exciting choice of material is to contact a local paper merchant and ask to be sent a set of sample books. If you are a private individual, try to give them the delivery address of a company, so that they are motivated to release their samples for free – they'll think it's a better opportunity for new business than delivering to a private address.

1.5 Symbols

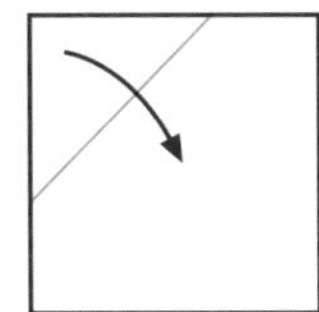
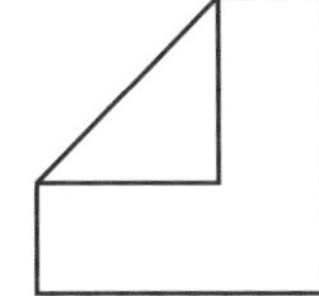

Valley fold

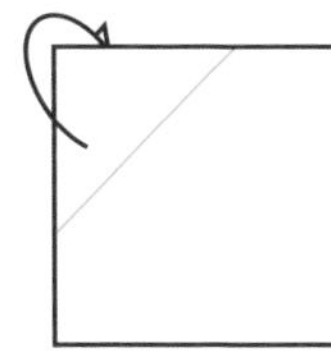
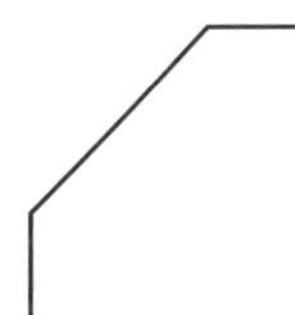

Mountain fold

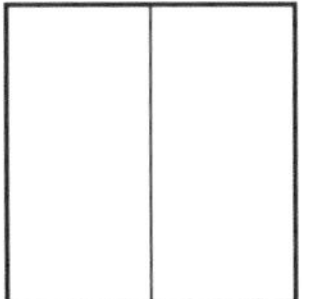

Existing crease

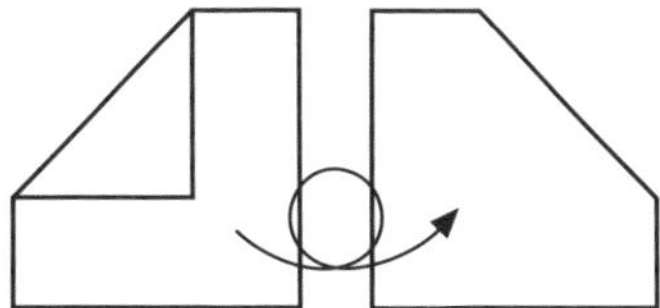

Turn over

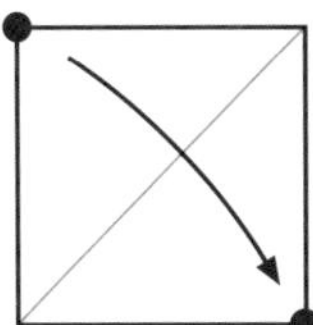

Fold dot to dot

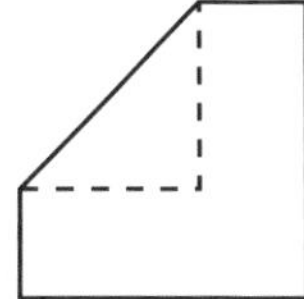

X-ray view

Glue

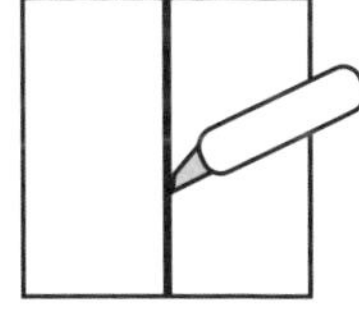

Cut

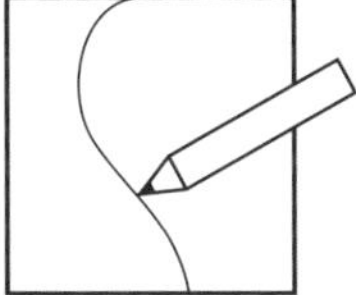

Draw

02:

FLEXAGONS

Introduction

The word 'flexagon' is a portmanteau word, made by combining 'flexible' and 'gon' ('gon' meaning a flat geometric figure, as in 'penta*gon*' or 'hexa*gon*'). Hence, flexagons are two- or three-dimensional configurations of cut and folded paper that can be flexed. Typically, a flexagon will have a surface which, after flexing, will be hidden inside the layers of the paper to reveal a new surface that in turn can be flexed out of view, to be replaced by the original surface or by a new one ... and so on. Alternatively, instead of flexing faces in and out of view, a flexagon can also realign different sections of a single face in relation to each other, thus scrambling and reassembling an image.

If that sounds a little difficult to visualize, it's testimony to how enigmatic flexagons are. They almost seem to be escapees from a multi-dimensional universe, difficult to describe, amazing to see in action and addictive to play with.

The appearance and disappearance of a succession of surfaces makes a flexagon ideal for carrying texts and images that work best when viewed in sequence. Intriguingly, many flexagons will show the same surface in two or more configurations, enabling texts and images to form, scramble and then form again.

The book brings together some of the very best two-and three-dimensional flexagons. Most are easy to construct, though you will need to make them carefully. Only by making them and then playing with them will you come to understand their many nuances and how you can best use them.

If flexagons are new to you ... prepare to be mystified and amazed.

2.1 Tri-hexaflexagon

This is the classic, original flexagon, created in 1939 by Arthur Stone, a British-born graduate student of mathematics at Harvard University. Although simple to construct, the permutations of its flexing patterns are fascinating and complex. If you are new to flexagons, start here.

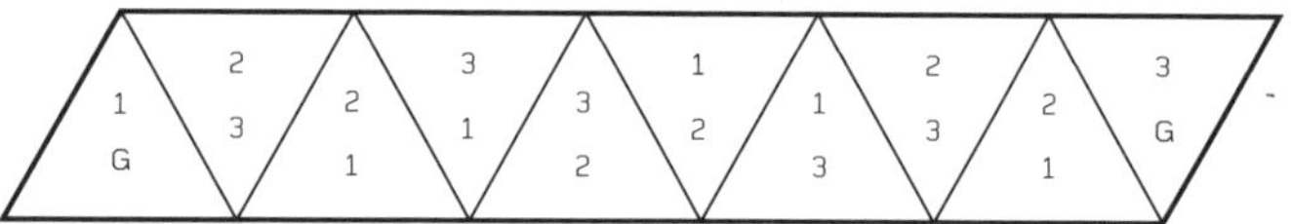

2.1 _ 1
Make a paper strip of ten equilateral triangles (all the angles are 60 degrees). The side length of each triangle should be 4–5cm. Each triangle shows two numbers. Write the top number on the front of the triangle in which it is written and the bottom number on the reverse side of the same triangle. 'G' means 'Glue'.

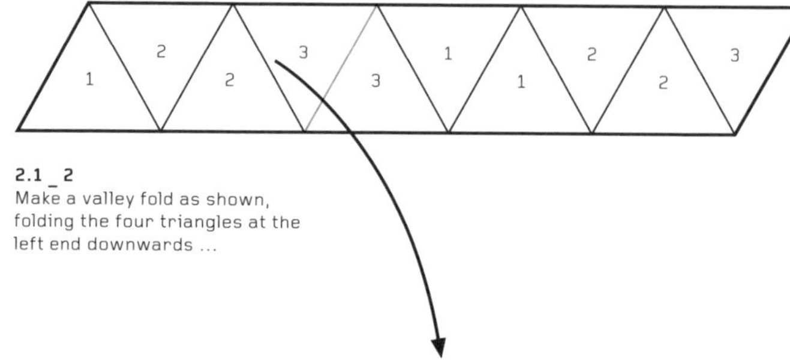

2.1 _ 2
Make a valley fold as shown, folding the four triangles at the left end downwards ...

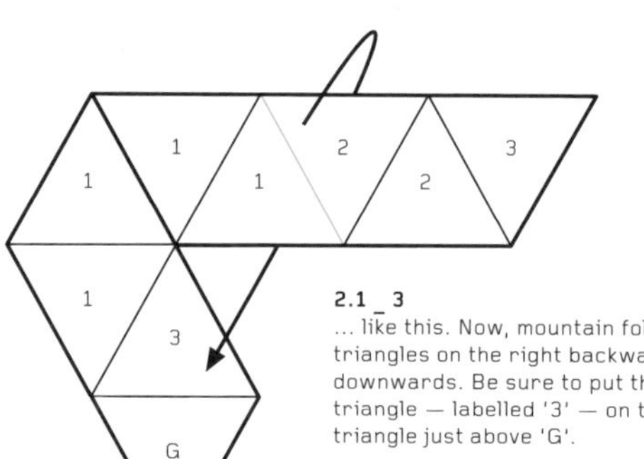

2.1 _ 3
... like this. Now, mountain fold the three triangles on the right backwards and downwards. Be sure to put the end triangle — labelled '3' — on top of the '3' triangle just above 'G'.

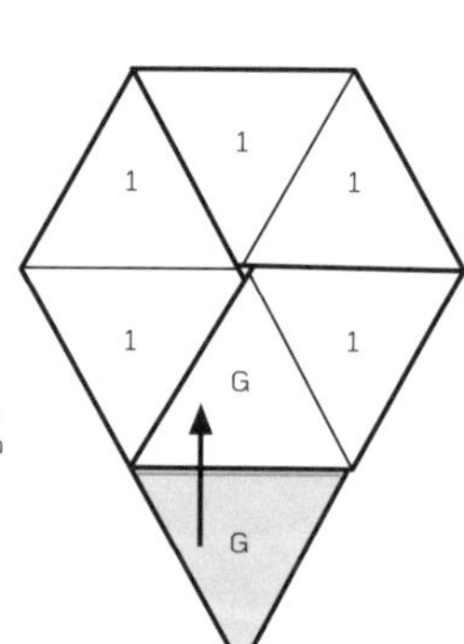

2.1 _ 4
Note how no '3' triangles are visible and the paper strip is loosely locked together. Glue the lower 'G' triangle and fold it onto the upper 'G', sticking them together. This will lock the paper into an endless hexagonal strip (the strip is called a Möbius strip).

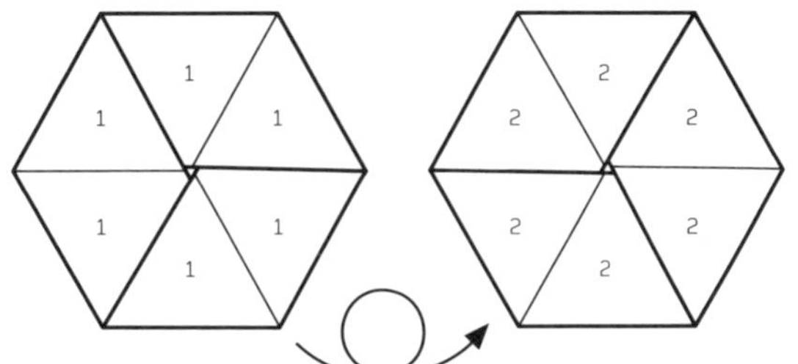

2.1 _ 5
The front face has six number 1s. The back face has six number 2s. If you have another configuration of numbers, check that you have numbered and folded the strip correctly.

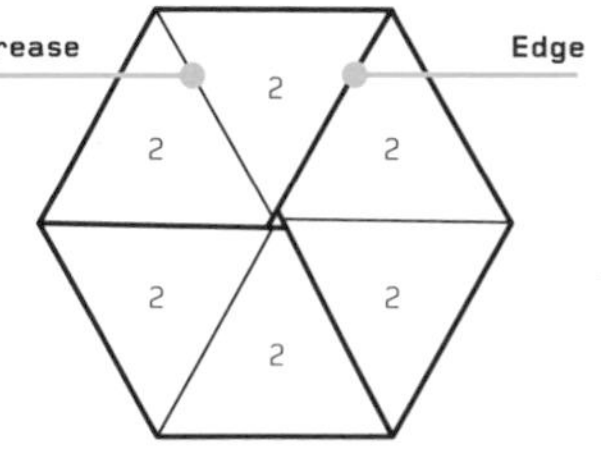

2.1 _ 6
On the 2s side, notice how the six lines that radiate from the centre like the spokes of a bicycle wheel are alternately an edge, then a crease, then an edge, then a crease, then an edge, then a crease, then an edge, then finally a crease. Every other edge is a crease and every other edge is a fold.

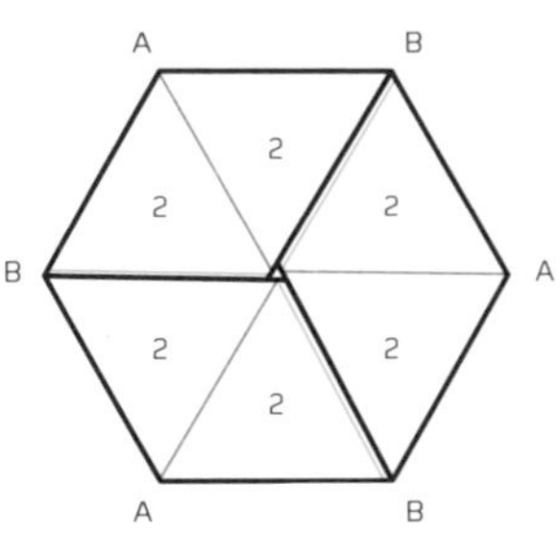

2.1 _ 7
Along every crease (A), make a valley fold. Along every edge (B), make a mountain fold. The hexagon will become three dimensional ...

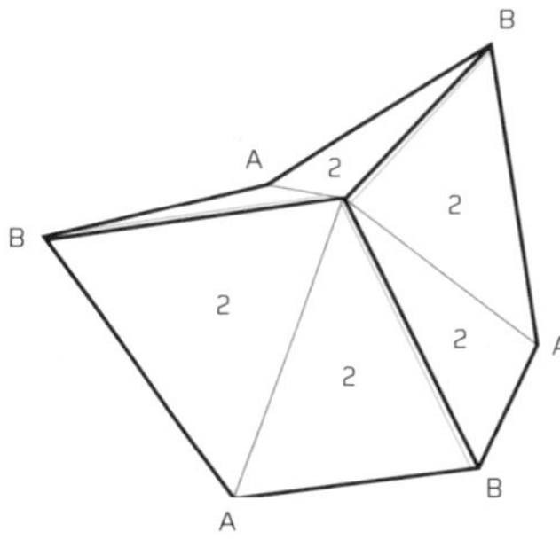

2.1 _ 8
...like this. Note how the A corners are dipping down and the B corners are rising up.

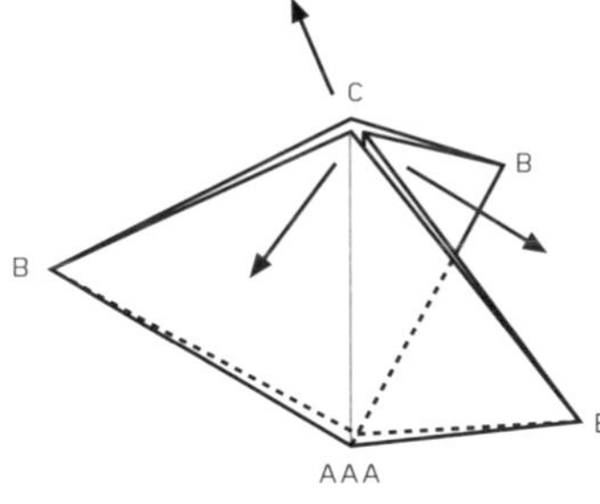

2.1 _ 9
Eventually, the three A corners will meet at the bottom and the three B corners will be at the ends of three flat fins. A new corner (C) has been created at the top. Open out the three parts of corner C ...

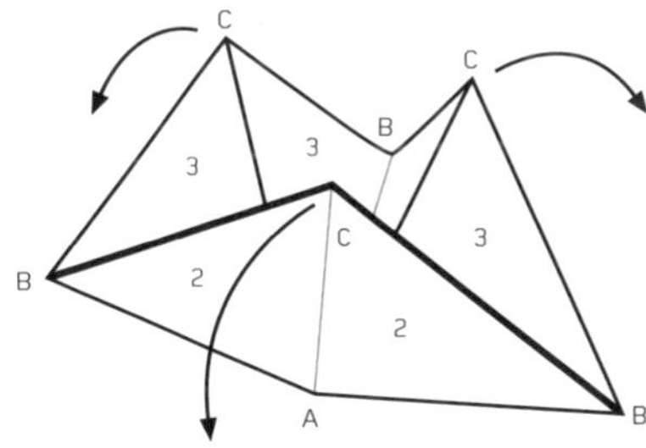

2.1 _ 10
... like this. C will split into three parts. Flatten the hexagon further by separating the C corners more and more.

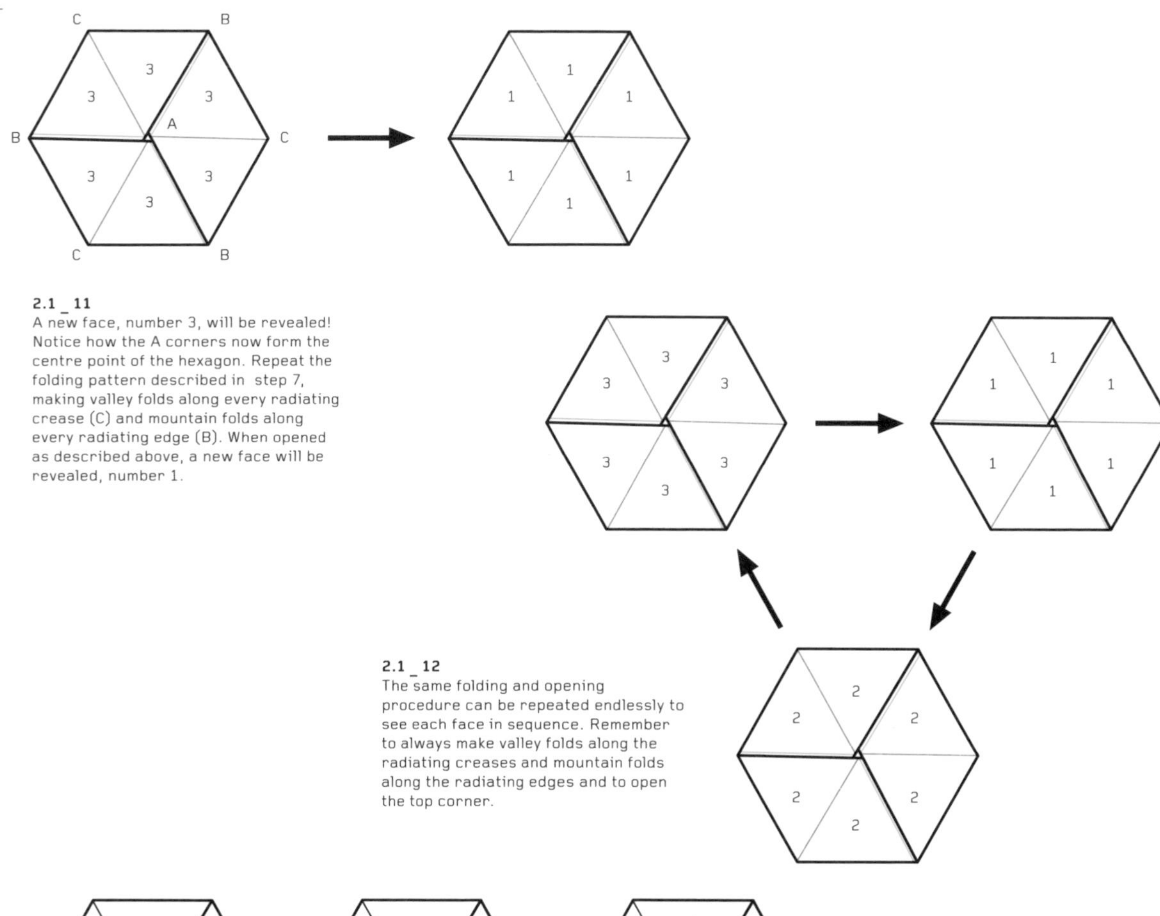

2.1 _ 11
A new face, number 3, will be revealed! Notice how the A corners now form the centre point of the hexagon. Repeat the folding pattern described in step 7, making valley folds along every radiating crease (C) and mountain folds along every radiating edge (B). When opened as described above, a new face will be revealed, number 1.

2.1 _ 12
The same folding and opening procedure can be repeated endlessly to see each face in sequence. Remember to always make valley folds along the radiating creases and mountain folds along the radiating edges and to open the top corner.

2.1 _ 13
Instead of numbering each face, make patterns on each of them. You could also write texts or a three-part cartoon or message. The choice is yours.

2.1 _ 14
The three centre images show the three patterned faces made in the previous step. If any of them is turned over, another patterned face will be revealed – one of the three shown in the ring of outer images. These three new patterns can also be flexed in an endless cycle; however, the three new patterns will be scrambled versions of the original patterns. In this way, the three faces make a total of six patterns! Take a few moments to play with your flexagon to understand what is happening, remembering to turn it over from time to time.

The possibilities for creating and scrambling images and text are huge. There are many possibilities for sequential narratives or puzzles, simple or complex, as you choose.

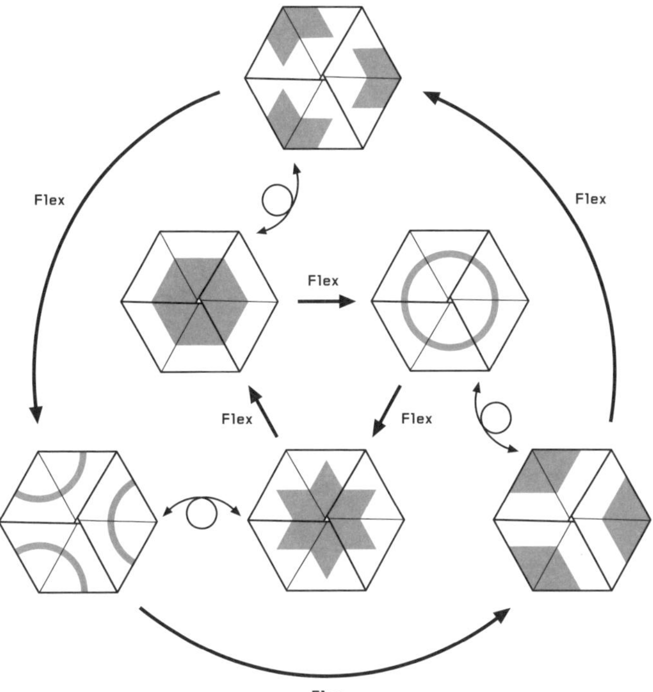

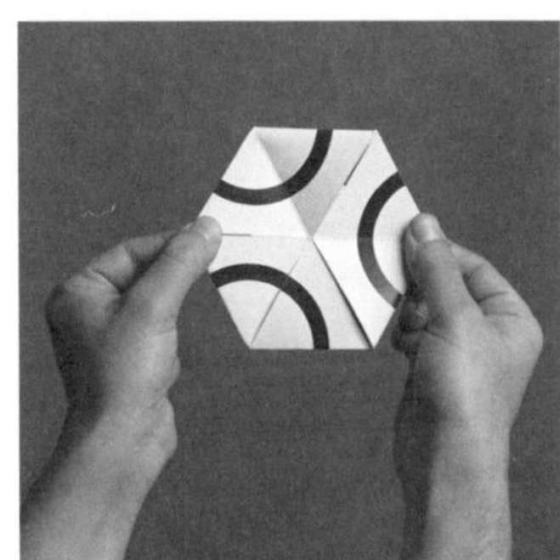

2.2 Square Flexagon

This three-faced flexagon is similar to the first one, but it is simpler to make and has fewer combinations of surface patterns. Essentially, it is a double hinge, which works exactly like the double hinge on a door that can swing both inwards and outwards (like the swing door in a restaurant between the kitchen and dining areas).

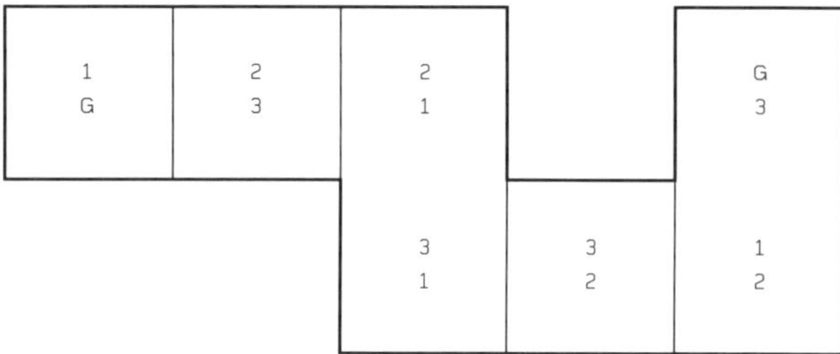

2.2 _ 1
Use paper to construct the configuration shown here, made of seven squares. The side length of each square should be about 4–5cm. Each square shows two numbers. Write the top number on the front of the square in which it is written and the bottom number on the reverse side. 'G' means 'Glue'.

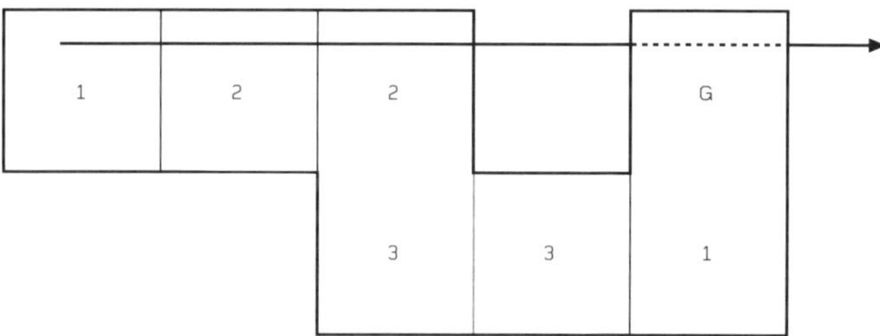

2.2 _ 2
Valley fold as shown, folding the four squares on the left across to the right. However, be careful to pass the squares behind the 'G' square at the top right ...

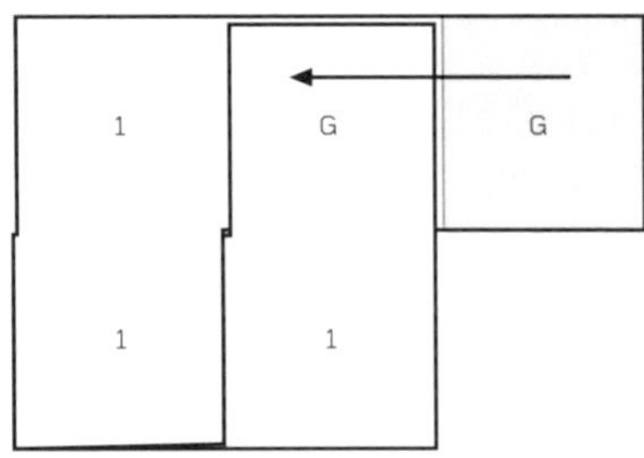

2.2 _ 3
... like this. Put glue onto the 'G' square on the right and fold it onto the 'G' square on the left, gluing them together. This closes the strip and makes an endless loop of squares.

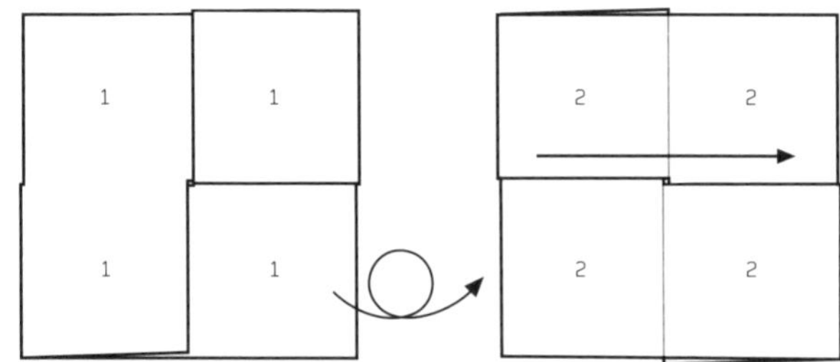

2.2 _ 4
On one side, four 1s will be visible. On the other side, there are four 2s. Fold the two 2s on the left across to the right.

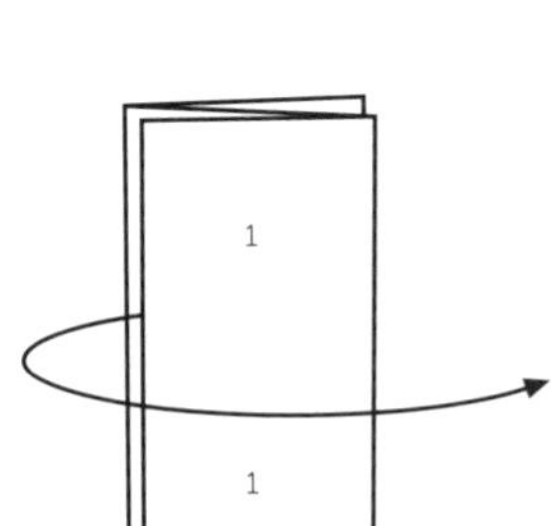

2.2 _ 5
The fold made in the previous steps is down the left-hand edge; however, the layers there will separate, so that the two 1s will fold across to the right ...

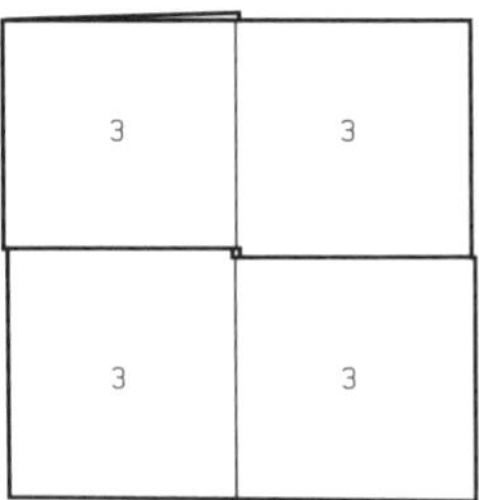

2.2 _ 6
... like this, to reveal four 3s! The face with 2s has vanished.

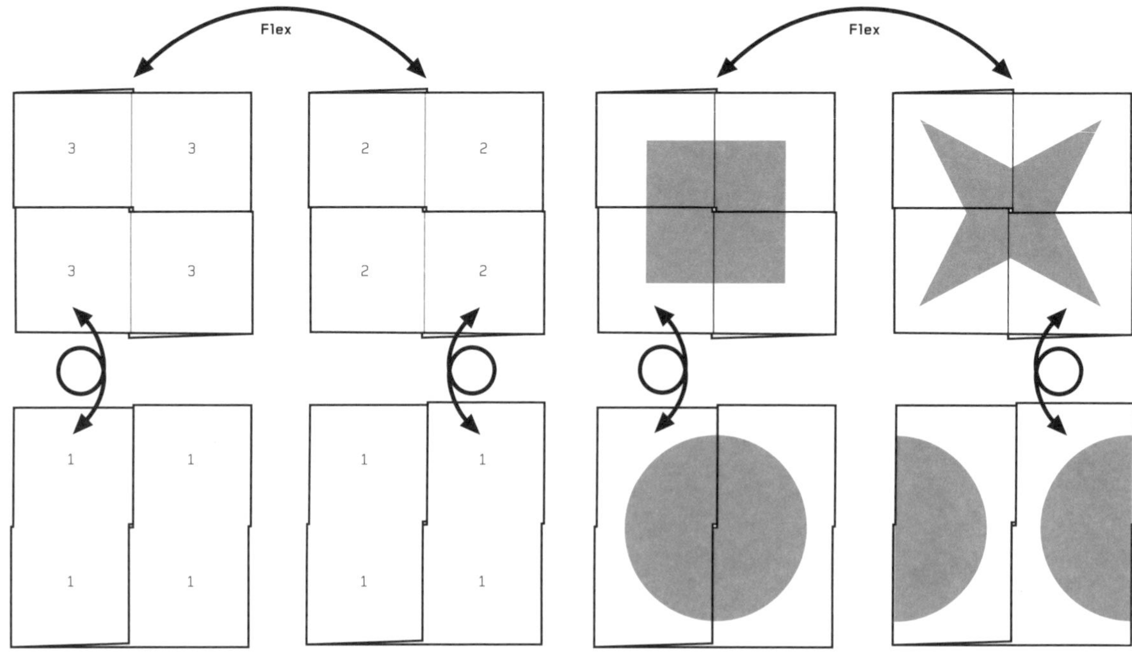

2.2 _ 7
By flexing in the way described above, it is possible to flex between the 3 and 2 faces. If the flexagon is turned over, the 1 face is always in view, whichever number (3 or 2) is on the other side.

2.2 _ 8
If surface graphics are substituted for the numbers 3 and 2, then a square will always be a square and a star will always be a star. However, the circle (on the side with the 1s) will either be an intact circle or two disconnected semicircles, depending on what image is on the other side of the flexagon at the time.

2.3 Windmill Base Manipulations

This is one of the few flexagons that is an example of pure origami. It is simply a folded square. Origami aficionados will immediately recognize it not as a model, but as the traditional Windmill Base, one of several bases traditionally used as the starting point for many models.

2.3 _ 1
Begin with a square of paper, 10–15cm on each side. Fold and unfold both diagonals.

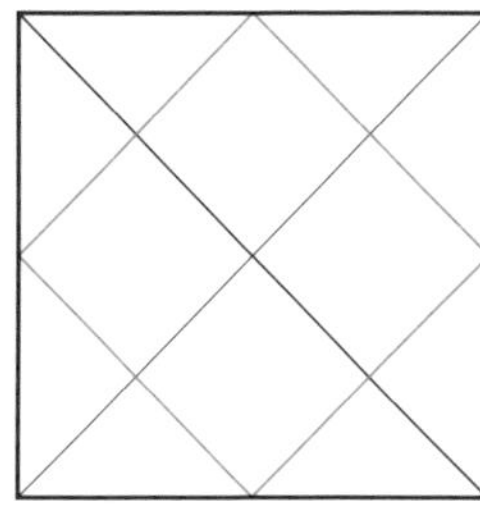

2.3 _ 2
Fold each corner to the centre point. Unfold.

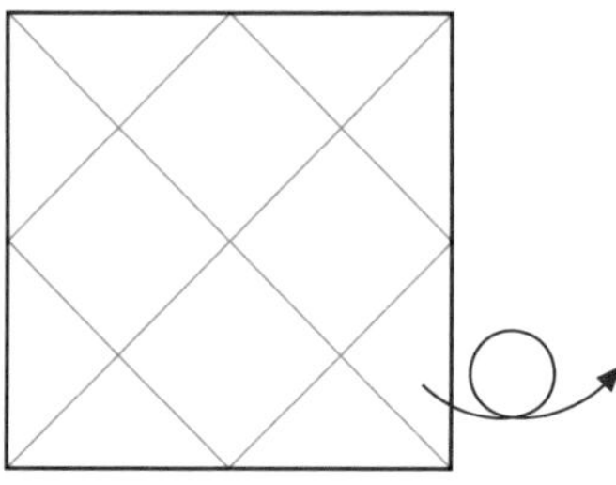

2.3 _ 3
Turn the paper over.

2.3 _ 4
Seen from this side, the existing folds are all mountains.

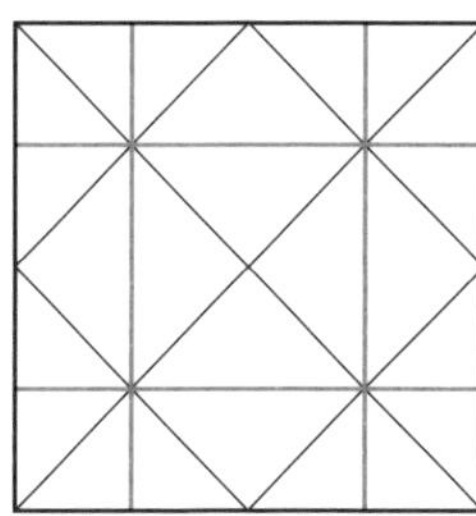

2.3 _ 5
Fold each edge to the centre point. Unfold each one before folding the next.

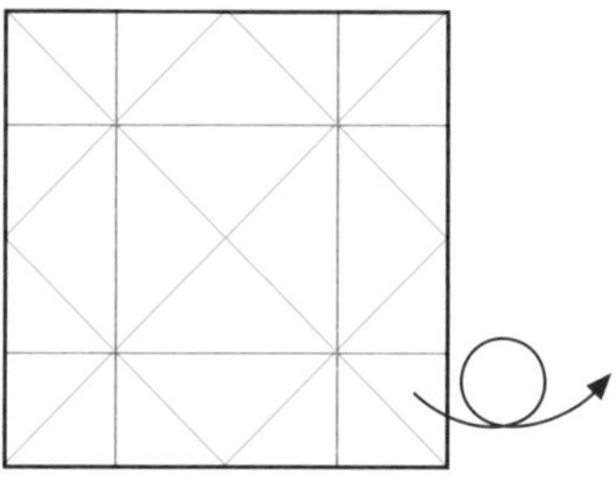

2.3 _ 6
This is the completed crease pattern. Turn over again.

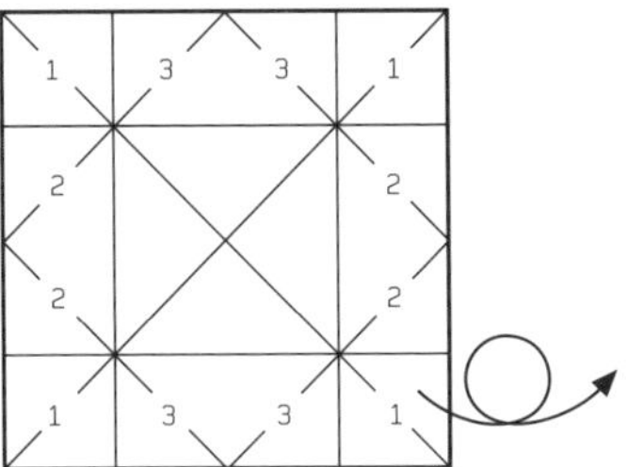

2.3 _ 7
Write numbers where shown.
Turn over again.

2.3 _ 8
Check the pattern of mountains and valleys.

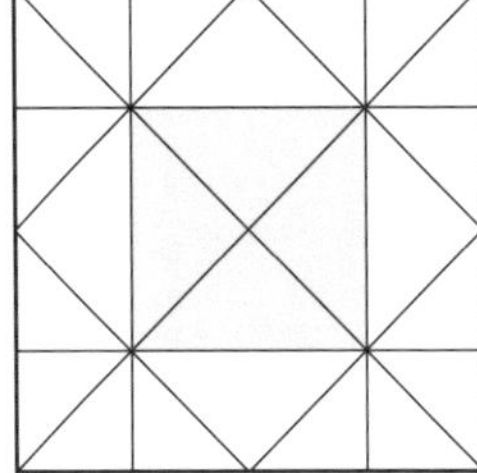

2.3 _ 9
Glue the centre square.

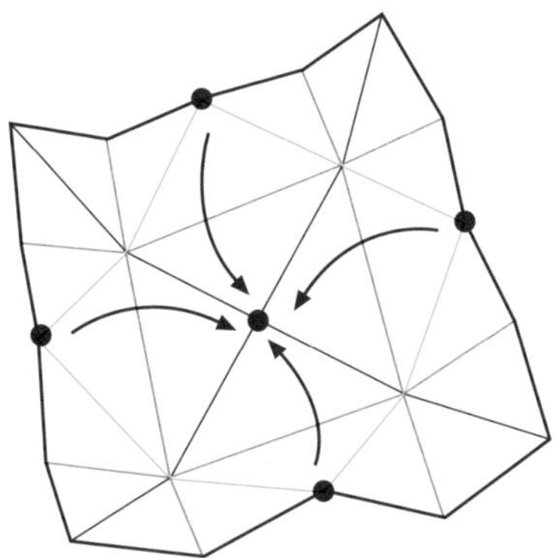

2.3 _ 10
Begin to collapse the creases, folding the four outer dots towards the central dot ...

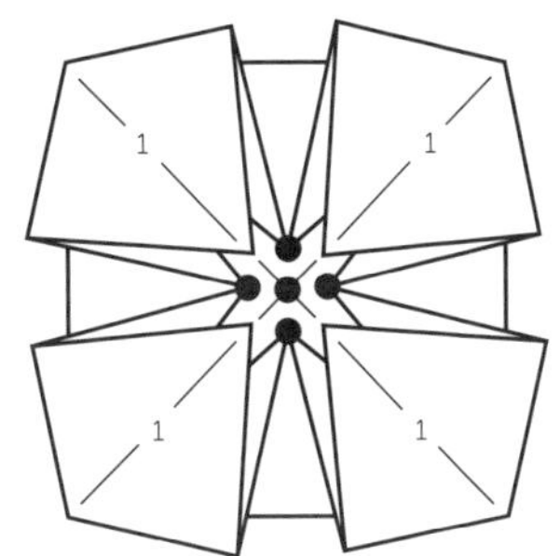

2.3 _ 11
... like this. Eventually, all five dots will merge together and the paper will be glued flat, though with loose triangles on the top side.

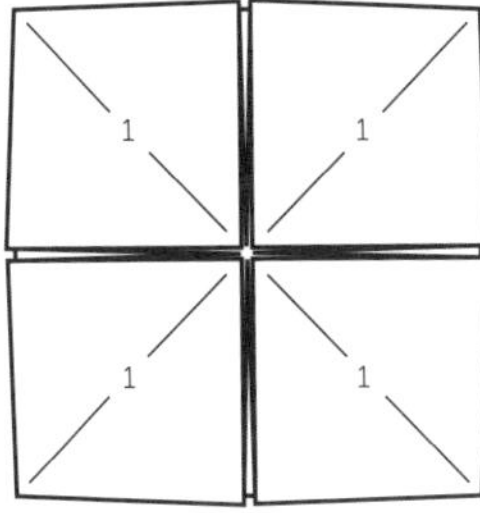

2.3 _ 12
This is the completed flexagon, ready to be flexed. Check that the eight triangles are loose enough to fold to and fro.

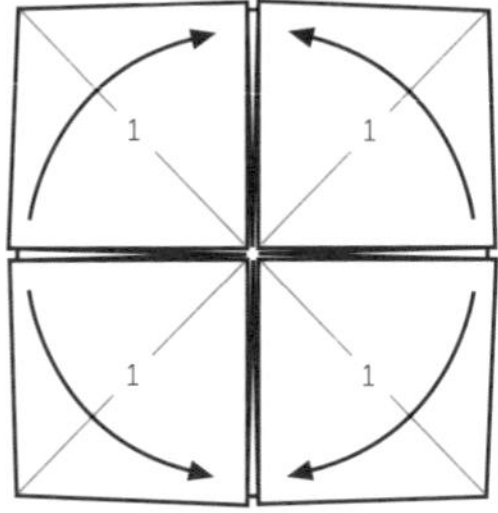

2.3 _ 13
Fold the loose corners at the left and right edges up to the top or down to the bottom of the paper. This will hide all the 1s …

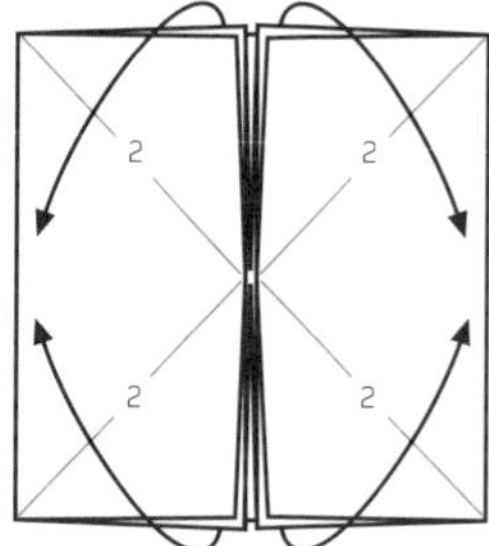

2.3 _ 14
… to reveal 2s. Now, move all the loose layers at the top and bottom edges to the left or right edges. This will hide all the 2s …

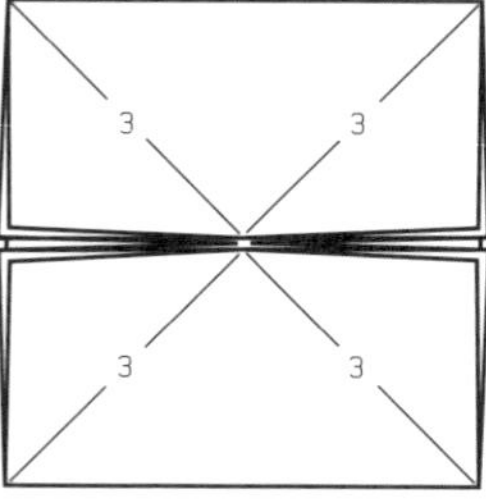

2.3 _ 15
… and reveal the 3s. It will be apparent that there are 3 different faces (1, 2 and 3); however, because each face is divided into four squares, it becomes possible to reveal not just three faces, but 81 different combinations of the four squares on the three faces. These 81 combinations mean that all manner of intricate puzzles, messages, illustrations and secret combinations can be created. Just let your imagination run riot!

2.4 Shapeshifter

Unlike the previous flexagons in this chapter, this example not only reveals new faces, it also changes its shape. It is perhaps the simplest example of a family of flexagons in which the faces rotate from front to back in opposing pairs around a central point, in an endless cycle.

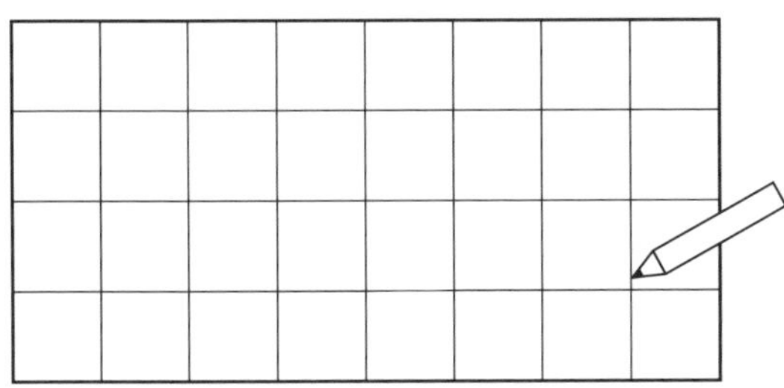

2.4 _ 1
Draw an 8 x 4 grid of squares. The size of the squares and the weight of the paper are both very open.

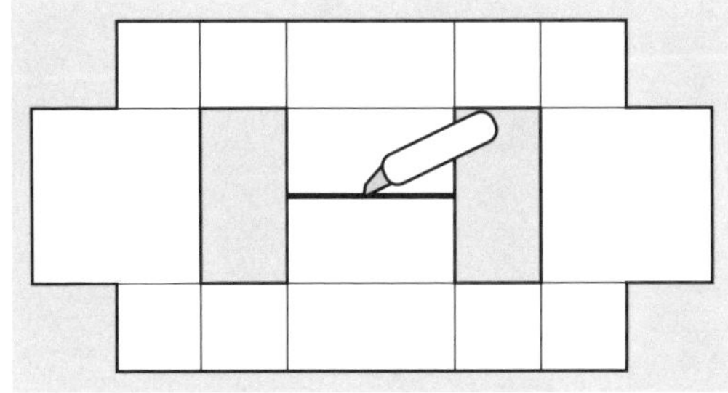

2.4 _ 2
Cut off the corner squares and remove two groups of two squares in the interior. Connect the rectangular holes with a straight cut.

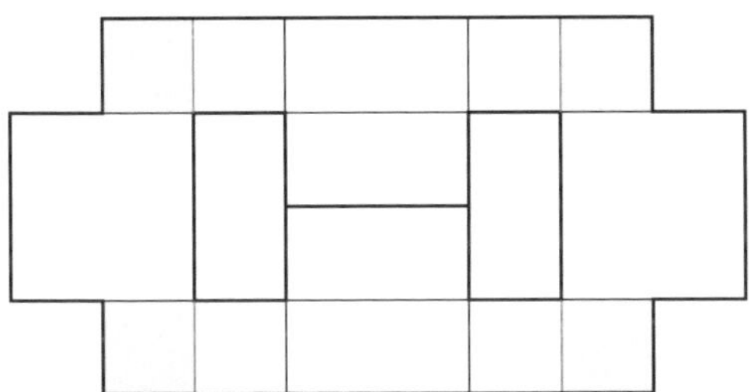

2.4 _ 3
Apply glue to the four corner squares. In preparation for the flexing which begins in step 6, crease and unfold along the lines shown – the other lines can be erased and need not be folded.

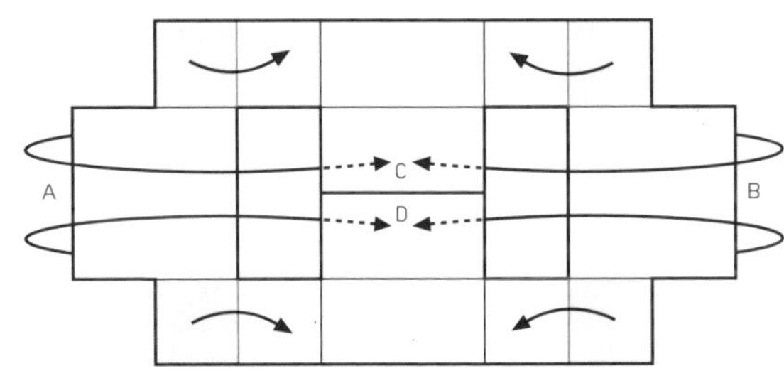

2.4 _ 4
Fold A then B to the middle, as shown, but tucking them behind C and D. The glued corners will hold everything in place.

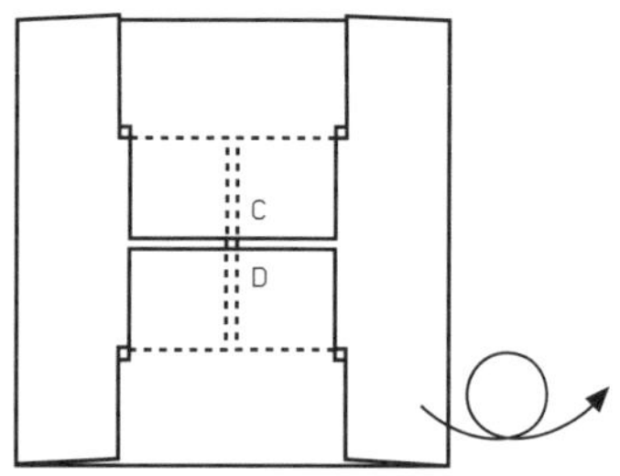

2.4 _ 5
This is the completed flexagon. Note how C and D are still visible. Turn it over.

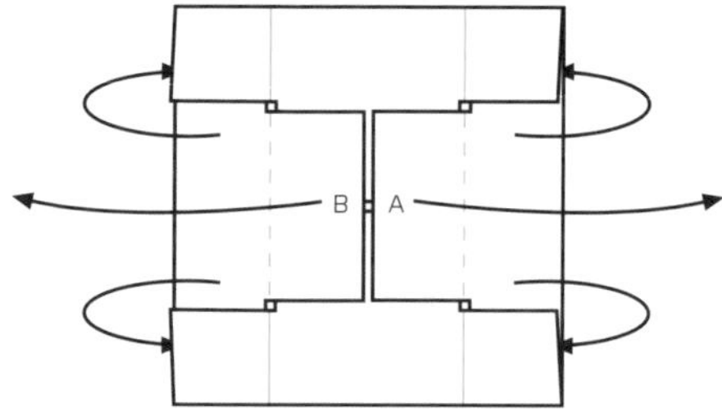

2.4 _ 6
The flexagon can now be taken through its flexing sequence. First, make two mountain folds as shown, rotating A and B to the outside ...

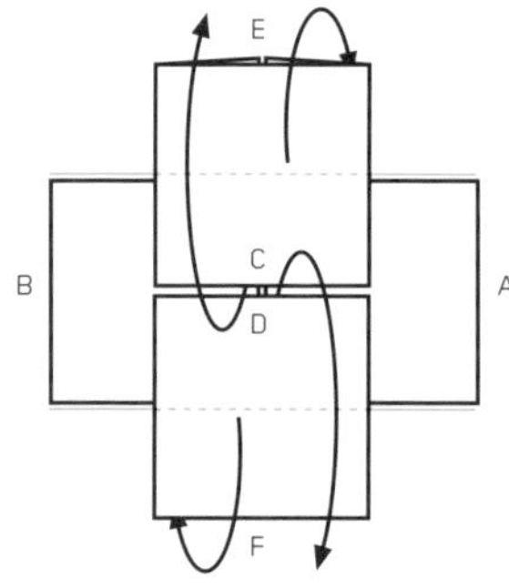

2.4 _ 7
... like this. Rotate E and F behind, allowing C and D to flip to the top and bottom edges ...

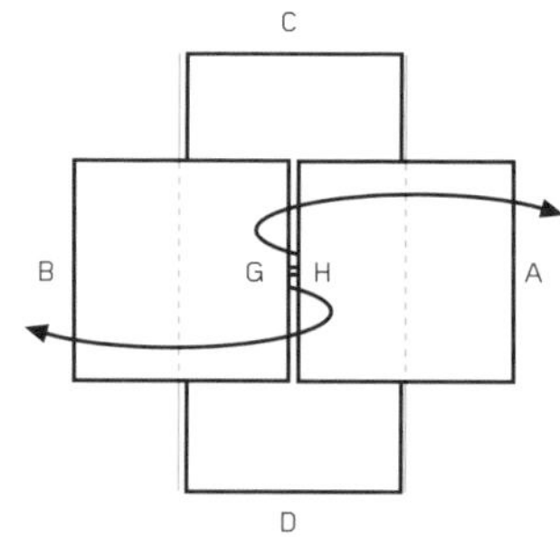

2.4 _ 8
... like this. Similarly, rotate B and A behind, allowing G and H to flip to the left and right edges ...

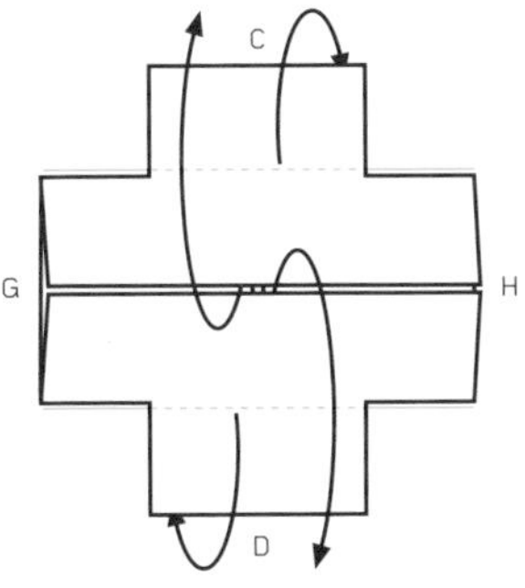

2.4 _ 9
...like this. Finally, rotate C and D behind, returning the flexagon to it starting shape ...

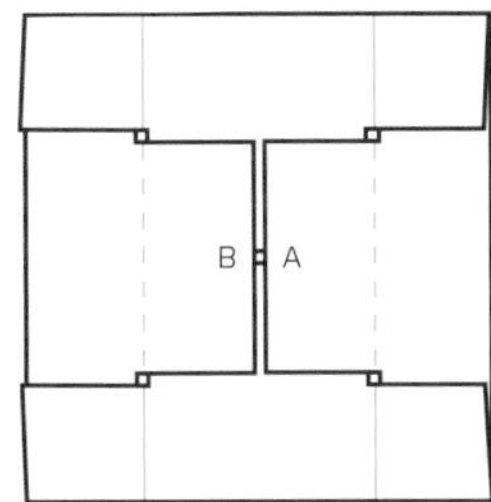

2.4 _ 10
... like this. The flexing cycle can now be repeated endlessly, beginning with step 6. To understand the many interesting possibilities for applying text and images, experiment widely with the Shapeshifter. Once the folds are worked loose, it's an addictive flexagon to play with and a very simple 'no choice' flexing cycle – each move leads inevitably to the next, then to the next.

2.5 Pivoting Cubes

This is the simplest example of a number of three-dimensional flexagons made with cubes or cuboids. The flexing is very simple, enabling the cube to adopt just two positions, yet the possibilities for different faces to be revealed, concealed or scrambled is pleasingly complex. The result is an addictive toy that is easy to operate and with many surprises in the flexing.

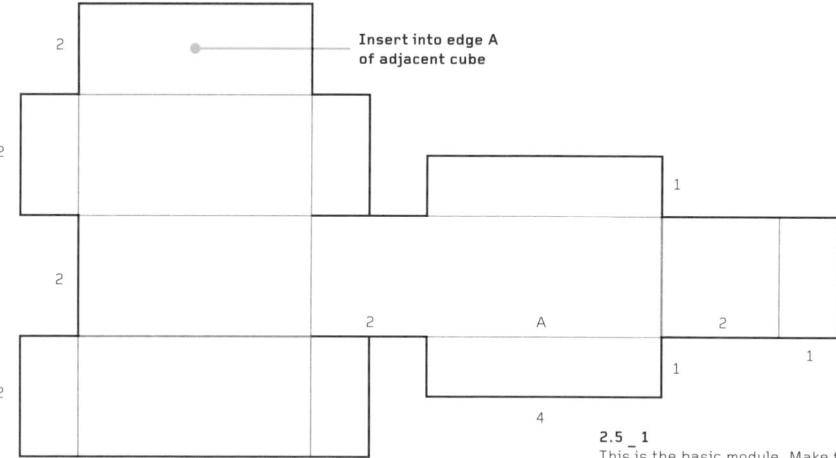

2.5 _ 1
This is the basic module. Make four, using 200–250gsm card. The size is not important, but it is crucial to keep the dimensions in the relative proportion of 1, 2 and 4 given in the diagram ('1' is the unit length, '2' is twice the unit length and '4' is four times the unit length). Carefully made, the card will fold up to make a 2 x 2 x 4 box, which will lock tightly without glue.

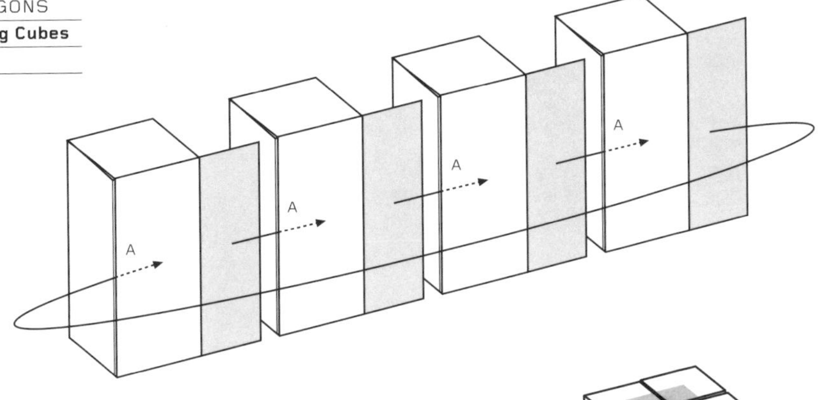

2.5 _ 2
When the four boxes have been made, apply glue to the shaded tabs. Slide each tab into a neighbouring box through the open edge at A (see step 1). Slide the fourth tab into the first box, thus closing the boxes into an endless ring. Alternatively, instead of gluing the boxes together, they may be joined with clear sticky tape or even with graphic stickers as large as the surface.

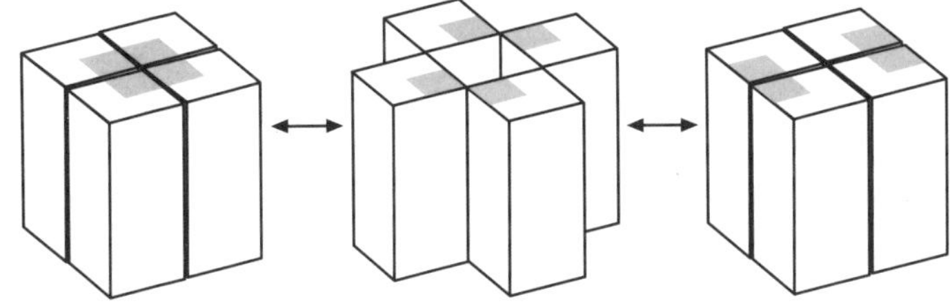

2.5 _ 3
The centre drawing shows the result. Before the glue is set, flex the boxes to and fro to check that everything is in alignment and the closed cubes will nest together fully in both positions. The boxes will flex to create two different configurations of squares on the top and bottom faces. Flexing will also create a series of reveals and concealments around the four sides.

2.6 Flexicube

The flexicube is a true design classic. It is simple in concept, exceptionally ingenious, easy to flex without instructions, it offers many intriguing options for surface graphics and is a totally addictive toy. The eight cubes take a little while to make, but time spent making them will be well-rewarded.

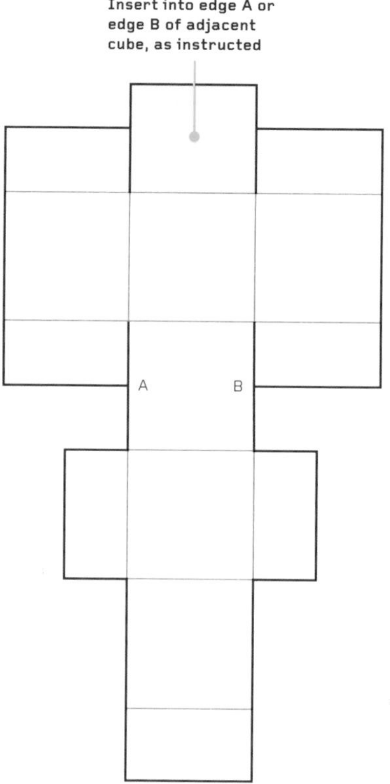

2.6 _ 1
Using 250gsm card, make eight cubes as shown here. The side length of the cubes should be about 3–5cm. The depth of the seven tabs is half the length of a square. Note the shaded tab 'A' at the top, which will lock the cube edge-to-edge to an adjacent cube. Instead of making them from card, the cubes could also be cut from solid wood or another material, and joined with strong tape as described in the next step.

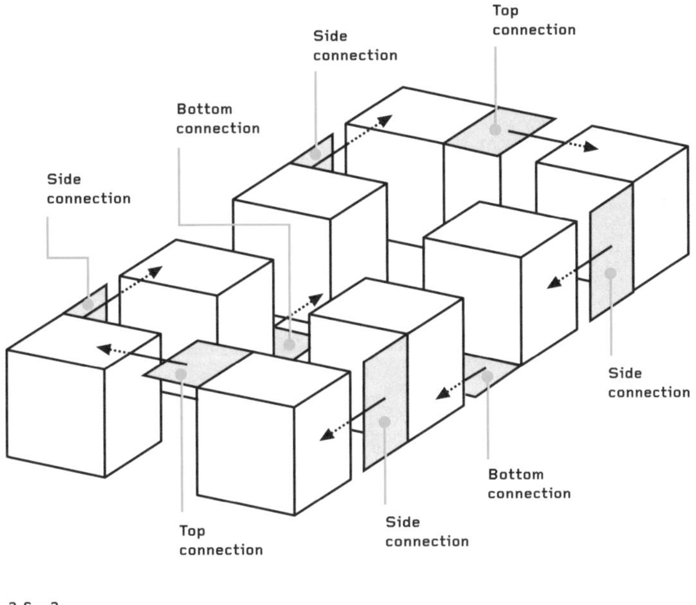

2.6 _ 2
The cubes connect to each other following a precise pattern. Begin by applying glue to just one shaded tab. Before inserting it into a second cube, check that the tab on that second cube is correctly orientated to be inserted into a third cube ... and so on, for all eight cubes. When joined together, the eight cubes will form a 4 x 2 solid brick, which can be flexed as described below.

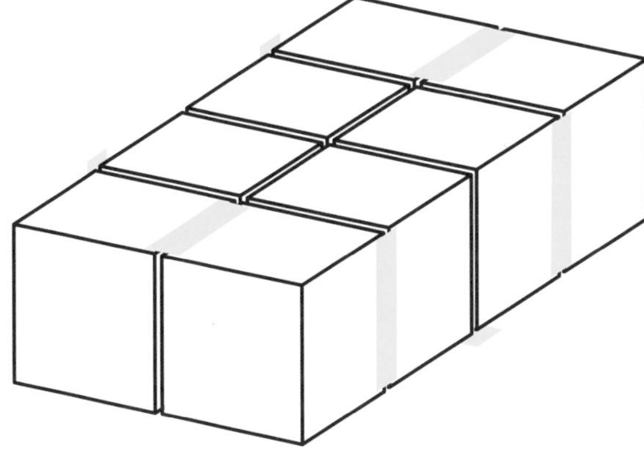

2.6 _ 3
These are the assembled cubes. The orange lines show where the cubes join.

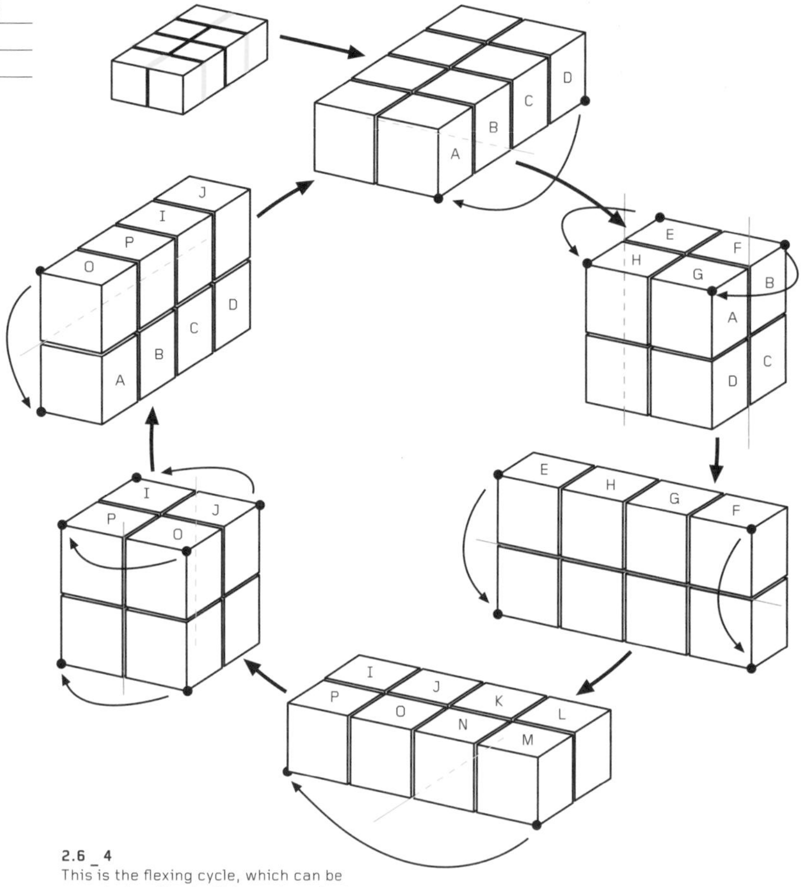

2.6 _ 4
This is the flexing cycle, which can be repeated endlessly. It is much easier to perform in the hand than to explain on the page, so if it looks complex, it is not – even a first-timer will be performing the cycle fluently in just a few seconds. The most remarkable of the many extraordinary flexing phenomena is that the 2 x 2 x 2 cube turns itself completely inside out!

03:

MODULAR SOLIDS

Introduction

Modular solids are polyhedra made from separate pieces of card ('modules'), which lock together without glue. The unfolded modules can be flat-packed for mailing or for holding in a special presentation wallet until assembled by the recipient to create the final three-dimensional form. Any of the envelopes in chapter 4 would be ideal for this purpose. The transformation of 2-D modules to 3-D solids gives them a real '*wow*!' factor.

It's a simple puzzle to fit the pieces together, so you may not need to give instructions for their assembly with the kit. If the surface graphics continue from one module to the next, this will give a strong visual clue as to how the pieces align with each other, helping someone to assemble them quickly and fluently. Once assembled, the solids make great objects for display, helping to keep your message or information in view and thus, to be remembered.

The simplest polyhedron to make is a cube – everyone knows what a cube looks like and how the faces, edges and corners relate to each other. For this reason, this chapter focuses on modular cubes, though many of them could be morphed into cuboid boxes of any proportion. The chapter concludes with two constructions that are not cubic, thus opening out the language of modular construction to other forms.

3.1 Six-piece Cubes

This six-piece cube was created by the author in the early 1980s and since then has become known widely as 'The Jackson Cube'. Although the units are very simple, it is cunningly awkward to assemble, but surprisingly strong when the units are locked together. The six flat faces are ideal for surface graphics, or the cube can be left almost blank as a puzzle cube.

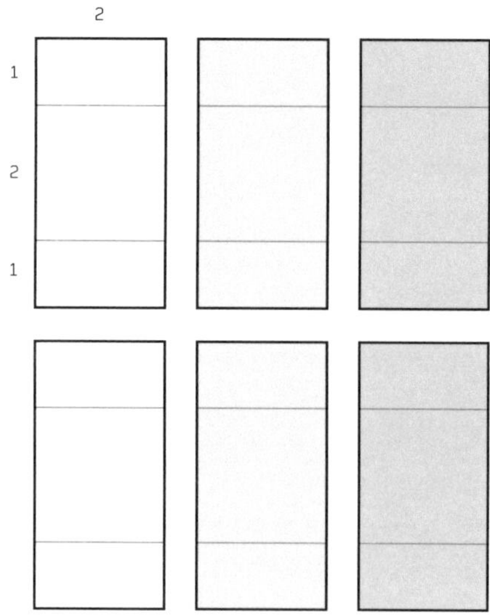

3.1 _ 1
Use six pieces of 200–250gsm card. Each piece is a 2 x 1 rectangle with two parallel folds that create a square in the centre of the rectangle. The illustration shows pairs of units in three different colours, though this is not essential.

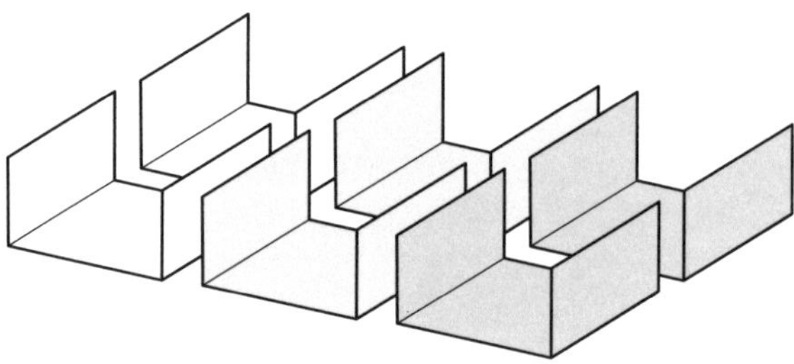

3.1. _ 2
Bend each fold to 90 degrees (it is better to first fold them flat to 180 degrees, then to open them to 90 degrees).

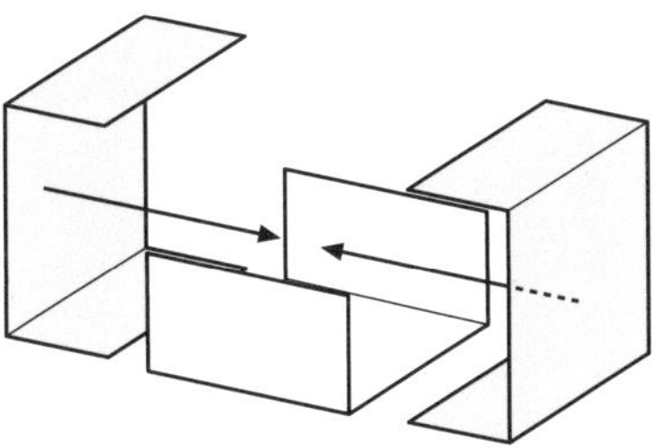

3.1 _ 3
Lay a white unit on its back. Stand up two light-grey units on their tabs and slide them onto the white square ...

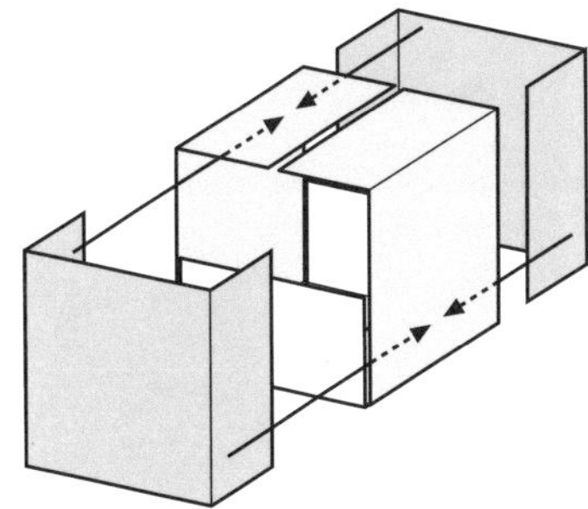

3.1 _ 4
... like this. Next, slide in the tabs of the mid-grey units ...

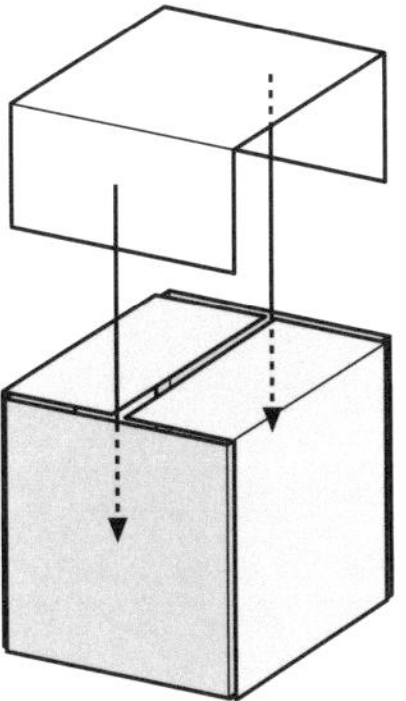

3.1 _ 5
... like this. Finally, slide in the second white unit. This will lock the cube together tightly.

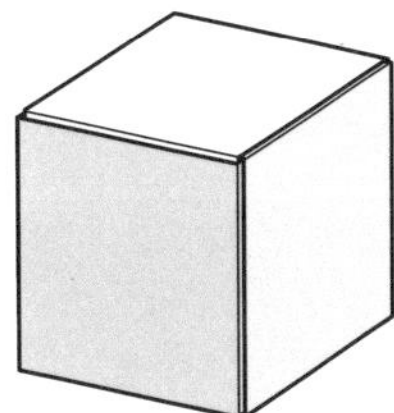

3.1 _ 6
Here is the assembled cube. To help assembly, the surface graphics can continue from one face to the next, so that someone unfamiliar with its construction can assemble it quickly. The same construction system can be used to create boxes with other proportions, not just a cube.

3.2 Three-piece Cubes

The Jackson Cube, above, is made from six units, each unit creating a square face of a cube with extra tabs to lock the units together. The same system can be used if two squares are joined together to create a unit, thus making three double units. There are two ways to do this, one simple and one less so. No photographs are shown of the first method, because with only ever three faces visible to the camera, the pattern of the colour distribution around the six faces is not clear.

First method:

3.2 _ 1
On 200–250gsm card, draw two squares.

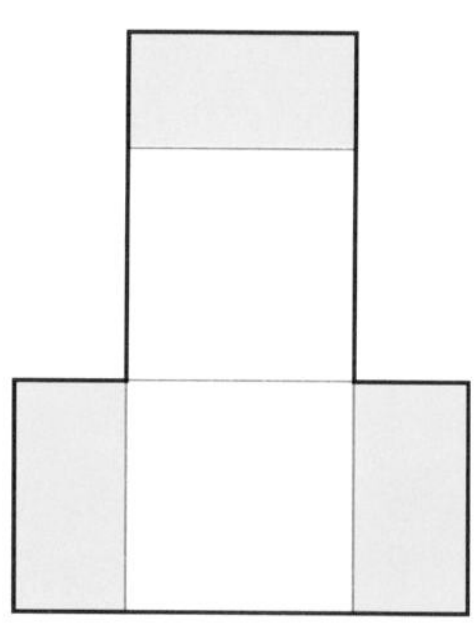

3.2 _ 2
Draw three locking tabs, here shown in orange. Add four folds.

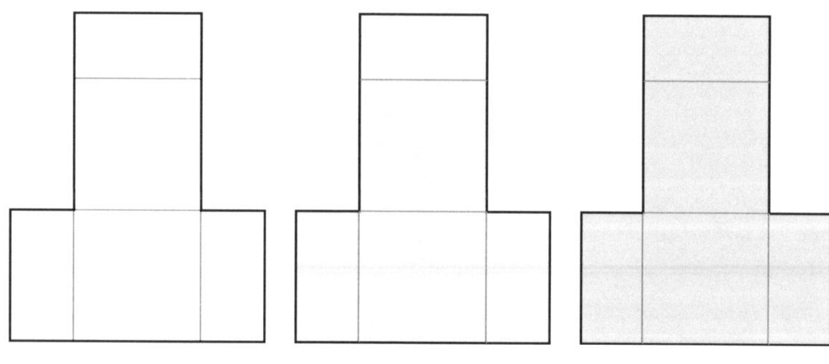

3.2 _ 3
Make three identical units, here shown in different colours.

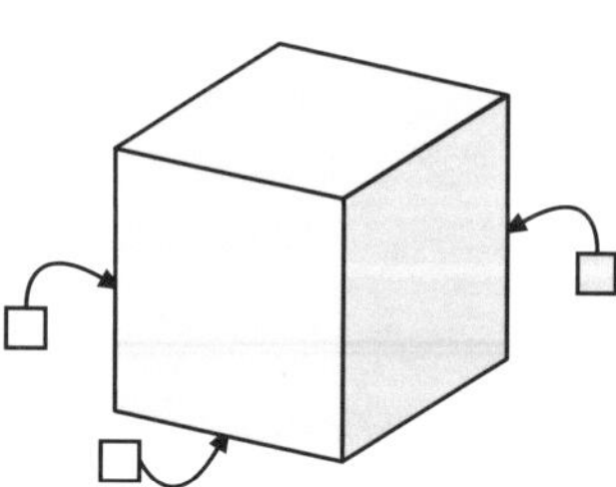

3.2 _ 4
Assemble the three units, following the principles of the six-piece Jackson Cube (see page 36). The small squares show the colour of the hidden faces.

Second method:

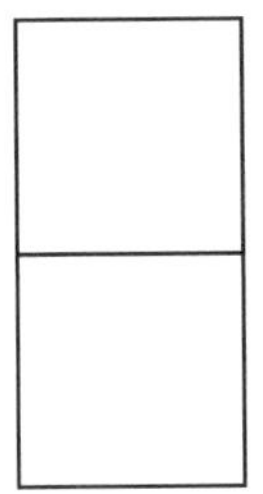

3.2 _ 5
Again, on 200–250gsm card, draw two squares.

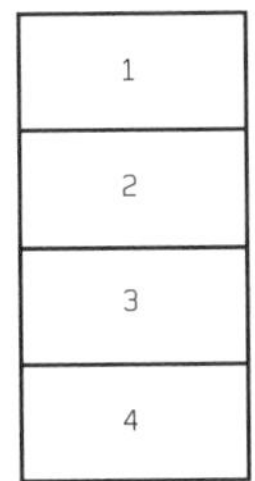

3.2 _ 6
Divide each square in half across the middle.

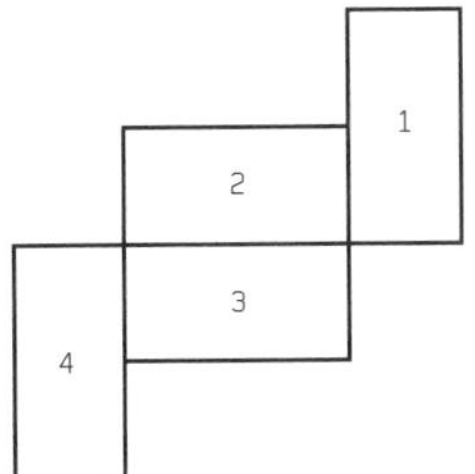

3.2 _ 7
Move the rectangles numbered 1 and 4 to the sides, as shown.

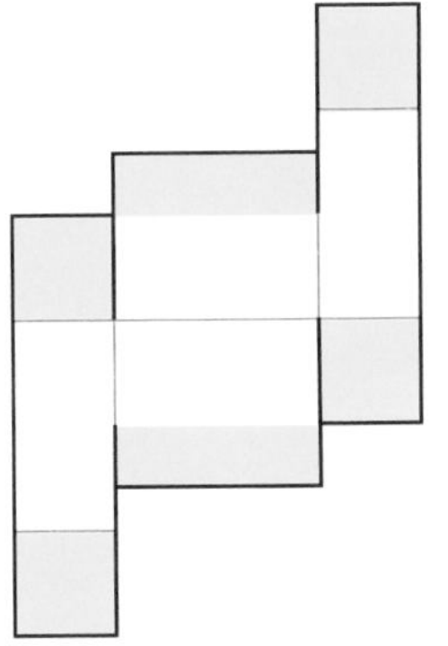

3.2 _ 8
Add four square tabs and two rectangular tabs, as shown. Create five folds.

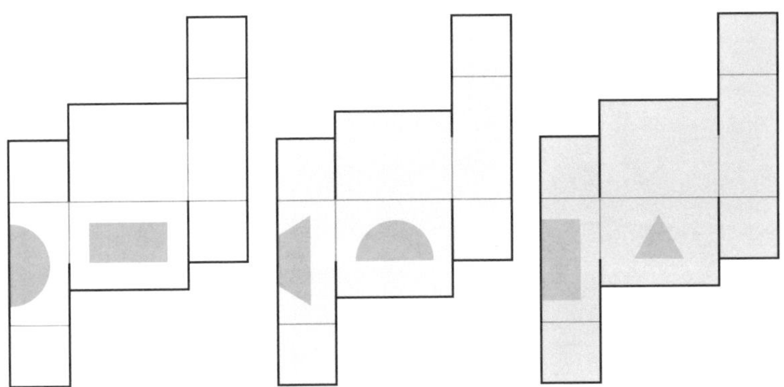

3.2 _ 9
Make three units, here shown in different colours. The simple geometric shapes will help you find the locking pattern.

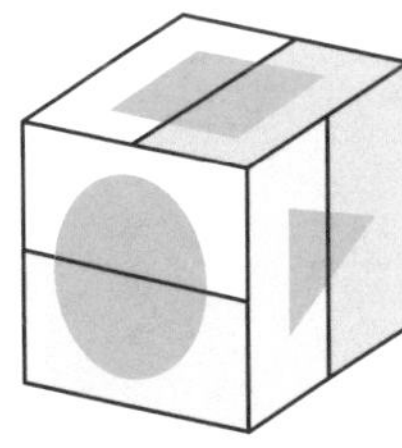

3.2 _ 10
The units are assembled. Note how each square face is divided into two rectangular pieces, also out of sight at the back. Each unit is divided into four rectangles, but the visible surface of each unit still equals two faces (one third) of the cube.

3.3 Two-piece Cubes

In the same way that the system which creates the six-piece Jackson Cube can be used to create two three-piece cubes (see above), it can also be used for two-piece cubes. This time, each unit is three square faces. There are other ways to divide up the three squares than the two methods shown here. No photographs are shown of the cubes, because with only ever three faces visible to the camera, the pattern of the colour distribution around the six faces is not clear.

Method One:

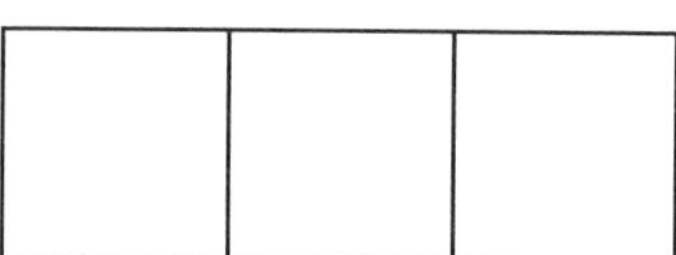

3.3 _ 1
Using 200–250gsm card, draw three squares in a line.

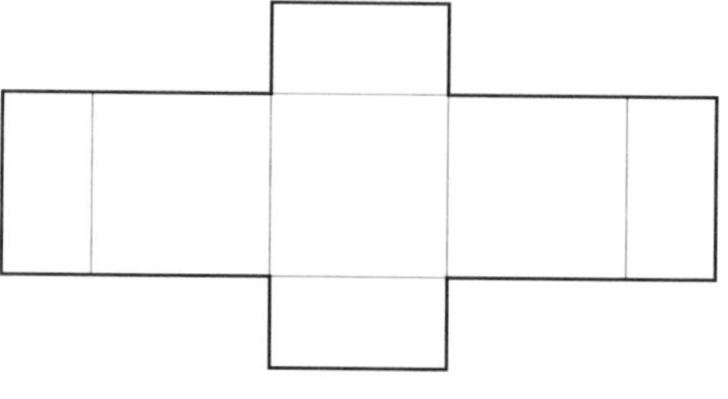

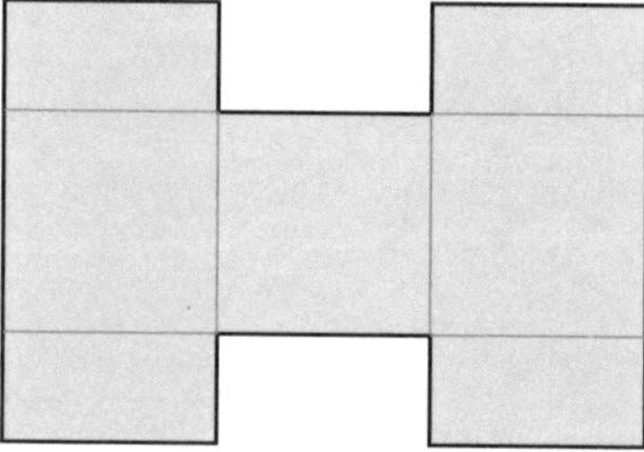

3.2 _ 2
Add four rectangular tabs to each unit. Also add six folds. Note how, unusually, the units are not identical.

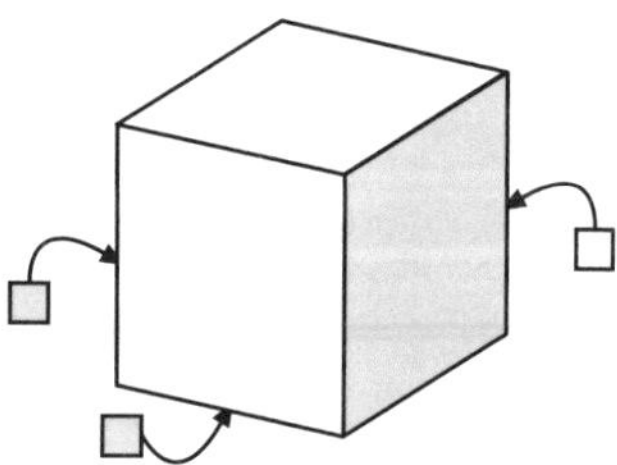

3.2 _ 3
Assemble the units as before, locking the tabs inside. The small squares show the colour of the hidden faces.

Method Two:

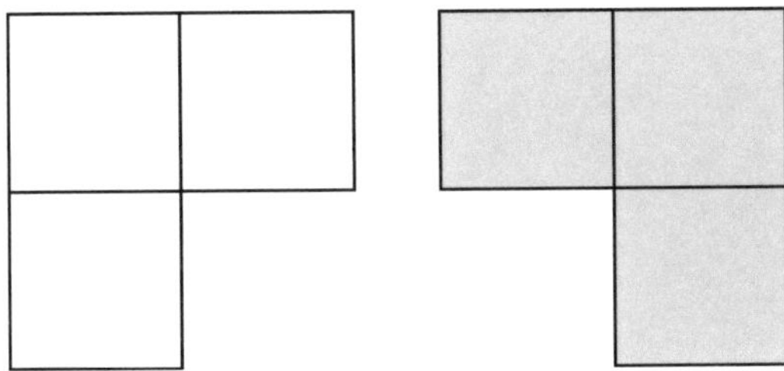

3.3 _ 4
Using 200–250gsm card, this time draw three squares in an 'L' shape. Do this twice, so that each is the mirror image of the other.

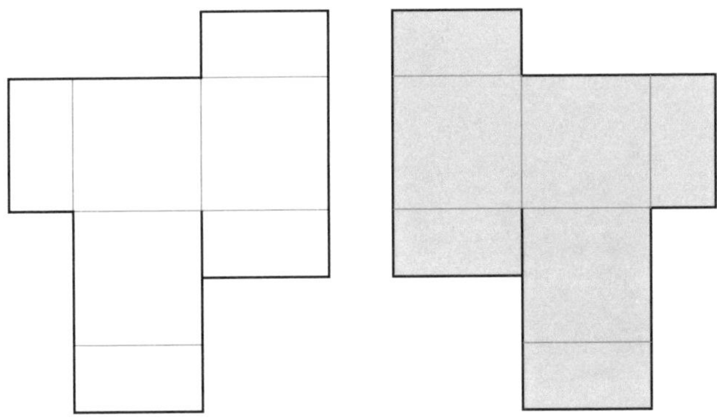

3.3 _ 5
Add four rectangular tabs to each module, as shown. Also add the folds.

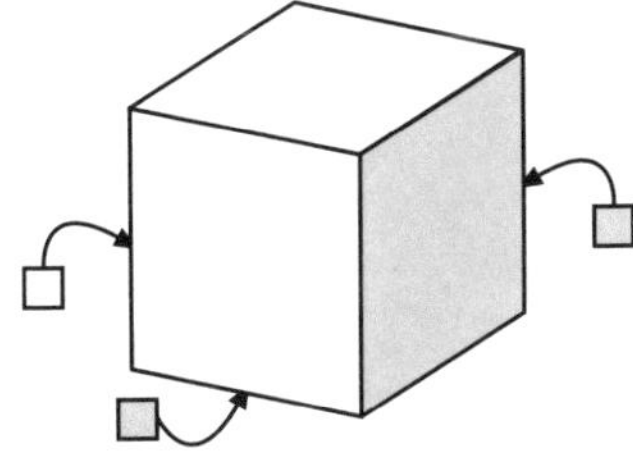

3.3 _ 6
Assemble the units as before, locking the tabs inside. The configuration of the faces of each unit around the cube is different to method one. The small squares show the colours of the hidden faces.

3.4 Jigsaw Cubes

The principles of the cubes shown previously in the chapter can be altered slightly so that the tabs are not folded, but instead project outside the cube. The example shown here is of the six-piece version but it can also be applied to the three-piece and two-piece cubes. The units are not folded.

3.4 _ 1
Using 200–250gsm card, draw a square.

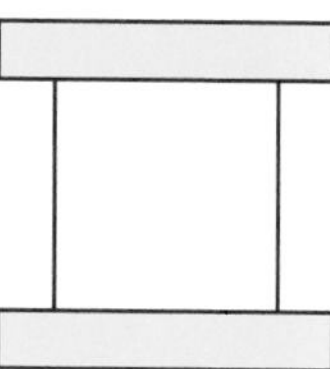

3.4 _ 2
Add two tabs to the square. Note how they project a little way over the sides of the square. This projection is crucial to the locking of the pieces.

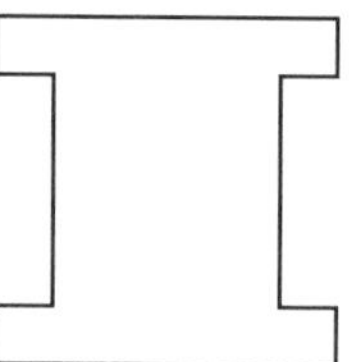

3.4 _ 3
This is the final unit. Note the absence of any folds.

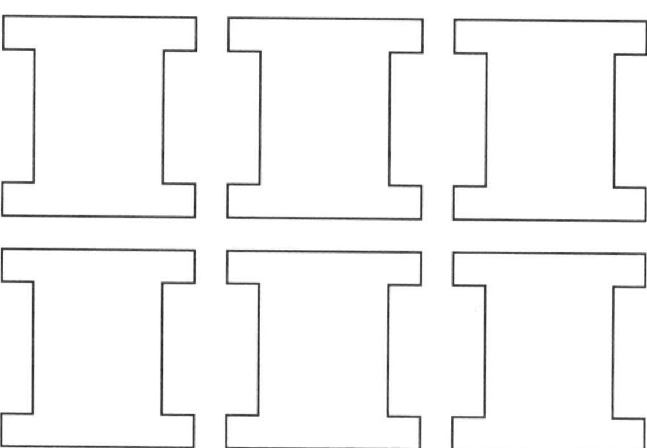

3.4 _ 4
Make six identical units. Assemble them using the locking pattern of the six-piece Jackson Cube (see page 36).

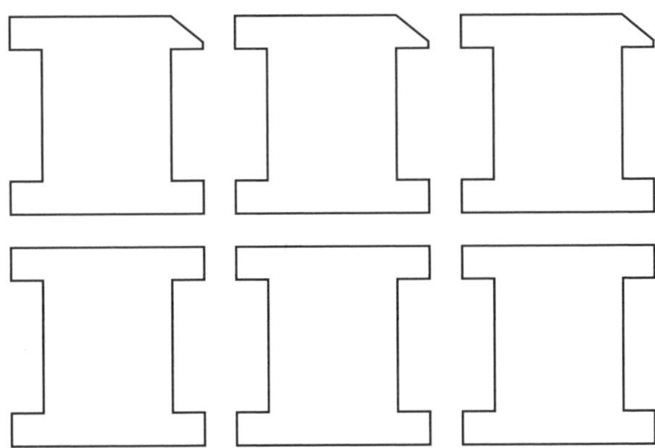

3.4 _ 5
Three of the corners may also be shaved off, so that when placed together at one corner of the cube, the cube can stand on a stable triangular foot.

3.4 _ 6
The external tabs can take on all manner of exotic shapes, to create cubes of great originality and beauty. The tabs can also be made huge, so that the cube is only a small part of a large structure. It is even possible to make figurative sculptures, such as a plant in a pot or a steam train. Your imagination can really run riot here!

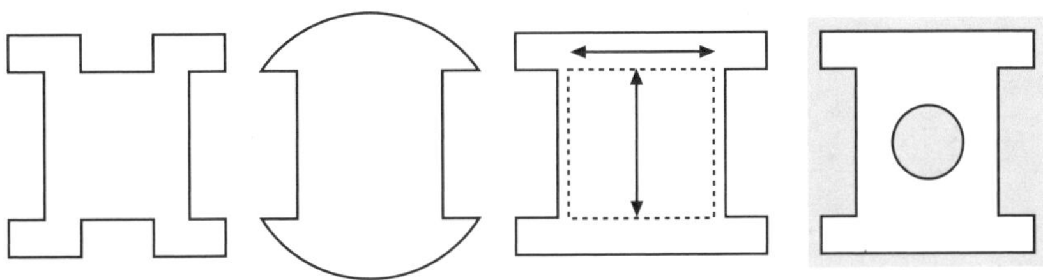

3.5 Tetrahedron

The ideas presented so far in this chapter will all create boxy structures. The system presented here will make a simple tetrahedron, but will also make many other beautiful and complex solids, which can be assembled quickly and strongly.

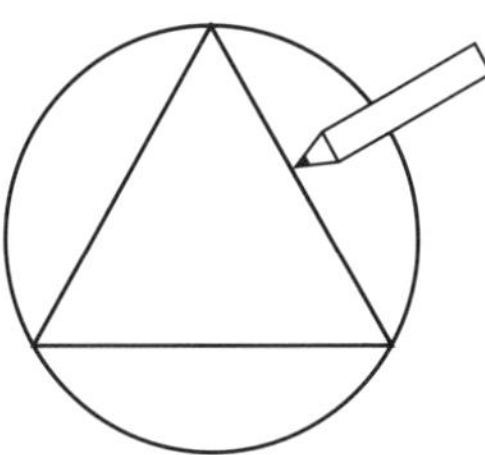

3.5 _ 1
Using 200gsm card, draw an equilateral triangle (the angles are all 60 degrees) inside a circle.

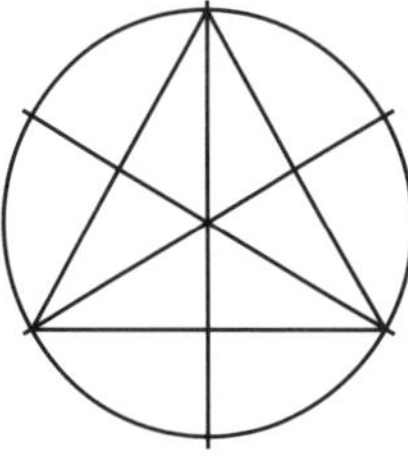

3.5 _ 2
Add construction lines, as shown.

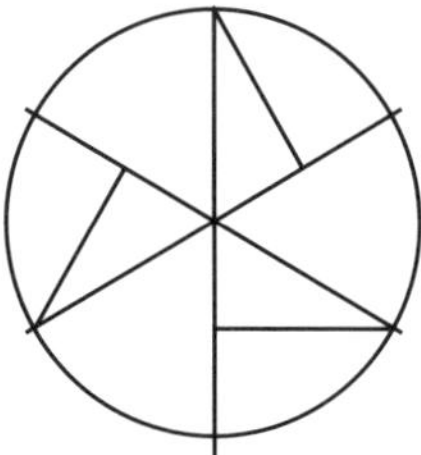

3.5 _ 3
Erase some of the lines of the triangle.

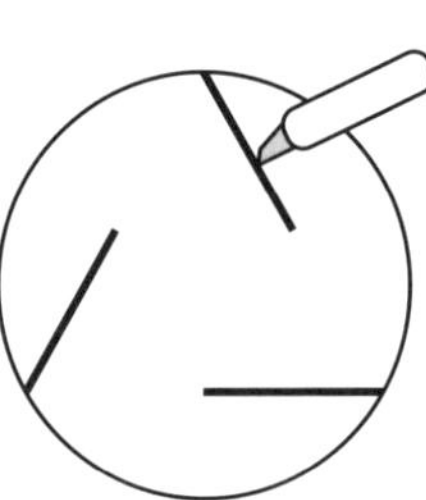

3.5 _ 4
Erase further lines, until only three lines remain, as shown. Cut only those lines.

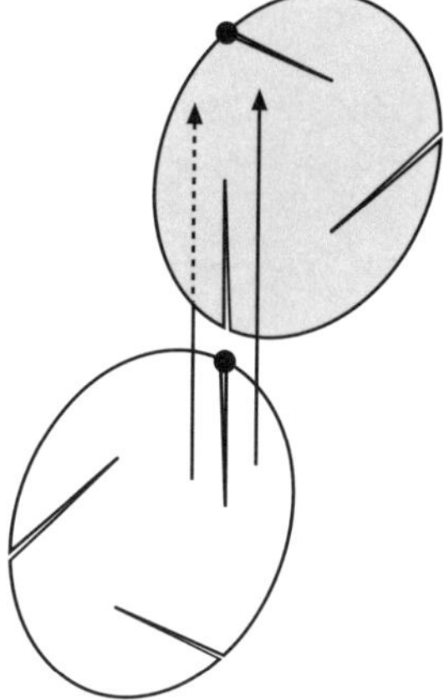

3.5 _ 5
To make a tetrahedron, make four units. For clarity, they are shown in different colours, but this is not essential. Lock two units together by engaging the cuts. One dot will touch the other ...

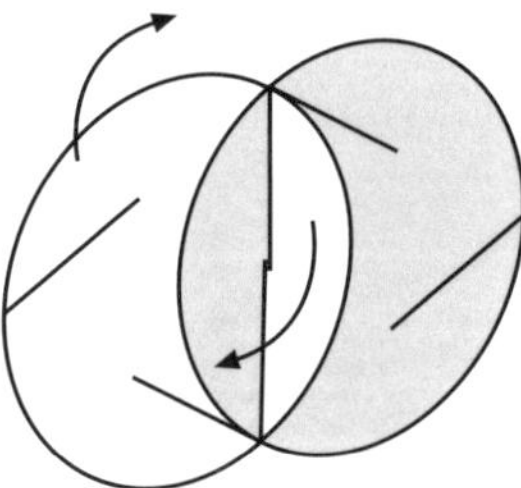

3.5 _ 6
... like this. If the two circles are lying flat, as though lying flat on a table, twist one so that they create an angle between them, like a letter 'V'.

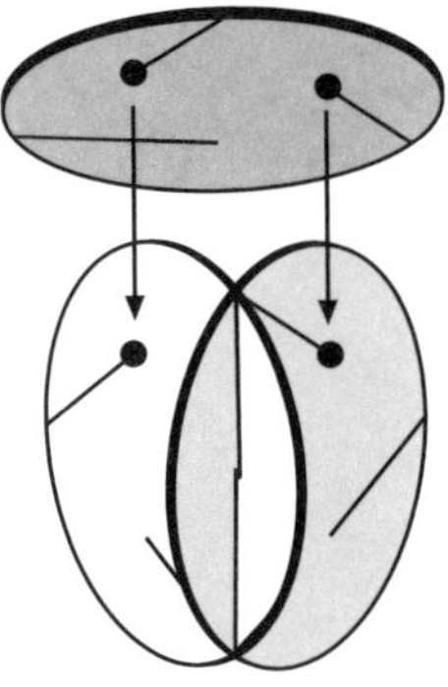

3.5 _ 7
Now introduce a third unit, engaging it with both the white unit and the light-grey unit.

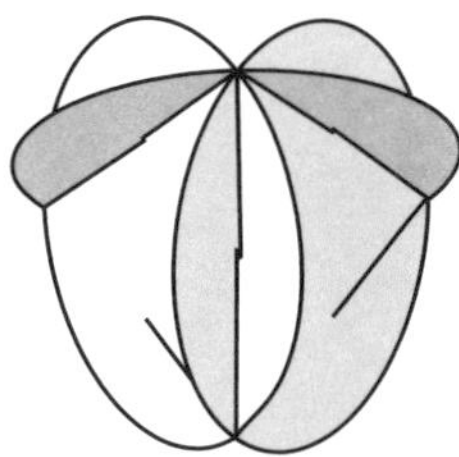

3.5 _ 8
This creates a solid corner at the top, where the three units meet as equal partners. Lock in the fourth unit (not shown), closing the triangular hole at the bottom.

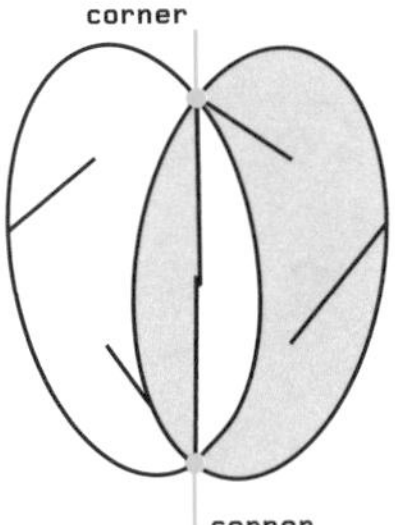

3.5 _ 9
Many different solids can be made, both regular and irregular. The key to creating different solids is knowing how many units to lock together at a corner. For the tetrahedron above, three units lock at each corner. This illustration shows the positions of two corners, marked by the orange circles.

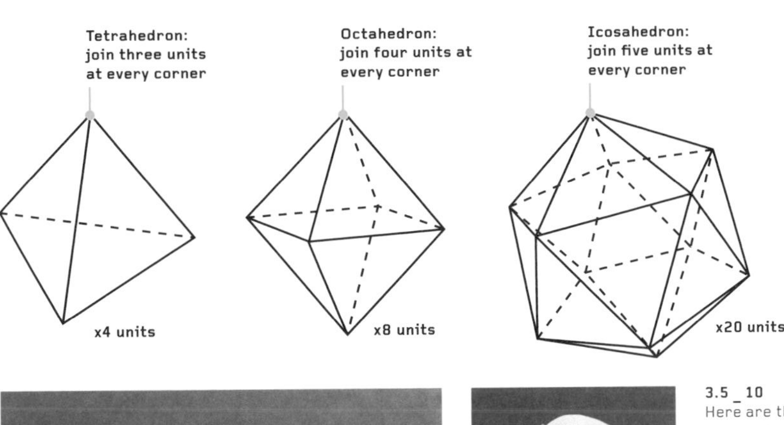

3.5 _ 10
Here are three platonic solids. The tetrahedron has already been made. To make the octahedron and icosahedron, lock four units and five units respectively at each corner. It is also possible to make an infinite number of forms resembling eggs, cylinders and knobbly potatoes by locking different numbers of units together at each corner.

3.6 A4 Pyramids

The humble and ubiquitous sheet of A4 paper is a rectangle with a precise mathematical proportion, which gives it enormous potential for geometric construction. One of the loveliest is its potential to create cubes and pyramids, in whole or in part. In turn, these create simple, effective structures on which to print surface graphics.

A Little Geometry

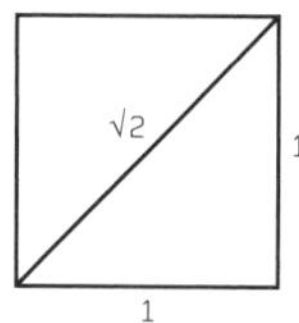

3.6 _ 1
Your understanding of the structures described here will be enhanced if the geometry of A4 paper is explained. According to the Pythagorean theorem, if a square has a side length of 1, the diagonal will have a length of $\sqrt{2}$ (or 1.414...).

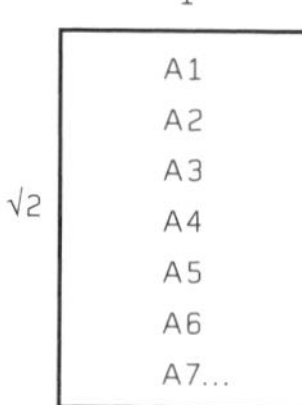

3.6 _ 2
The sides of A4 paper are proportioned 1:$\sqrt{2}$. It is the same proportion for all the A sizes of paper (and also all the B and C sizes). This simple proportion makes a lot of beautiful geometric constructions possible.

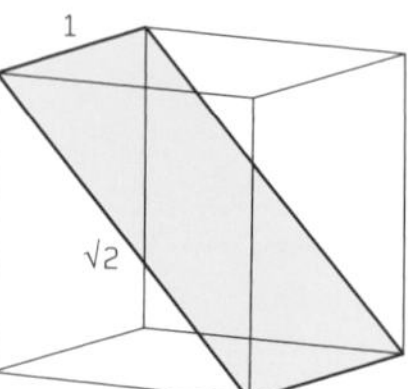

3.6 _ 3
Thus, a sheet of A4 paper (in orange) can be stretched across the interior of a cube.

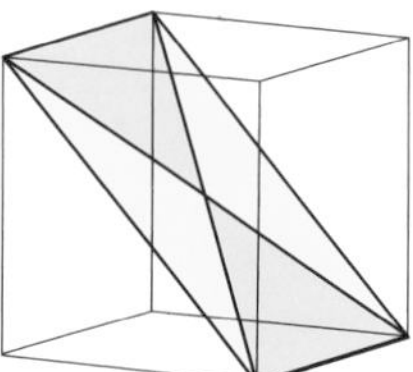

3.6 _ 4
Imagine that an 'X' is drawn on the A4 sheet, dividing it into four triangles.

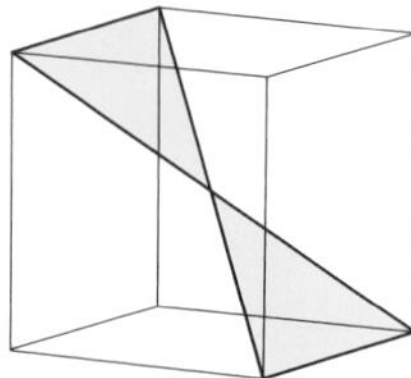

3.6 _ 5
Here, the long triangles have been cut away, leaving only the darker ones. The point where the triangles meet is also the centre point of the cube's interior.

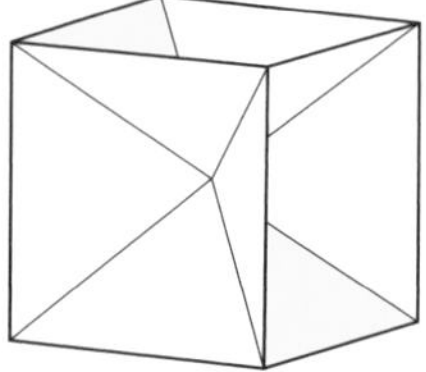

3.6 _ 6
The same stretching of A4 sheets can be done six times across a cube, to create a series of triangles that all meet at the centre point of the cube. In effect, six pyramids have been created, all meeting at their apexes.

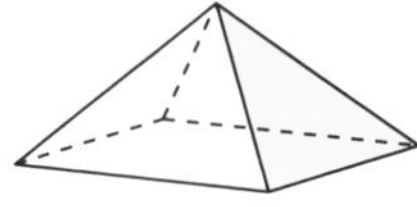

3.6 _ 7
This is one of the pyramids. Note how the triangular faces are the same as the triangles in step 5.

So, it can be seen that there is a direct relationship between 1:$\sqrt{2}$ rectangles (such as A4 paper) and cubes, and pyramids that pack together to create a cube. Interesting, don't you agree?

Structure One: Quarter Pyramid

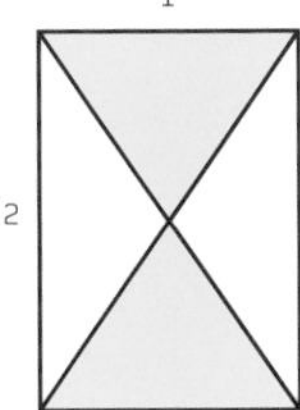

3.6 _ 8
The orange triangles create pyramids that pack inside a cube. Draw them on a sheet of 200gsm A4 card.

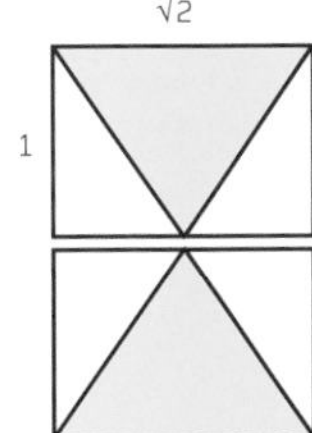

3.6 _ 9
Cut the A4 in half across the middle to create two A5 sheets.

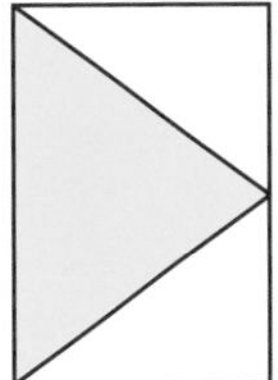

3.6 _ 10
This is the basic unit to make a quarter pyramid.

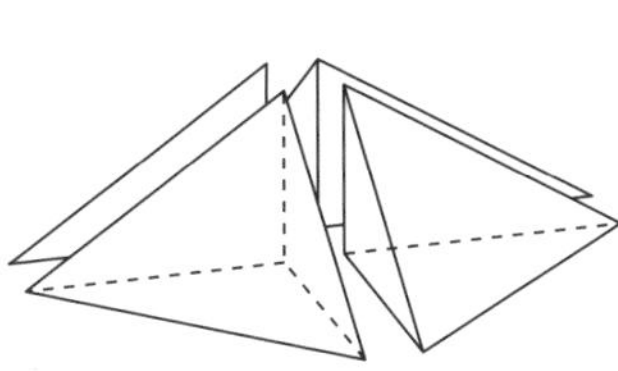

3.6 _ 11
Here, the pyramid has been cut into quarters. Note how each quarter contains one triangular face.

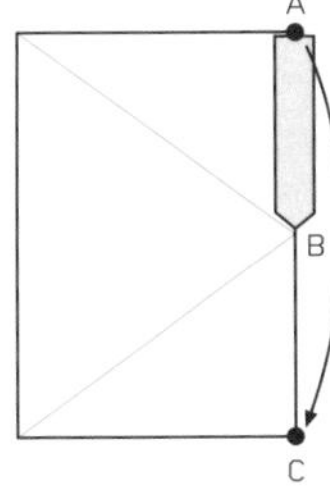

3.6 _ 12
Add sticky tape where shown. Then, with the help of two mountain folds, bring the two dots together. The card will not lie flat ...

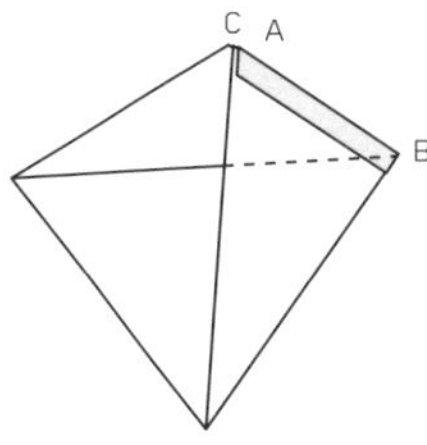

3.6 _ 13
... like this. The structure will remain three-dimensional. Note the open side at the left of the drawing. Turn the structure over to continue to step 14.

Structure One: Quarter Pyramid

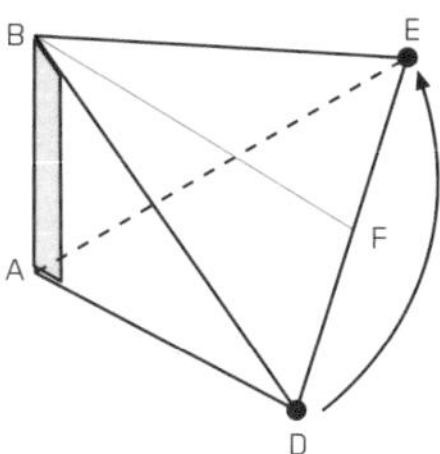

3.6 _ 14
With an additional valley fold, make the structure flat, so that the dots are brought together ...

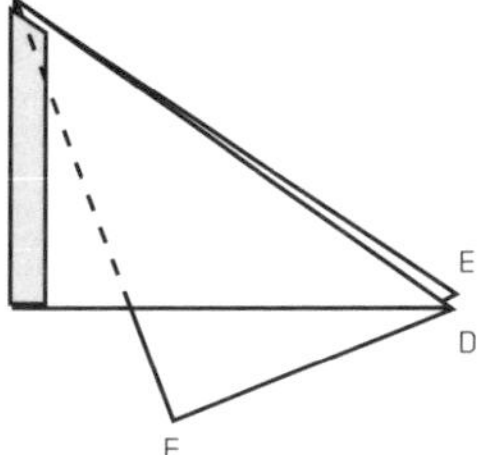

3.6 _ 15
... like this.

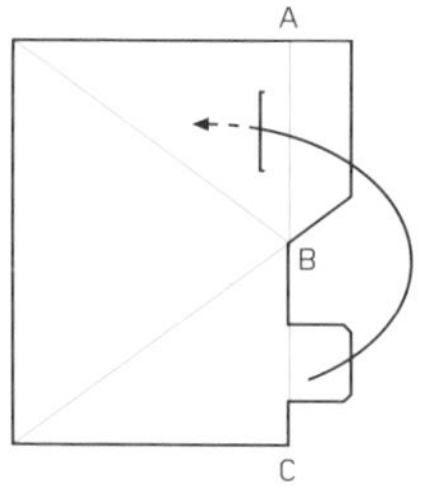

3.6 _ 16
The use of sticky tape to hold the structure together is simple and effective, but it might also be considered unaesthetic. Another way – shown here – is to engineer the locking, by creating extra locking tabs.

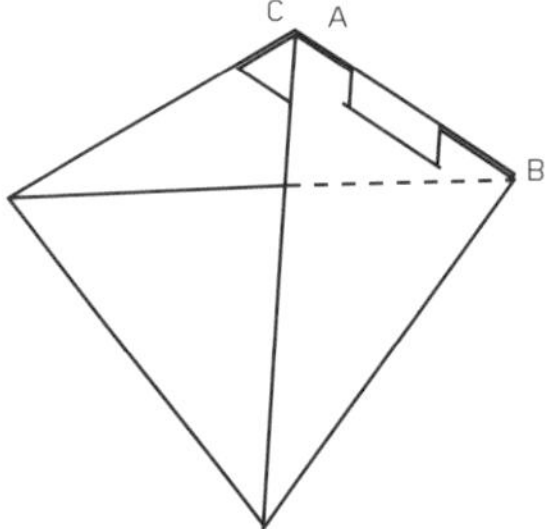

3.6 _ 17
Although more aesthetic than tape, the tabbing method does require more card than just the simple taped A5 sheet method, shown above. So, there are advantages and disadvantages to both methods. Make four quarter pyramids to create a complete pyramid.

Structure Two: Half Pyramid

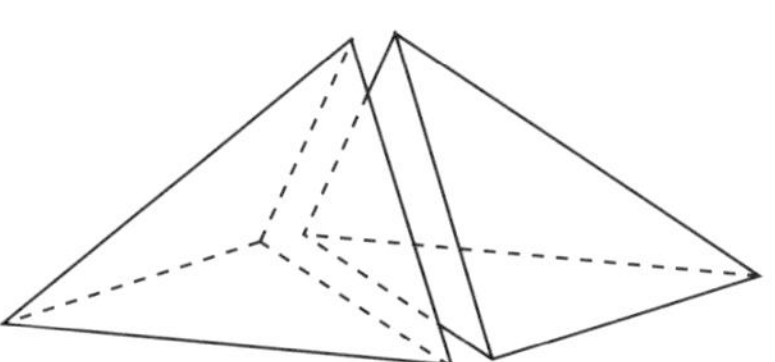

3.6 _ 18
Here, a complete pyramid has been split into two halves. Each half has two triangular faces.

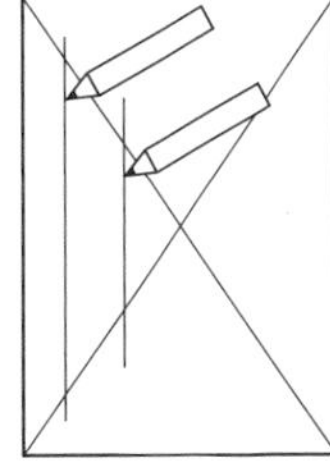

3.6 _ 19
On a sheet of 200gsm A4 card, draw the large 'X', then draw two parallel lines as shown. The exact placement of these lines is unimportant.

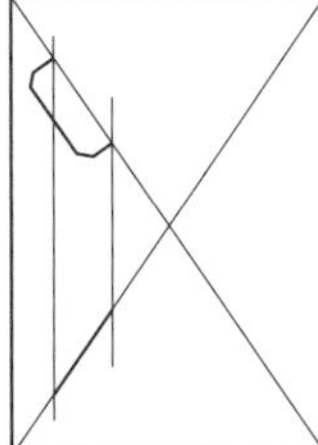

3.6 _ 20
Draw and then cut a tab and a slit, both of which begin and end exactly on the two lines drawn in step 19.

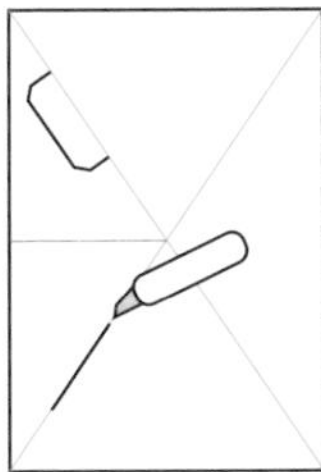

3.6 _ 21
Fold a mountain 'X' and add a short horizontal valley.

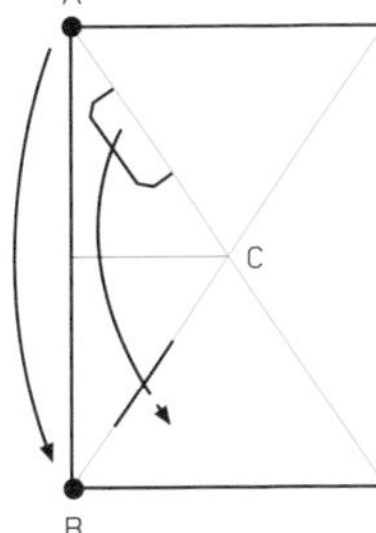

3.6 _ 22
Fold A to B, tucking the tab through the slit ...

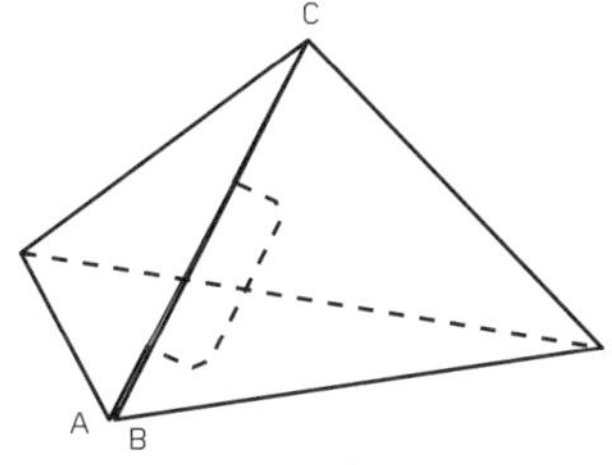

3.6 _ 23
... like this, to create a locked half pyramid. Make another identical half pyramid and put them together to create a whole pyramid.

Structure Three: Whole Pyramid

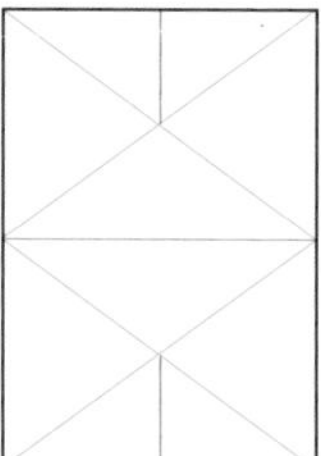

3.6 _ 24
Using 200gsm A4 card, create four mountain folds and three valley folds, as shown.

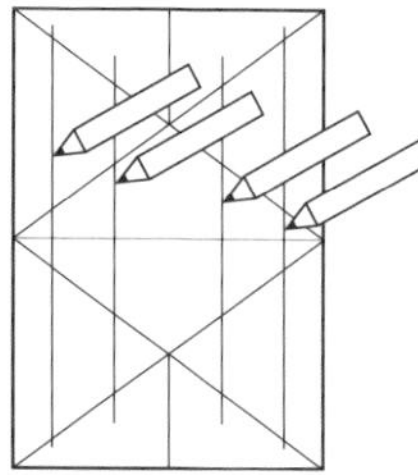

3.6 _ 25
Draw four lines, more or less as shown. Their exact placement is unimportant, but it is crucial that the left and right pairs of lines are placed symmetrically on the card.

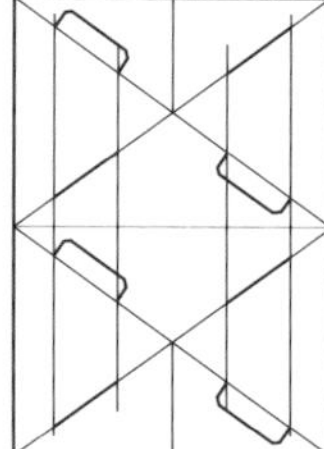

3.6 _ 26
Create four tabs and four slits, as shown, each of which begins and ends exactly on the drawn lines.

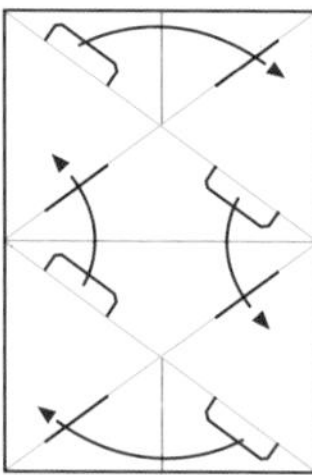

3.6 _ 27
Engage the four pairs of tabs and slits. This will lock the final whole pyramid into shape.

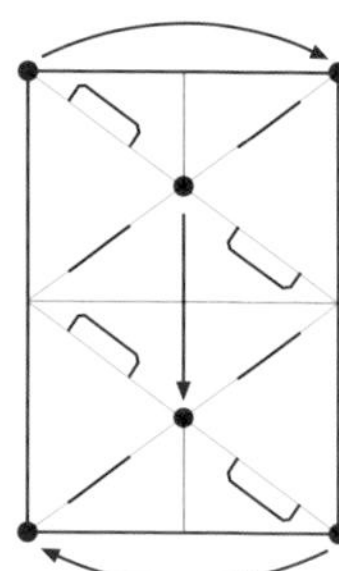

3.6 _ 28
While engaging the pairs of tabs and slits, it is helpful to remember to bring together these three pairs of dots.

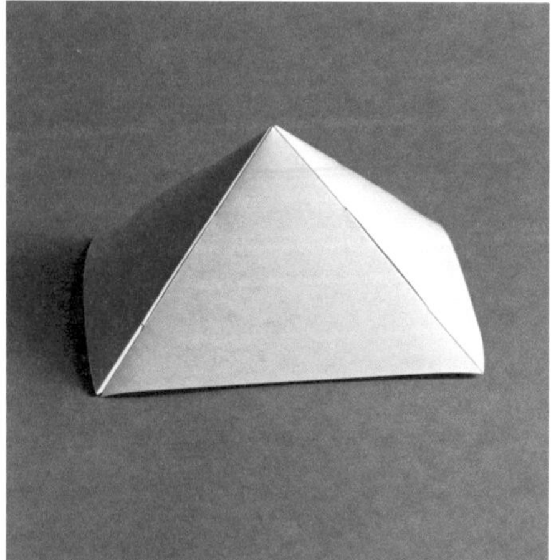

Structure Three: Whole Pyramid

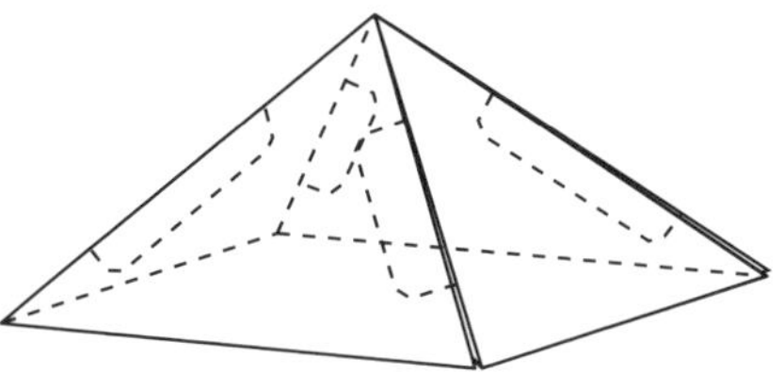

3.6 _ 29
Here is the final whole pyramid. It may take a little time to engage all the tabs into all the slits, but when complete, the whole pyramid will be very strong and clean.

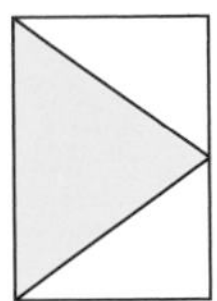

3.6 _ 30
There is a second way to create the whole pyramid. Note the triangle that makes the four triangular faces of the pyramid.

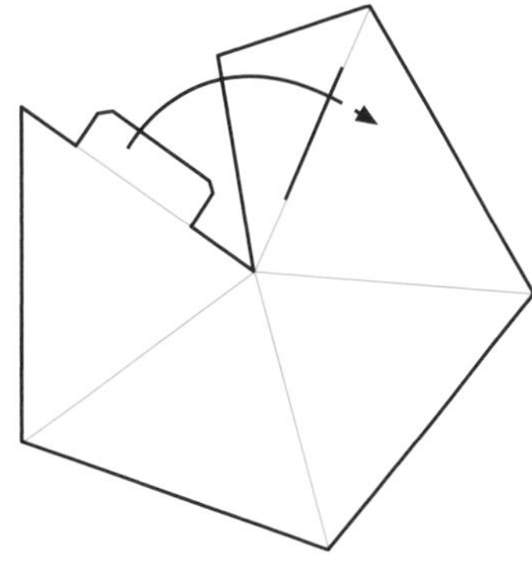

3.6 _ 31
Put four of these triangles together, so that they meet at a common point (if it looks like they create four sides of a pentagon, the geometry is not quite accurate). Add a tab at the left, a slit at the top right and also an extra small triangle. Make mountain folds, then engage the tab into the slit. The whole pyramid will form.

The advantage of this method of making a whole pyramid over the first method is that the pyramid will collapse flat for mailing and can be easily erected into three-dimensions. The disadvantage is that it is an engineered structure, not made from a simple sheet of A4 card.

04:

ENVELOPES

Introduction

As a culture, we are forgetting the art of giving. We are forgetting that even if what is given is mundane, the way it is given can make it seem out of the ordinary and make the recipient feel special.

To pack anything inside a regular, mass-produced envelope may be easy and inexpensive, but it is also very, very dull, particularly if you have tried hard with the contents to impress. The total presentation should be completed with an extra-special envelope – after all, first impressions are always important.

The envelopes in this chapter have been chosen not only for their ability to impress, but also for the speed with which they can be folded, should you be making them individually by hand. A finishing touch would be to make them from an interesting paper, perhaps textured or coloured. Simply to make them from regular copier-type paper is not special enough to truly make your presentation special, so make an effort to find the right paper or card.

Many of the 2-D designs in the book can be packed inside one of these special envelopes, so use this chapter in conjunction with a design from another.

An interesting experiment is to fold the designs as described in the book, but using fabric. Special fastenings can be incorporated, such as buttons, bows or Velcro®.

4.1 A4 Random Envelope

Whereas almost all designs need their cuts and folds to be placed exactly, this design can be made with a high degree of randomness, thus accelerating the speed with which it can be made. The same design can be made with a rectangle of any proportion, including a square.

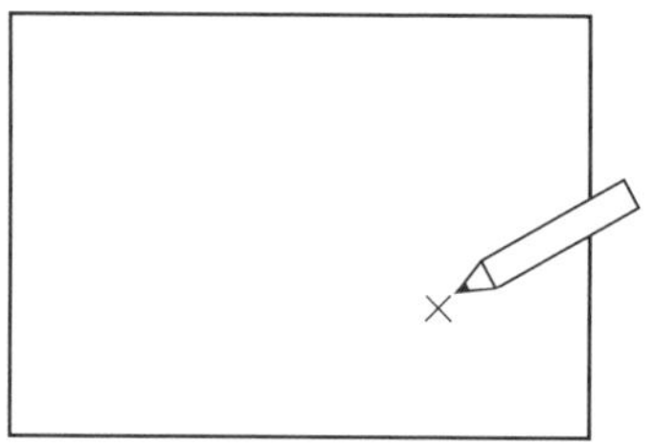

4.1 _ 1
Anywhere on an A4 sheet, make a small mark.

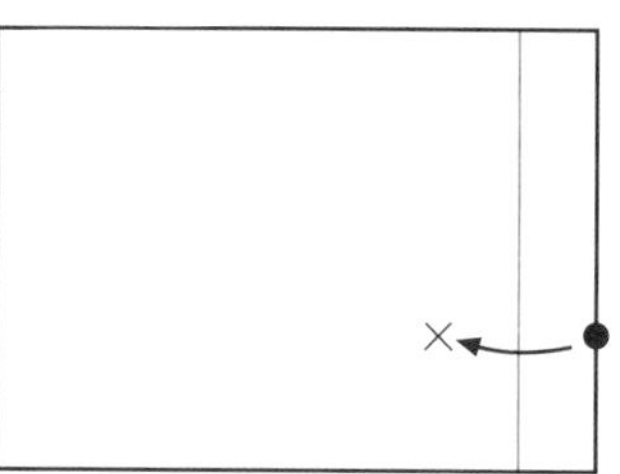

4.1 _ 2
Fold the right-hand edge to the mark.

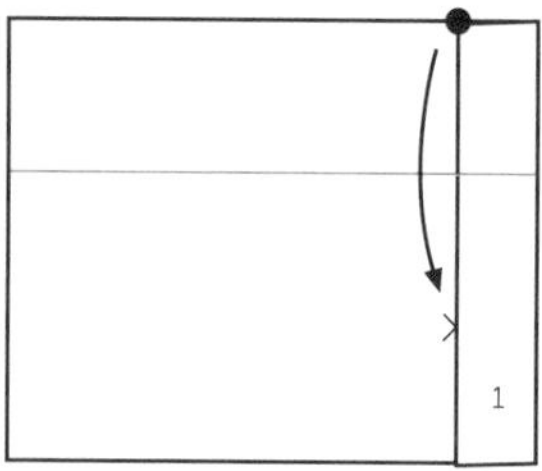

4.1 _ 3
Then, fold the top edge to the mark.

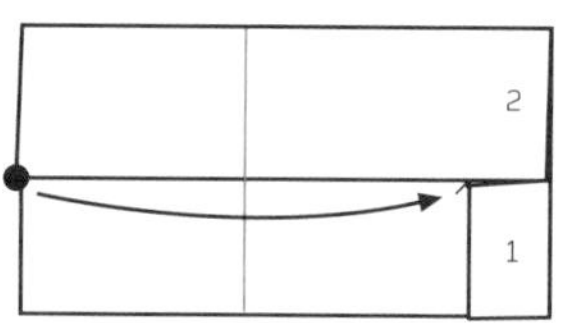

4.1 _ 4
Then, fold the left-hand edge to the mark. The '1' and '2' denote the order in which the edges were folded to the mark. Note that this third fold will touch the edge of the first fold.

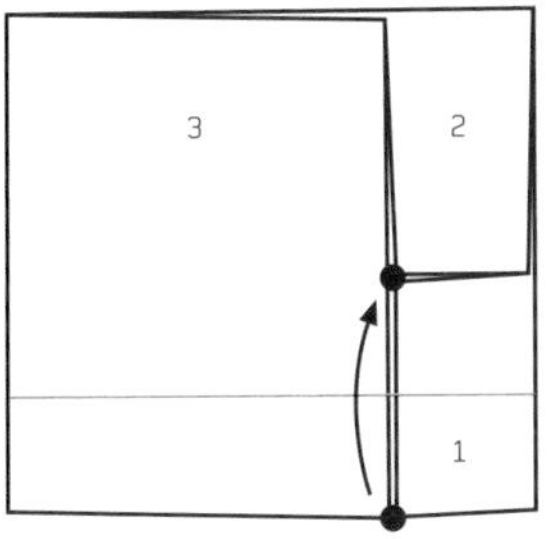

4.1 _ 5
Then, finally, fold the bottom edge up to the mark. The fold will touch the bottom edge of the second fold.

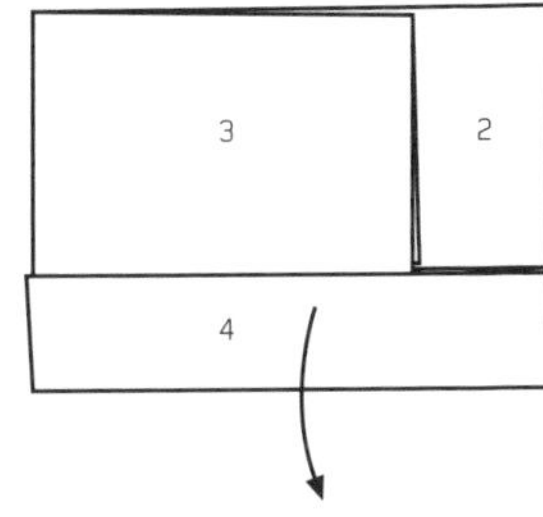

4.1 _ 6
This is the basic configuration of the envelope; however, it does not lock. To lock it begin by unfolding the fourth edge.

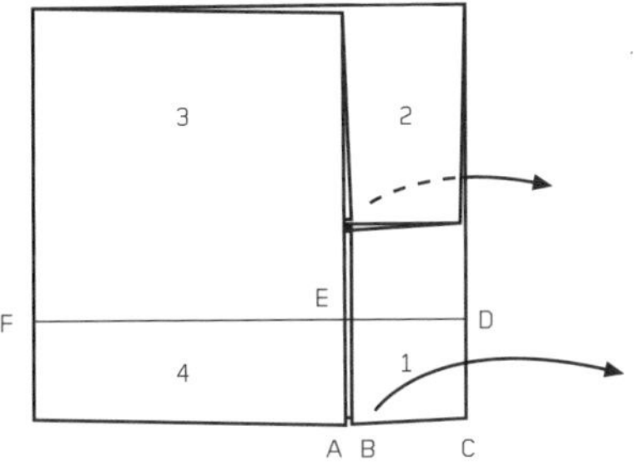

4.1 _ 7
Corner D is the corner where the first fold and the fourth fold meet. Lift up corner B a little ...

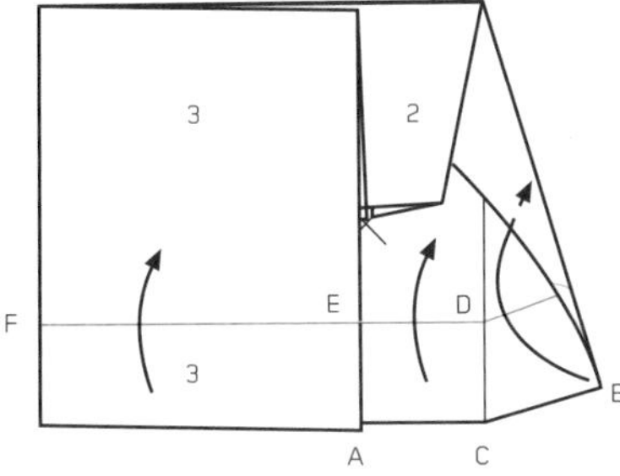

4.1 _ 8
... like this. Now, fold up edge 4 again, but unlike the first time (step 5), corner B is pushed forcefully up under the 1 edge ...

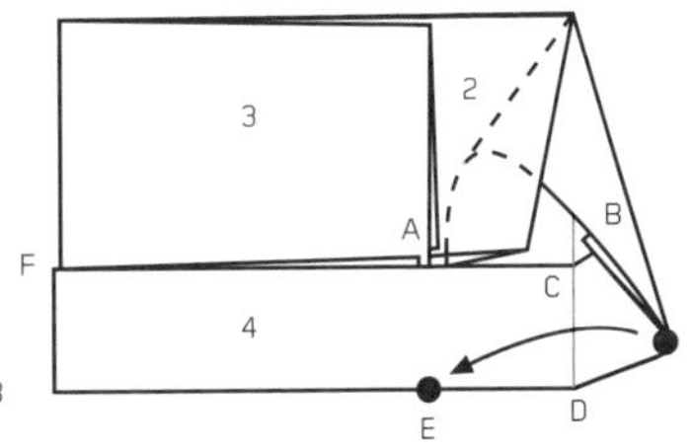

4.1 _ 9
... like this. Note the valley fold, which starts at F, continues through E and D to the black dot. It is one simple, straight fold. Flatten the paper, bringing the dots together.

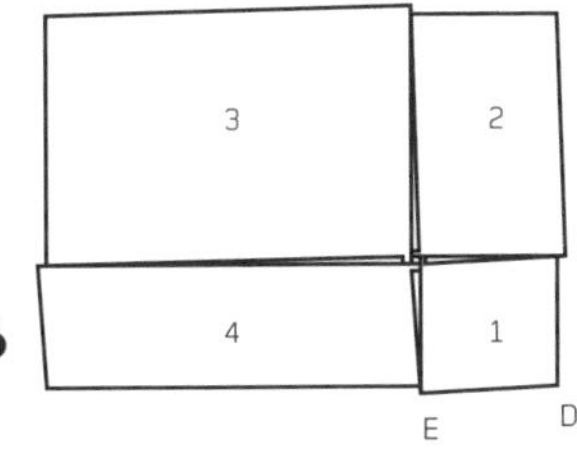

4.1 _ 10
The random envelope is complete. Note how each of the four flaps lies on top of one neighbour and under the other, without a beginning or an end.

4.2 A4 Angled Envelope

The random envelope (above) will always be half the dimensions of the paper it was made from. Thus, an A4 sheet will make an A6 envelope. Sadly, an A6 envelope is too small to contain an A4 sheet folded into quarters (A6). So, here's an ingenious way to fold A4 to create an envelope a little larger than A6.

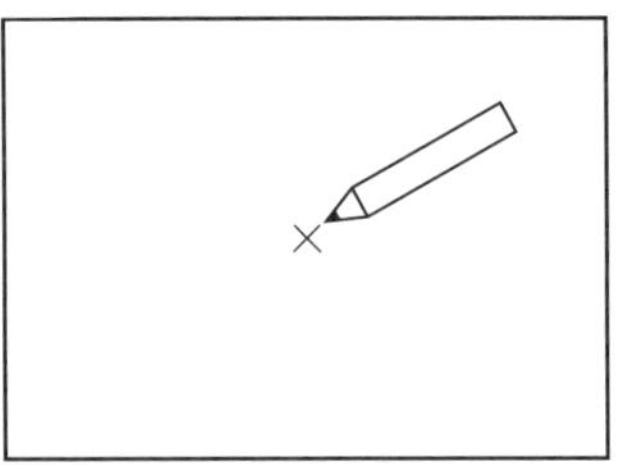

4.2 _ 1
Mark the centre of an A4 sheet.

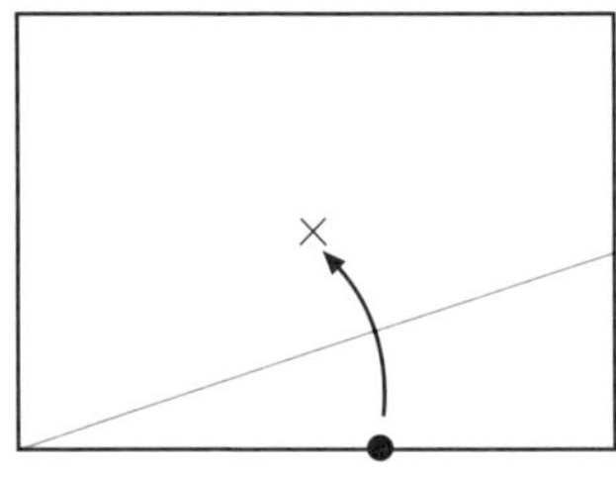

4.2 _ 2
Make a sloping fold which begins at the bottom left-hand corner, so that the bottom edge of the paper passes through the centre point of the A4 ...

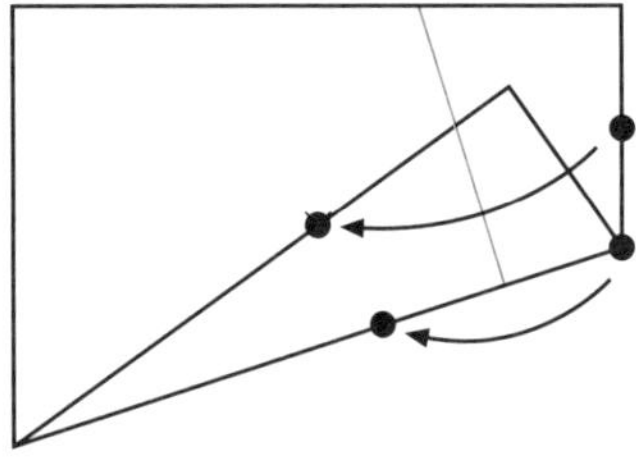

4.2 _ 3
... like this. Now, make a fold so that the right-hand edge touches the centre point, bringing the two pairs of dots together.

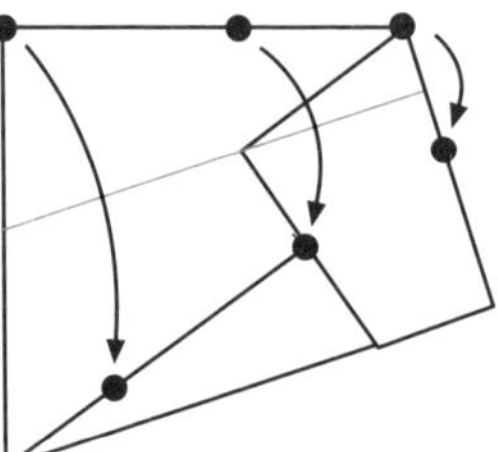

4.2 _ 4
Now bring the top edge down to the centre point, bringing the three pairs of black dots together.

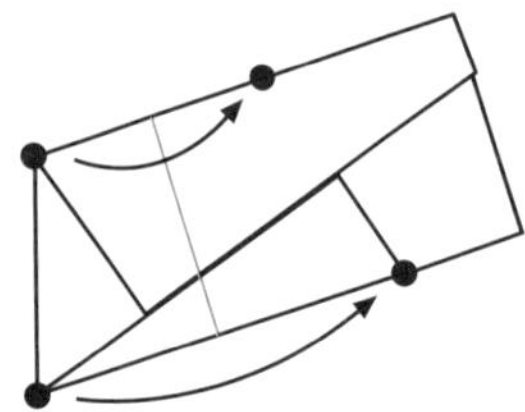

4.2 _ 5
Finally, fold the left-hand edge to the centre point, bringing the two pairs of black dots together.

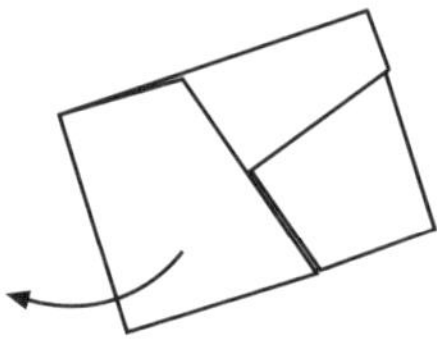

4.2 _ 6
This is the basic form of the envelope, but poorly locked. Note that all the corners are 90 degrees. Unfold the left-hand edge.

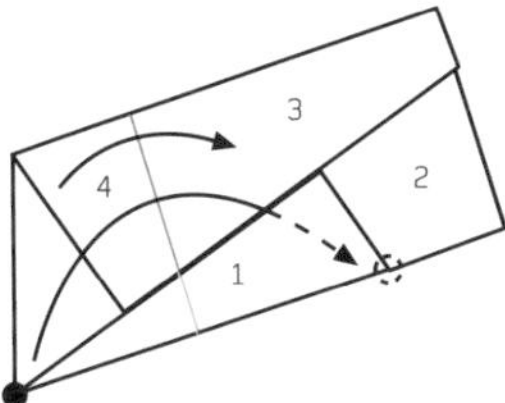

4.2 _ 7
This manoeuvre is the same as the one made in the random envelope, above. If you have not made the random envelope, it is recommended that you do so before attempting this step (see page 54). Count back to the first edge that was folded, marked with a '1'. Pull it open a little and force the corner with the black dot up inside it, to the position of the hollow circle.

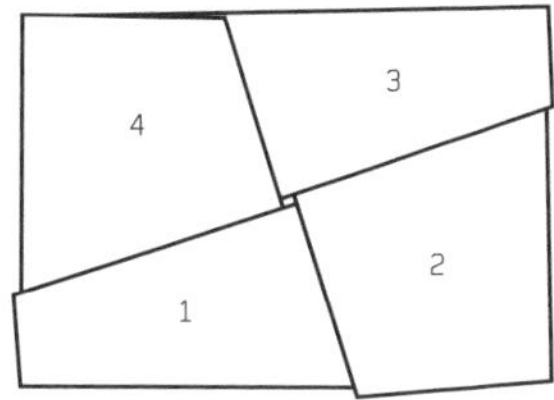

4.2 _ 8
This is the completed angled envelope.

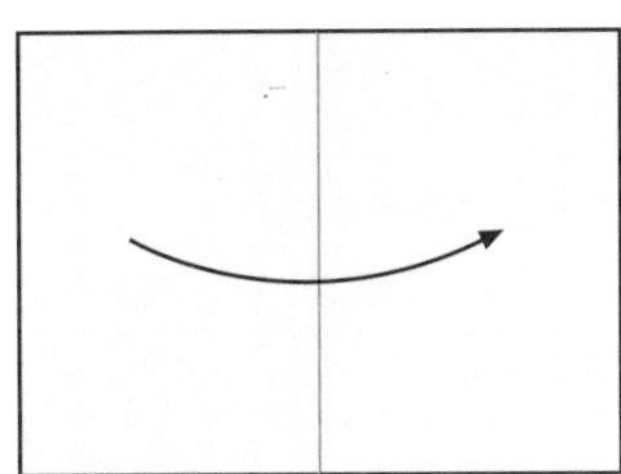

4.2 _ 9
If there is something you want to put into the envelope, such as a letter, invitation or flyer, fold a sheet of A4 in half …

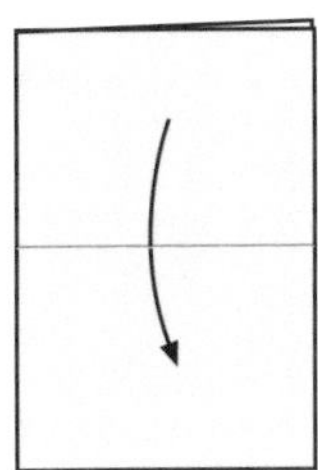

4.2 _ 10
… then in half again …

4.2 _ 11
… and notice how it will fit within the envelope, with a gap of a few millimetres all the way around it. The envelope is a little bigger than A6.

4.3 A4 Wrap

The special 1:√2 proportions of A4 paper were well explored in the pyramids (see page 46). Another example of the beautiful geometry hidden within the A4 is explored here with this simple wrap, developed further in the next project, the Japanese envelope.

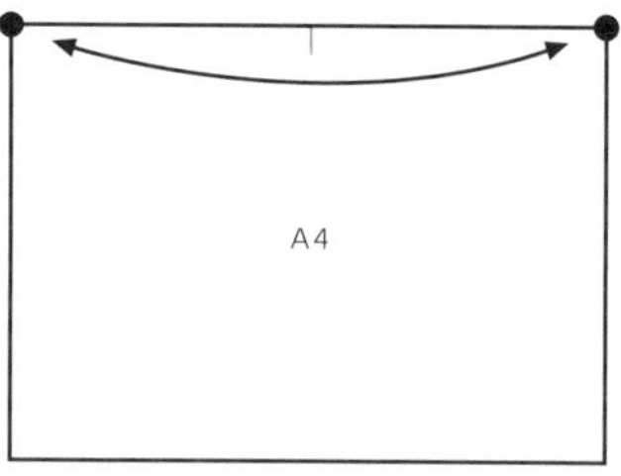

4.3 _ 1
Fold dot to dot, but only pinch the top edge.

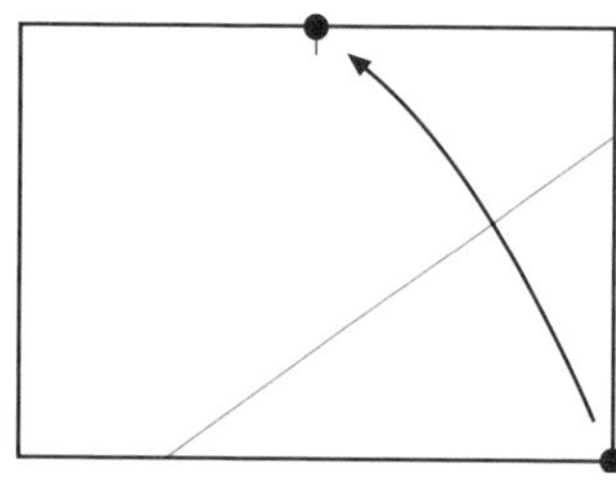

4.3 _ 2
Fold dot to dot.

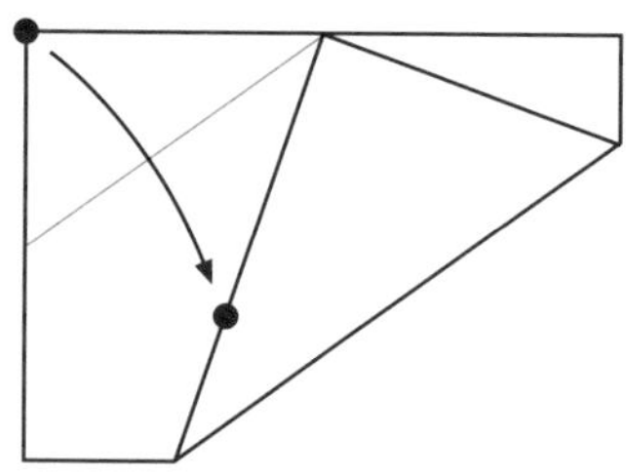

4.3 _ 3
Again, fold dot to dot. These shapes seem very random, but after this fold the geometry is very satisfying.

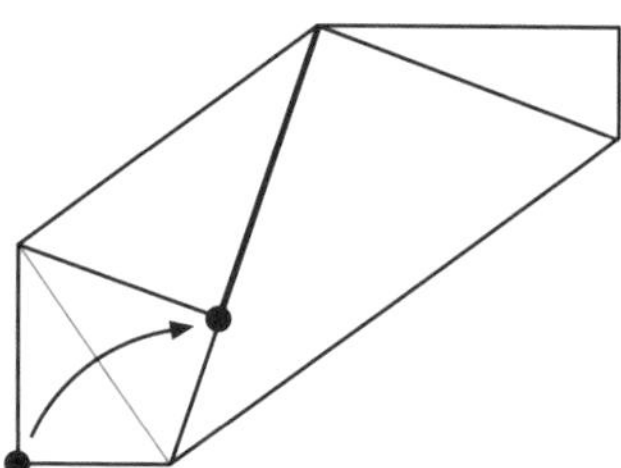

4.3 _ 4
Again, fold dot to dot. Note how the corner of the A4 will fold in to exactly fill the space!

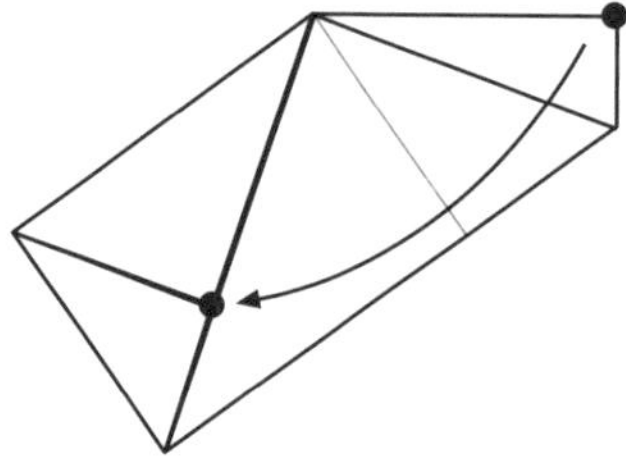

4.3 _ 5
Again, fold dot to dot, bringing three corners of the A4 together.

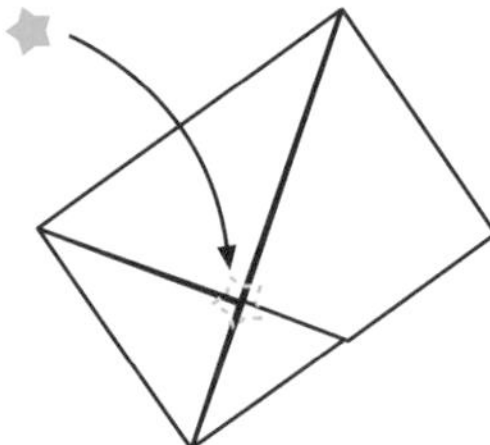

4.3 _ 6
This is the completed wrap. The lock is not strong, so if you want to place something inside, secure the loose corners with a sticker ...

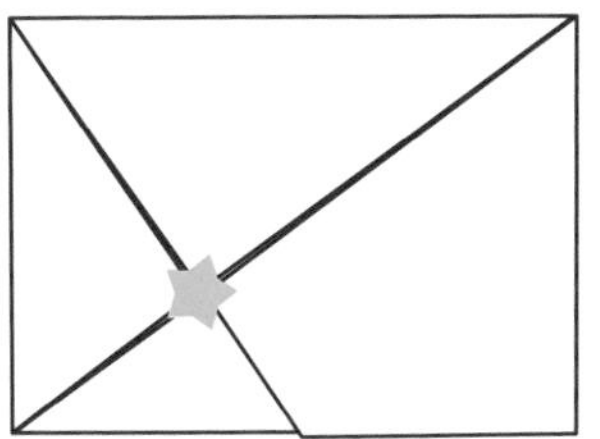

4.3 _ 7
... like this.

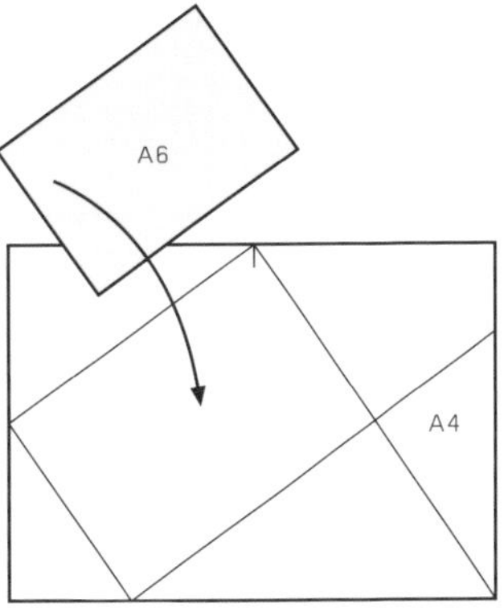

4.3 _ 8
An A4 sheet folded down to A6, or an A6 postcard, will fit nicely into the envelope ...

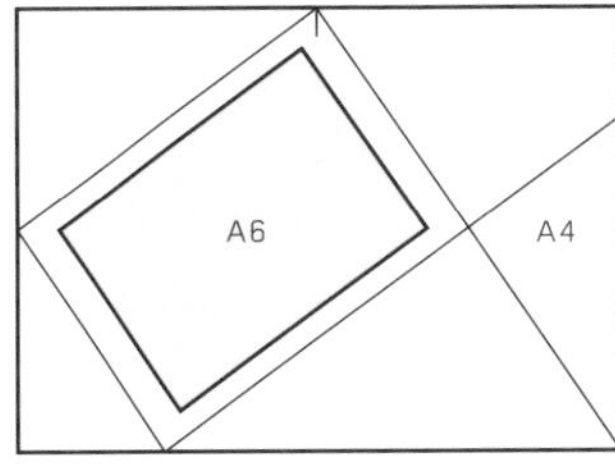

4.3 _ 9
... like this. The design is a masterpiece of simplicity and elegance, more 'discovered' in the paper than 'created' from it.

4.4 Japanese Envelope

This design is a continuation of the previous design, the A4 Wrap. It is described as 'Japanese' because it was first collected there. The unique aspect of its design is the ingenious use of a postage stamp to hold it closed, a feature not only wholly functional but also very charming.

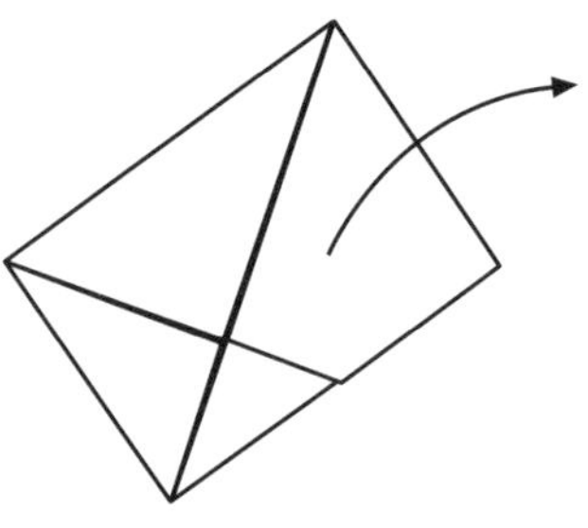

4.4 _ 1
Begin with the A4 wrap (see page 58). Unfold the right-hand flap.

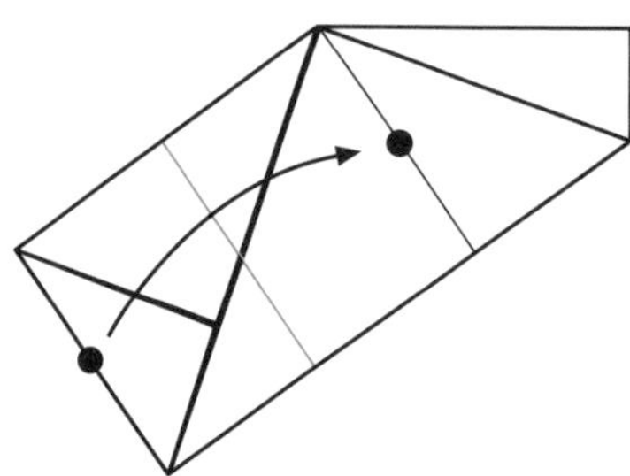

4.4 _ 2
Fold dot to dot.

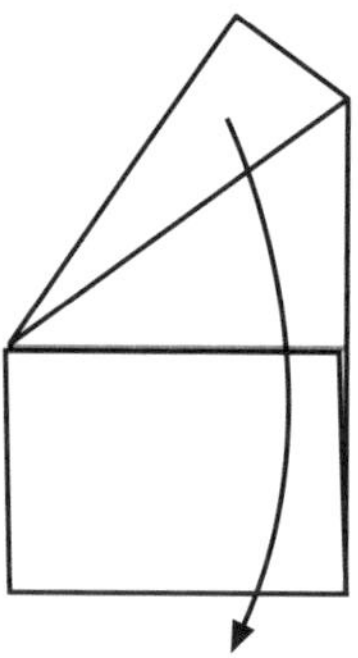

4.4 _ 3
Rotate the envelope to the position shown here, then refold the crease opened in step 1.

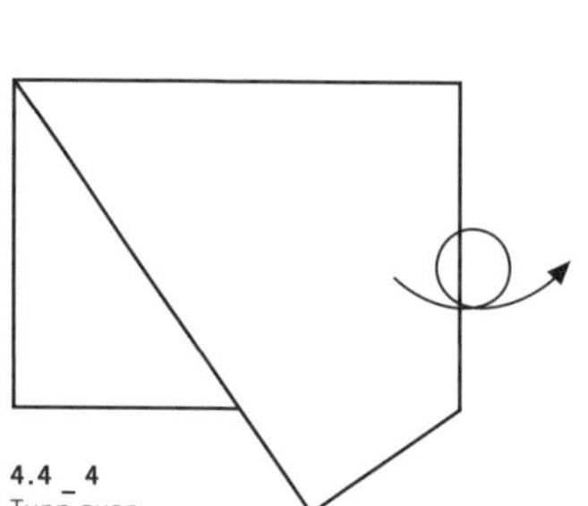

4.4 _ 4
Turn over.

4.4 _ 5
Fold the triangle over, flush with the top edge.

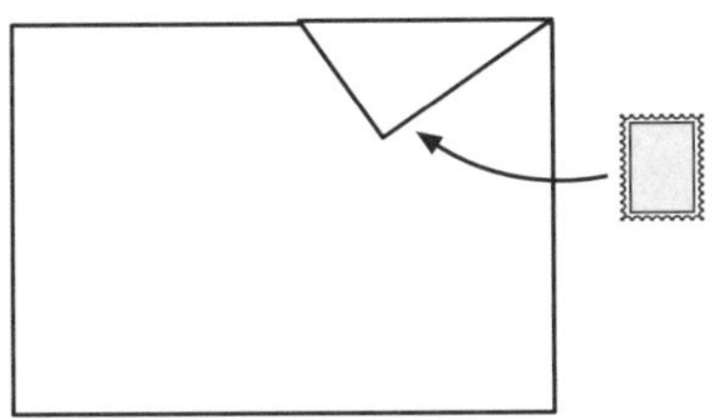

4.4 _ 6
Secure the corner of the triangle with a postage stamp!

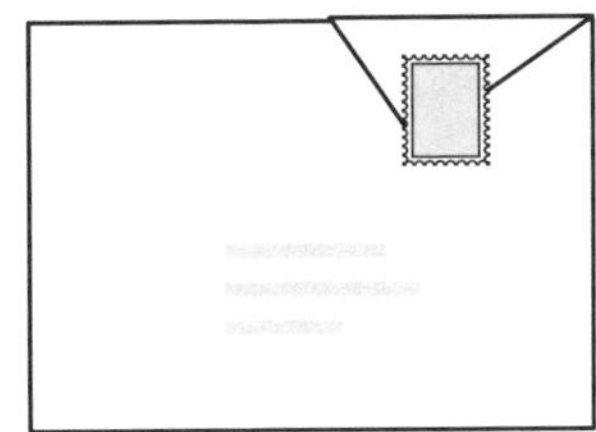

4.4 _ 7
This is the completed Japanese envelope. If the envelope is not being mailed, the corner can be secured with a sticker, or even left unsecured.

4.5 French Envelope

If the Japanese envelope (above) is poetic, this design, believed to be of French origin, can be described as prosaic. It is particularly easy to remember and will still lock, even if folded quite roughly. For these reasons, it is a favourite with children.

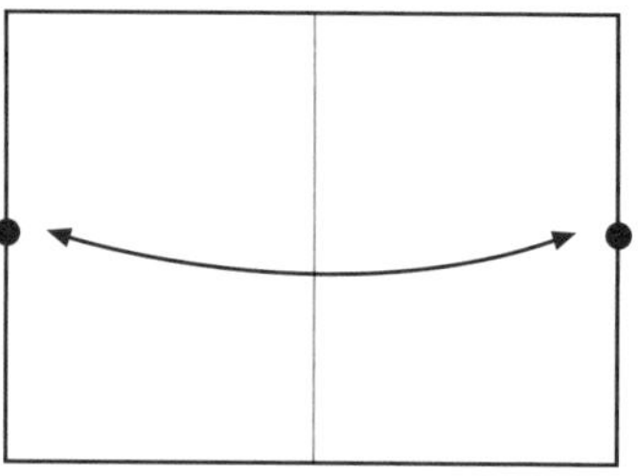

4.5 _ 1
Begin with an A4 sheet. Fold in half, dot to dot, then unfold.

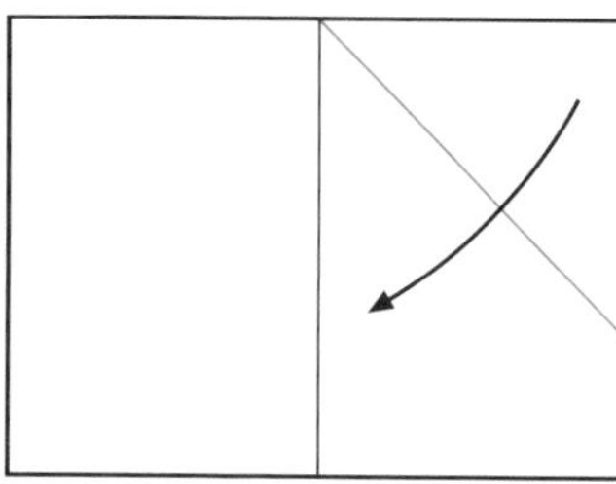

4.5 _ 2
Fold in the top right corner to the centre line. If you fold in the top left corner instead, the 'bites' out of two of the corners on the final envelope will be at the other corners.

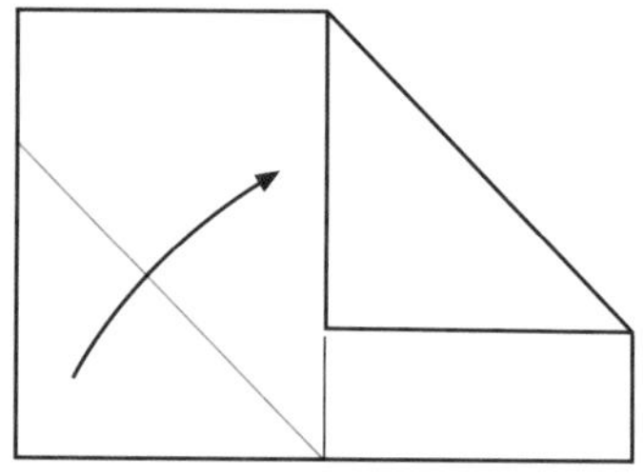

4.5 _ 3
Fold in the opposite corner to the top right corner, namely, the bottom left corner.

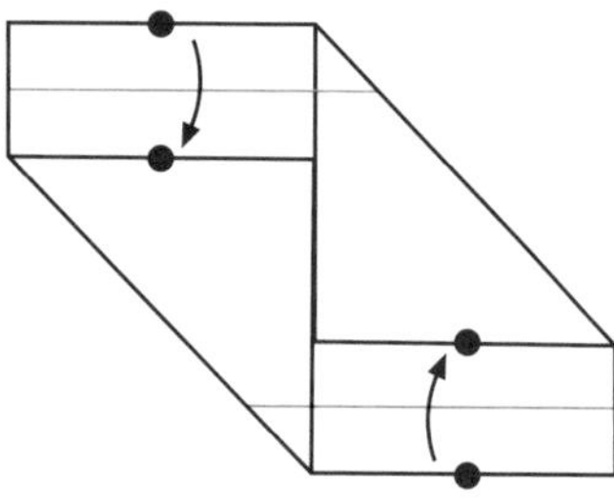

4.5 _ 4
Fold twice dot to dot, as shown. Folding the edges of the A4 to the edges of the triangles.

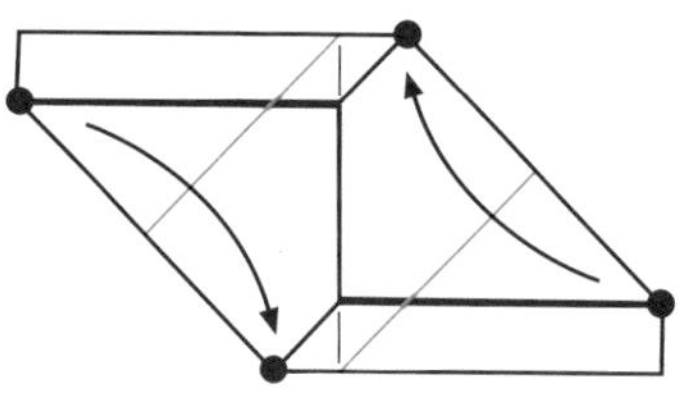

4.5 _ 5
Fold dot to dot, twice.

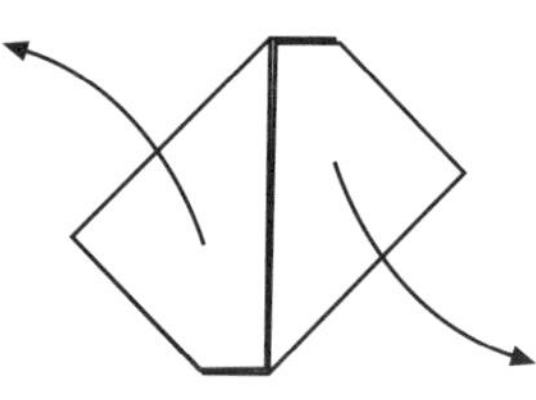

4.5 _ 6
Open the folds made in step 5.

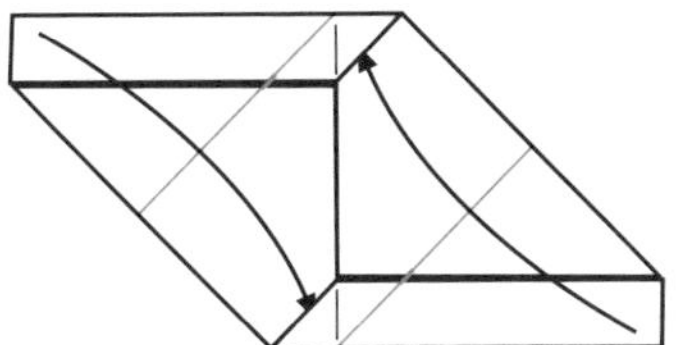

4.5 _ 7
Refold the folds made in step 5, but this time, tuck the corners under the sloping edges, thus trapping them in place ...

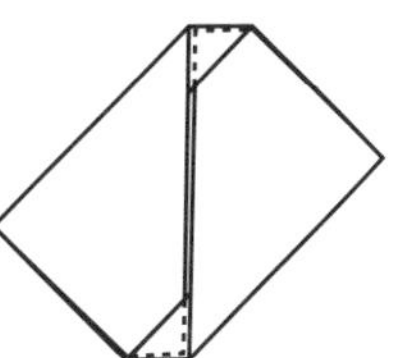

4.5 _ 8
... like this.

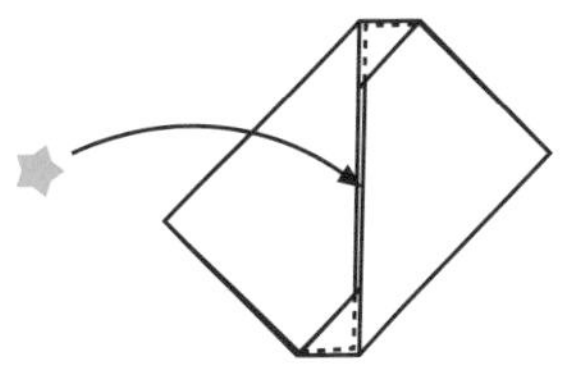

4.5 _ 9
You may wish to secure the flaps with a sticker, though this is not essential.

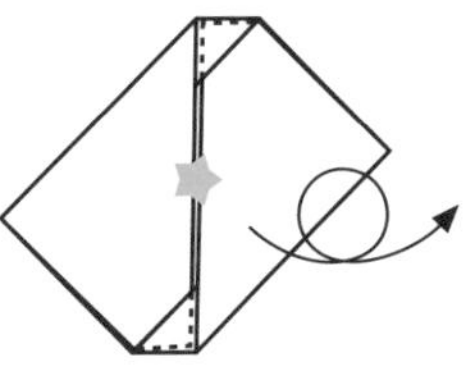

4.5 _ 10
Turn over.

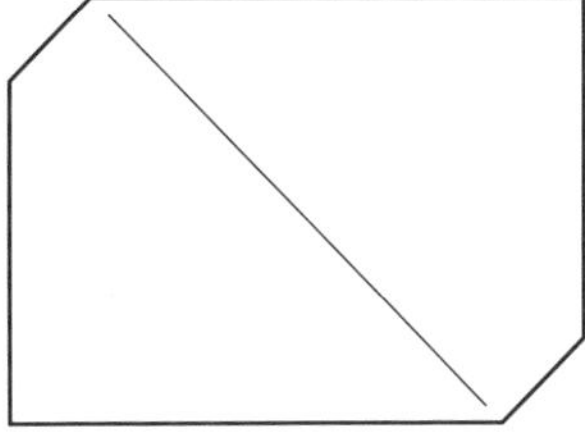

4.5 _ 11
The French envelope is complete.

4.6 Square CD Envelope

We have all been given a CD, and not had anything to put it in for safekeeping. The solution is usually to wrap it roughly in a piece of paper, as though packing a sandwich. Here is an alternative method for wrapping a CD, being safer, more secure and of course, more elegant.

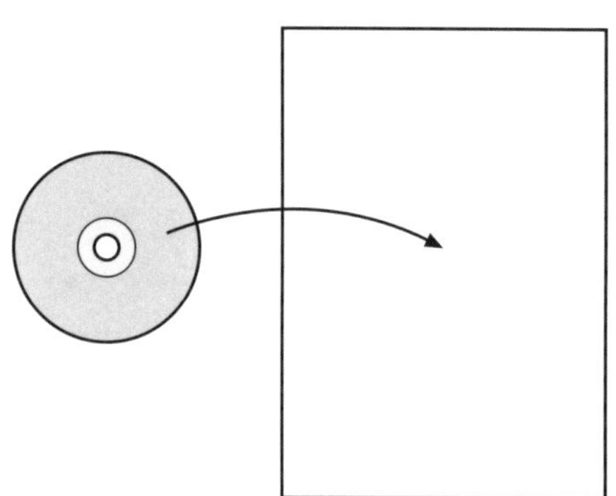

4.6 _ 1
Put a CD onto a sheet of A4.

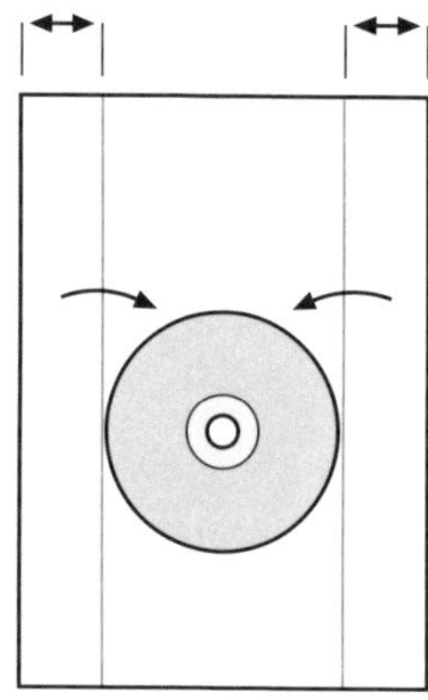

4.6 _ 2
Move it around until the spaces to the left and right are equal, though it is not crucial if they are a little unequal. Fold the long edges of the A4 over the CD.

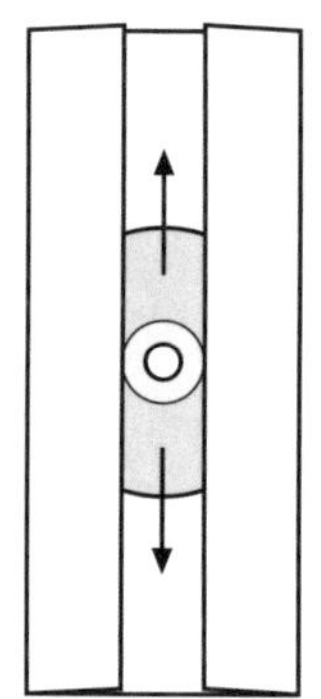

4.6 _ 3
Slide the CD up and down inside its sleeve, until ...

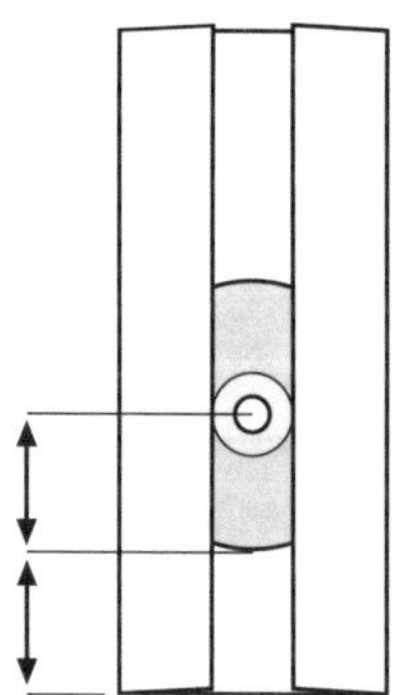

4.6 _ 4
... the distance from the centre of the CD to the bottom of the CD is the same as from the bottom of the CD to the bottom of the A4.

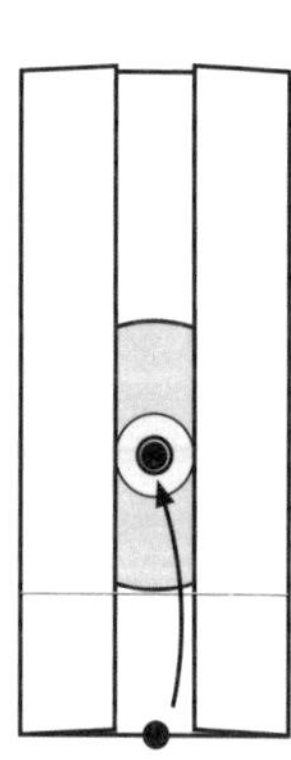

4.6 _ 5
Then, fold up the bottom edge of the A4. It should touch the middle of the CD.

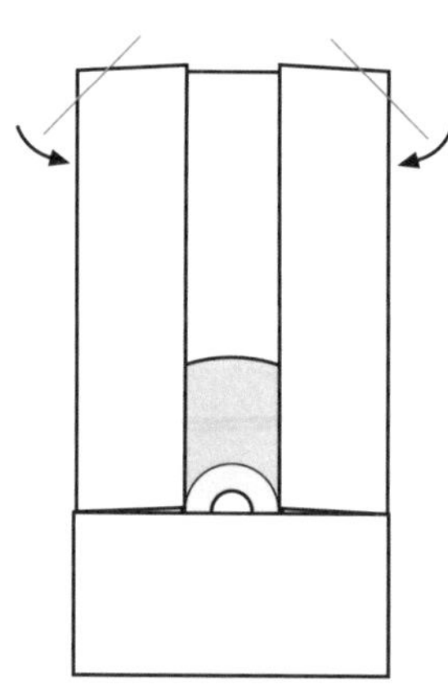

4.6 _ 6
Turn in the top corners, just a little.

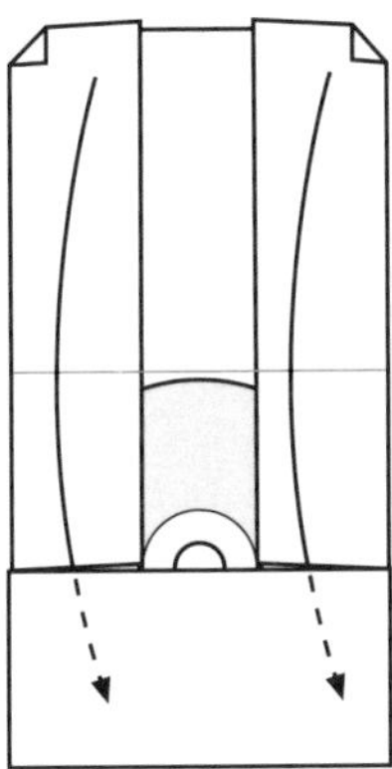

4.6 _ 7
Fold down the top edge of the A4, making a crease across the top of the CD. Tuck the top edge of the A4 into the two hidden pockets, left and right ...

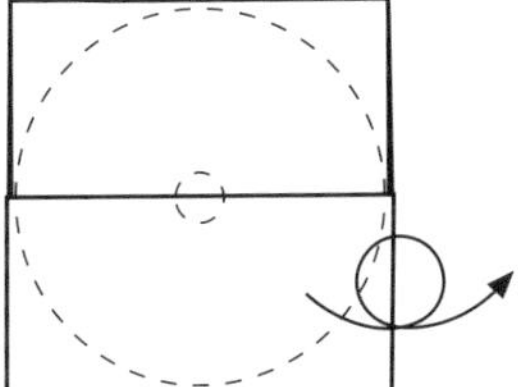

4.6 _ 8
... like this. Turn over.

4.6 _ 9
The square CD envelope is complete. This front side is pleasingly clear of all folded edges, allowing any surface graphics to be applied, or printed, with ease.

4.7 Engineered Envelope

All the previous examples in the chapter have been origami envelopes made from A4 paper. This final envelope is engineered. Although clearly more time-consuming to make by hand and more expensive to make if die-cut, it is also stronger and more versatile than any origami envelope.

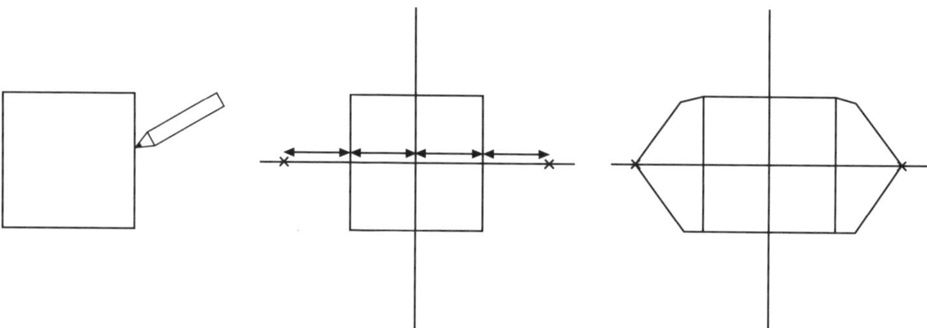

4.7 _ 1
On a sheet of 250–300gsm card, draw a square the size of the envelope you want to make.

4.7 _ 2
Draw centre lines through the square. Extend the lines left and right, marking the same distance outside the square as inside to the middle of the square.

4.7 _ 3
Use those marks as a guide and draw two identical shapes, as shown. Note that the short edges at the top are not horizontal.

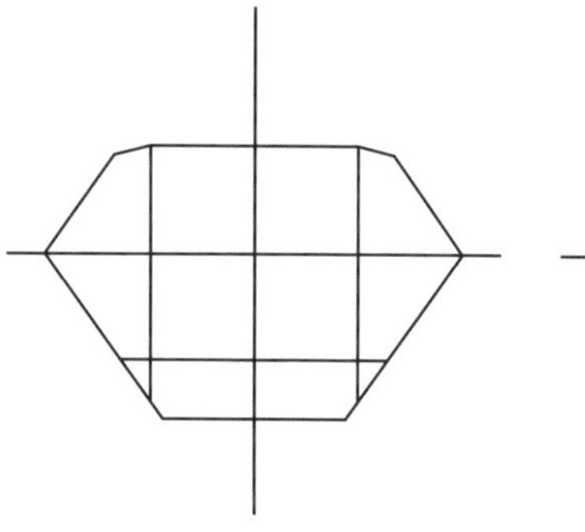

4.7 _ 4
Extend the long sloping lines downwards and create a new shape exactly as shown.

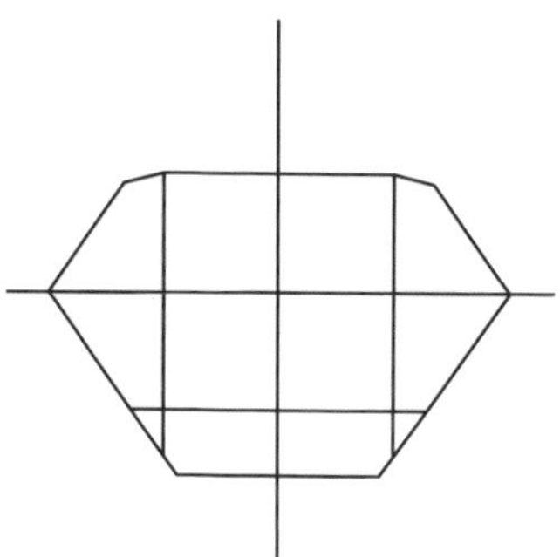

4.7 _ 5
Take note of the shaded shapes.

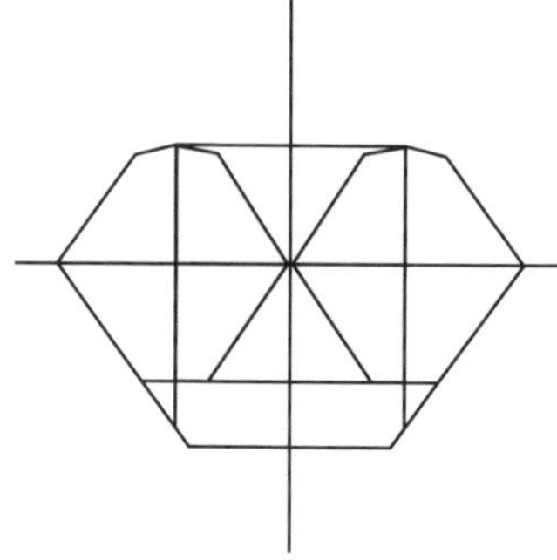

4.7 _ 6
Mirror the shaded shapes into the square. They should meet in the middle of the square.

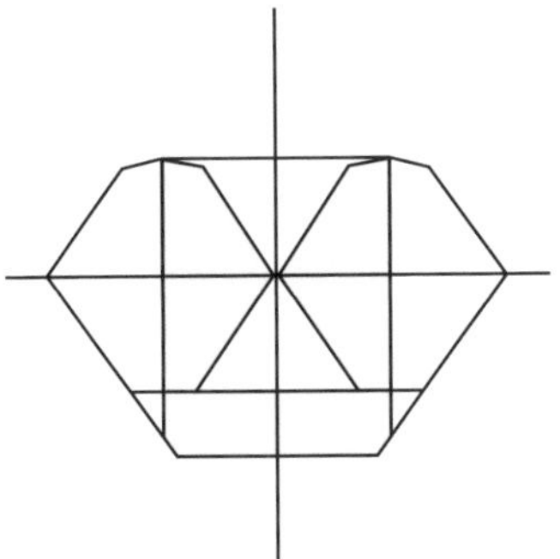

4.7 _ 7
Now take note of the shaded shape at the bottom.

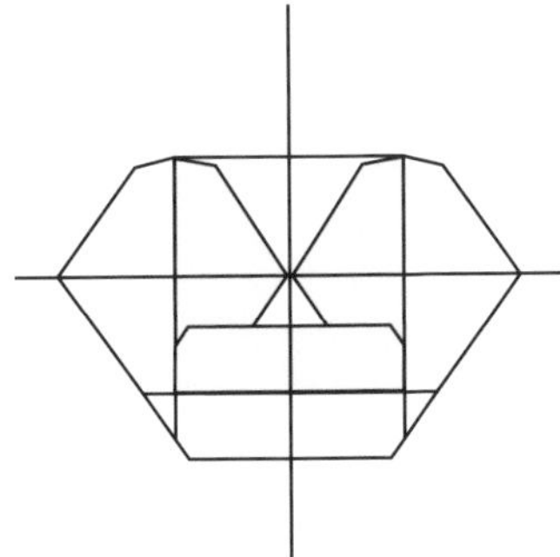

4.7 _ 8
Mirror that shape upwards into the square.

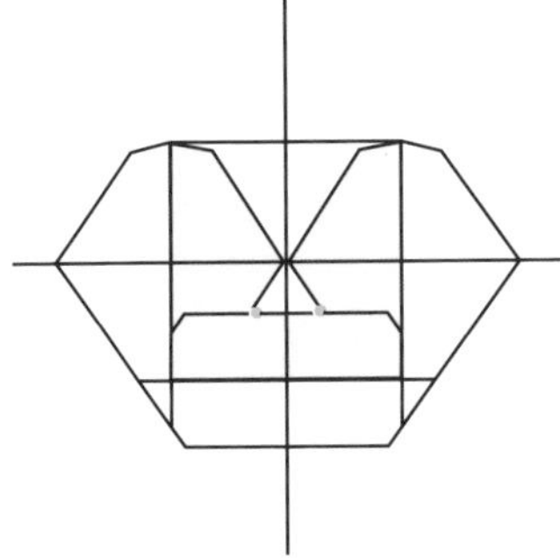

4.7 _ 9
Make two dots (shown in orange) exactly where shown.

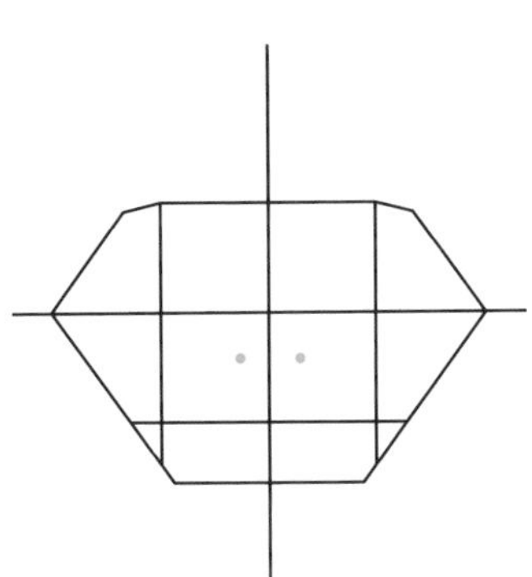

4.7 _ 10
Erase any drawing inside the square, but maintain the positions of the dots.

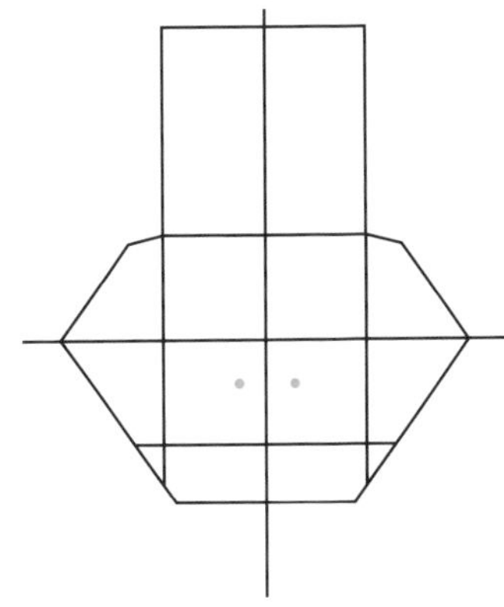

4.7 _ 11
Draw a square of the same size above the existing square.

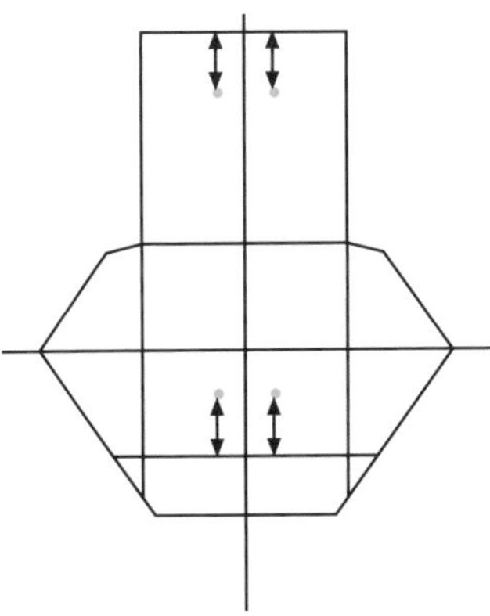

4.7 _ 12
Measure the distance of the two dots from the bottom edge of the lower square, then draw two more dots the same distance from the top edge of the upper square.

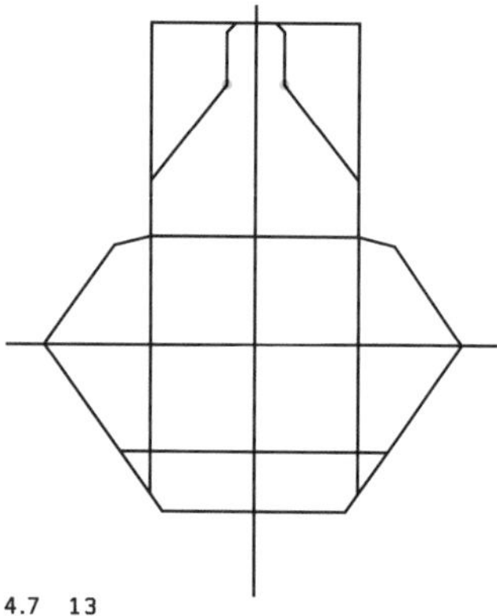

4.7 _ 13
Use the two new dots as a guide to draw the 'roof with a chimney' shape shown here.

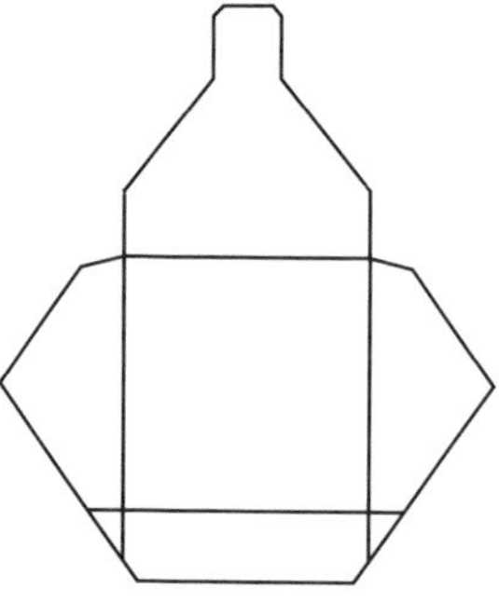

4.7 _ 14
Erase the lines of the upper square. This is the final shape of the envelope. Cut it out from the card.

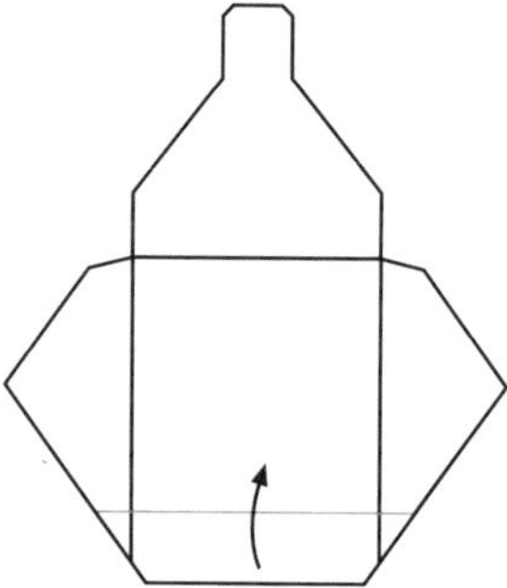

4.7 _ 15
The envelope can now be closed. Fold up the bottom edge.

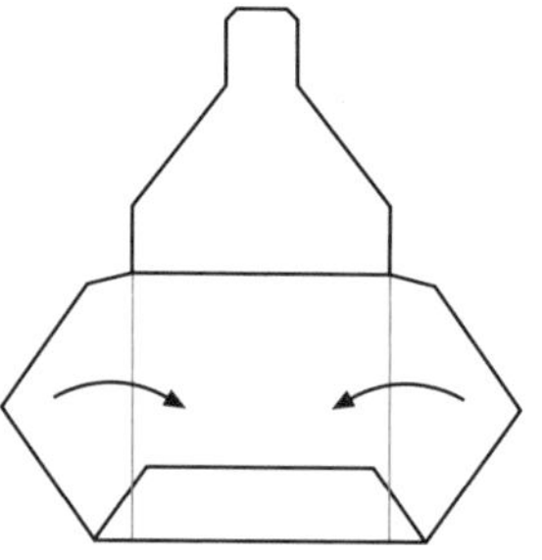

4.7 _ 16
Then, fold in the left and right corners.

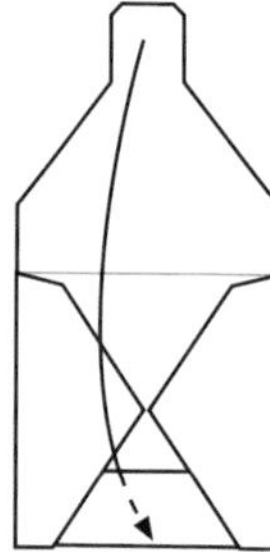

4,7 _ 17
Finally, fold down the top flap, tucking it into the pocket near the bottom edge. The envelope will lock shut.

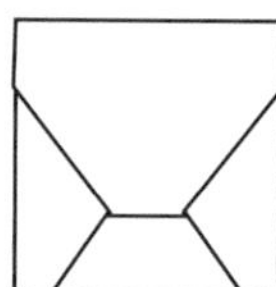

4.7 _ 18
This is the completed engineered envelope.

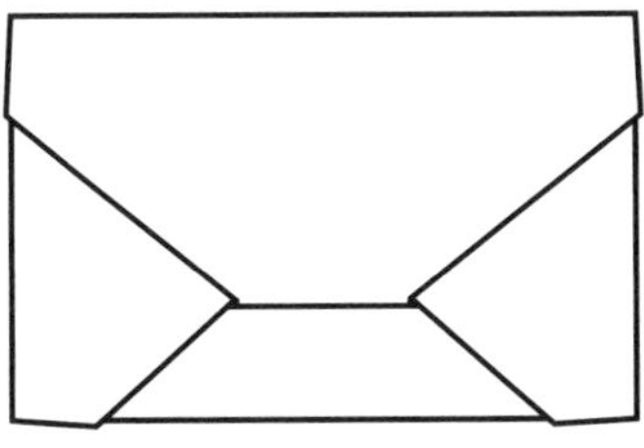

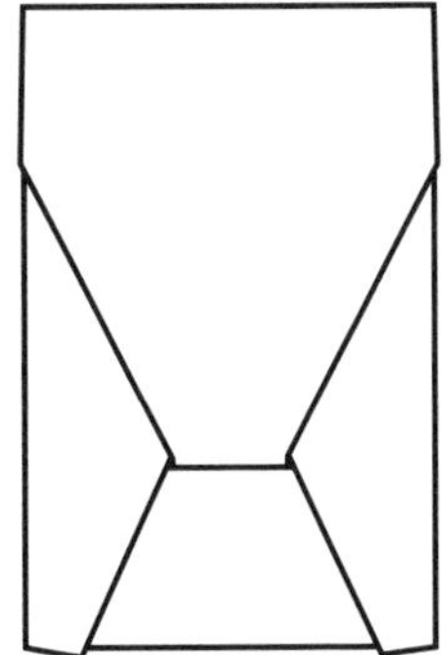

4.7 _ 19
Rectangular envelopes can be made as easily as the square envelope explained here. Simply follow the same method of construction, but instead of starting in step 1 with a square, start with a rectangle of your chosen size and shape.

05:

PUZZLES AND ILLUSIONS

Introduction

We all love a good puzzle or illusion. They make us pause and think, ask us to question what we consider possible and give us a few moments of personal contemplation.

As a type of promotional device, they have a great advantage because they invite prolonged interaction. They invite people to play with them, to question and to problem-solve ... and by doing so, encourage a greater involvement with what is presented on the object (a message, information, etc.). In turn, this makes what is presented more memorable, which of course, is the point of it all.

Puzzles and illusions can take many diverse forms. Those presented in the chapter have been chosen for their quality, fun appeal and the ease with which surface graphics can be applied. However, it is recommended that before creating a final design, you test it on as many people as possible to see if they can solve the puzzle or make the illusion. If they can't, you will need to make it easier in some way. If it seems too easy, complicate it slightly. There is little point in making something that is either too difficult or too easy, as it will only make people frustrated or not engage them sufficiently to make it worthwhile. It's a fine balance and it needs to be struck correctly.

5.1 Impossible Illusion

This is a true classic. It's very simple to make but utterly baffling. Even the smartest people will have difficulty remaking it, given paper and scissors. The upright rectangle appears to have grown from nowhere. It can be flattened left or right, but inexplicably creates a double layer when flat. Simply wonderful!

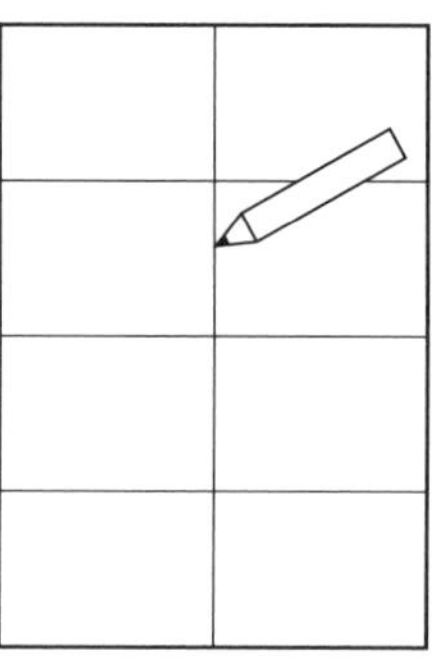

5.1 _ 1
With A4 paper or card, draw lines that divide the sheet into eight rectangles.

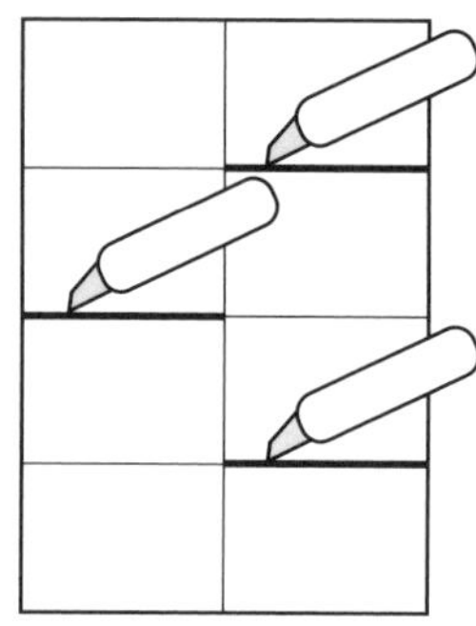

5.1 _ 2
Make three cuts, as shown.

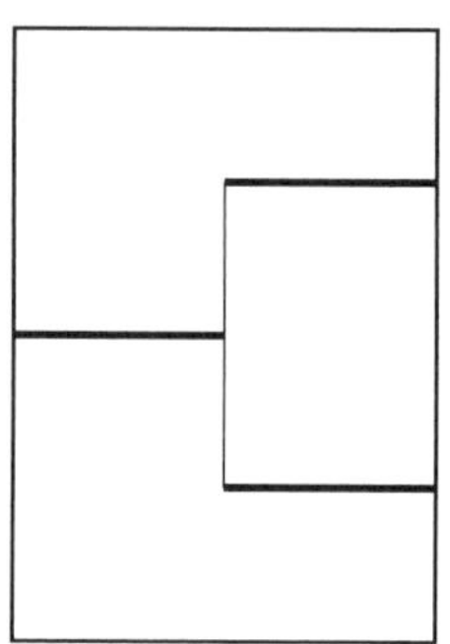

5.1 _ 3
Erase some of the lines.

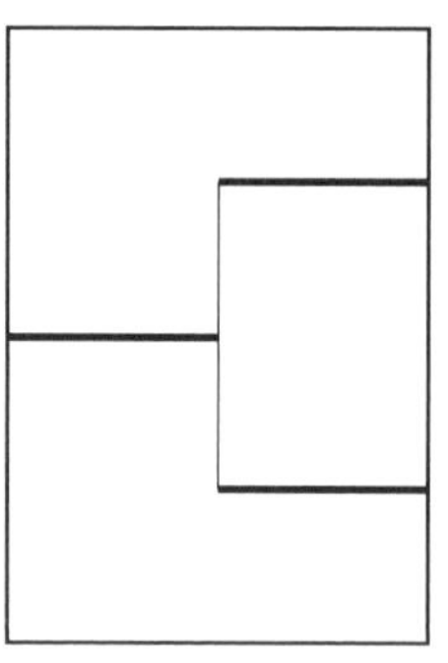

5.1 _ 4
Make a fold between the top and bottom cuts. Be very careful not to extend the fold towards the top and bottom edges of the paper.

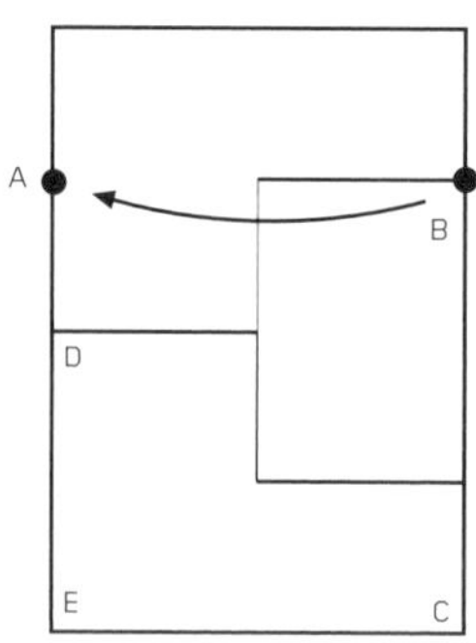

5.1 _ 5
Take note of the letter corners (you could even write them on the paper). Pick the paper up off the table. Make a short valley fold as shown, so that edge BC rises up towards you and edge DE rotates behind. Corner B will rotate towards A ...

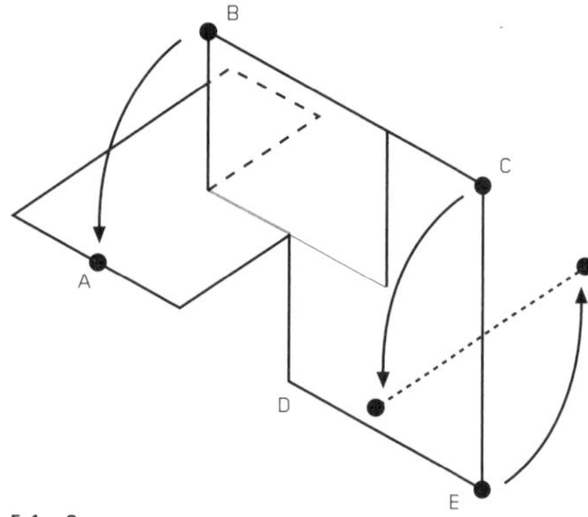

5.1 _ 6
... like this. The paper is now three-dimensional. Flatten the paper so that B touches A and C and E rotate to the horizontal ...

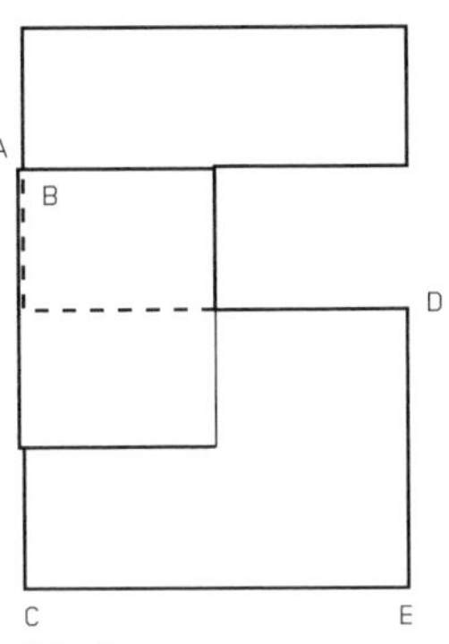

5.1 _ 7
... like this. Note how B is touching A and how corners C and E have swapped positions!

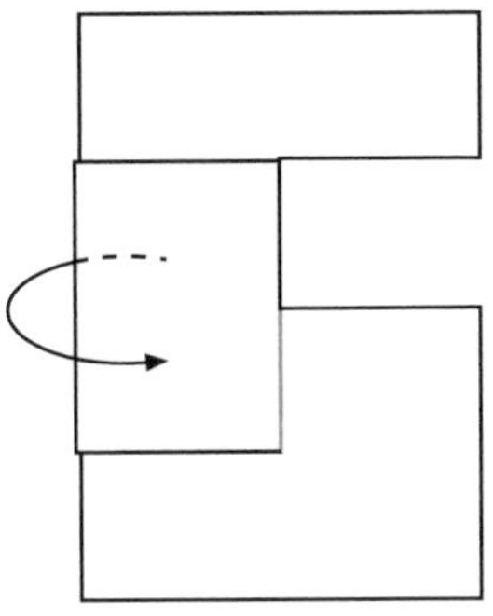

5.1 _ 8
Lift up the shaded rectangle so that it stands perpendicular to the remainder of the paper ...

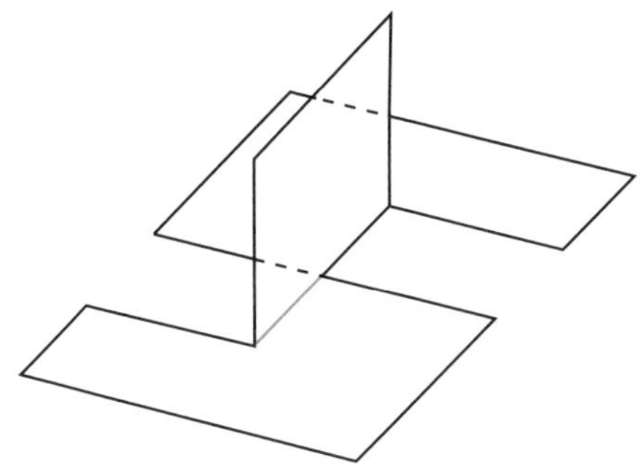

5.1 _ 9
... like this. There are many ways to incorporate printed materials onto the sheet. It can even be bound into a multi-page document. The placement and shape of the cuts can change and the illusion can be repeated many times down a long strip.

5.2 Negative/Positive Cube Illusion

Here's another wonderfully simple idea, but one which is also rather spooky. The cube appears to be a regular convex cube, but is actually concave. This means that when you move your eye, the perspective of the faces will shift the opposite way to what you expect. Your eye – and brain – are totally confused by what you see!

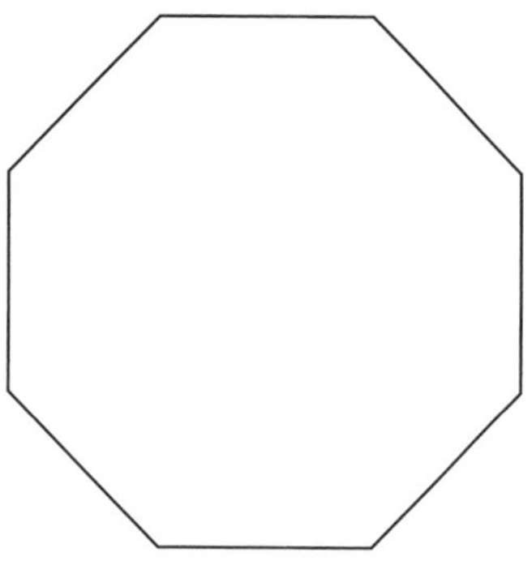

5.2 _ 1
Using card, make a regular octagon about 15cm across.

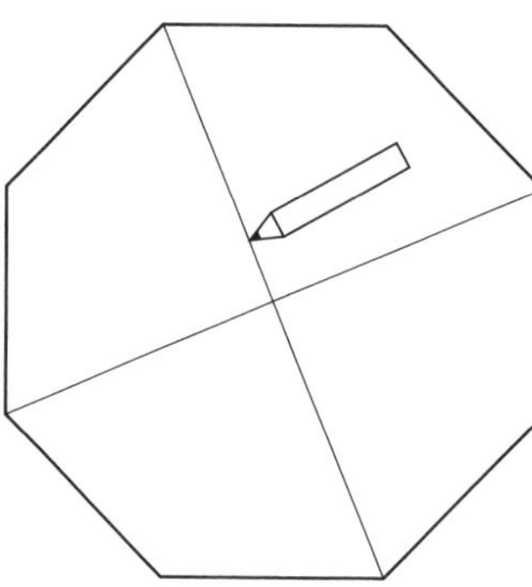

5.2 _ 2
Draw two lines perpendicular to each other that connect opposite corners.

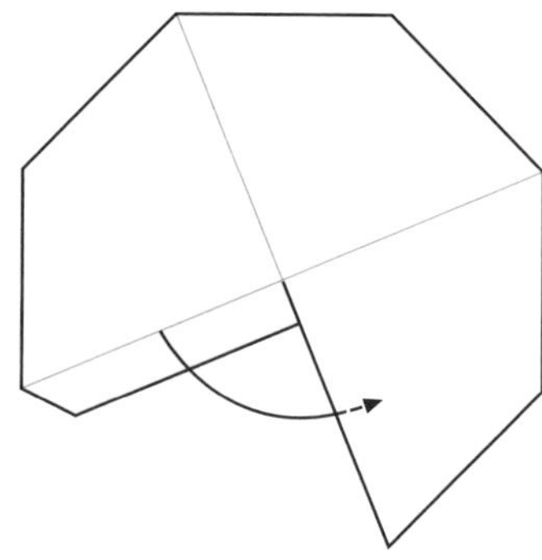

5.2 _ 3
Cut out one of the quarters, but leave a small glue tab. Make three valley folds. Apply glue to the tab and stick it to the neighbouring edge. The tab goes behind, out of sight.

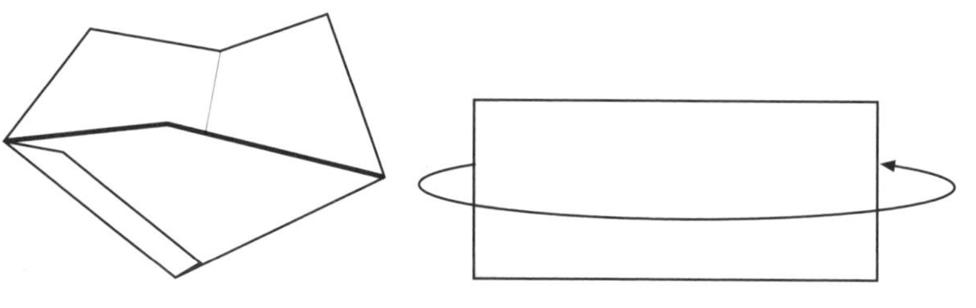

5.2 _ 4
This 'dish' is the result.

5.2 _ 5
Take another piece of card, the same width as the octagon and about as high as one side-length of the octagon. Glue one end, then bend it into a cylinder, gluing the ends together ...

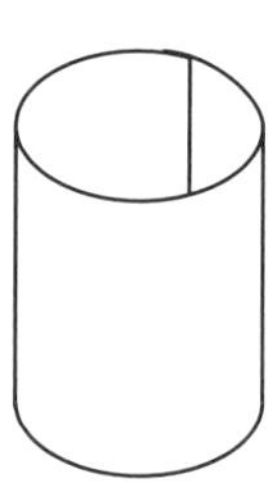

5.2 _ 6
... like this.

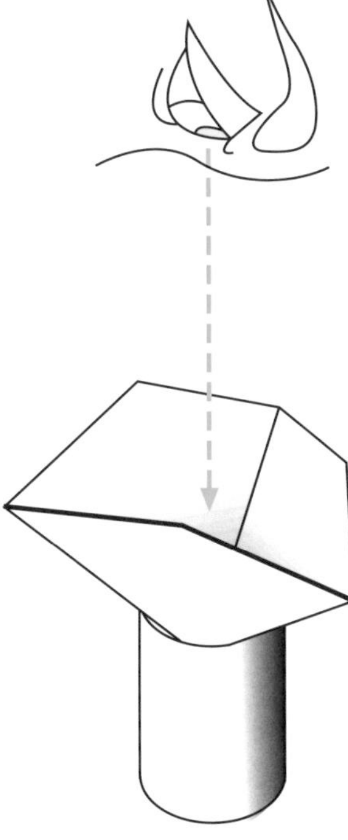

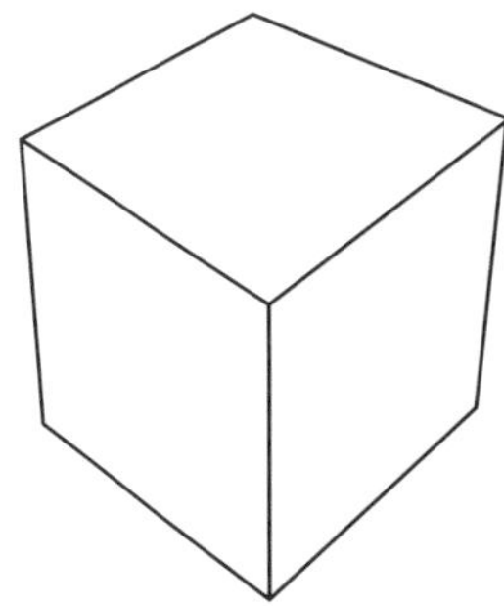

5.2 _ 7
Here's how to see the negative-positive effect.

Place the cylinder on the floor and place the cube level on top. Stand over it, looking straight down into the cube (the illustration shows an eye very close to the cube, but it's not necessary to be so close). Close one eye. After a little time, the negative cube will 'pop' and appear to be positive, like a solid cube. The illusion is extremely convincing! Move your head around to experience the weird perspectival effects.

5.2 _ 8
This is what the eye sees, first as a negative cube, then as a positive cube. The effect is easier to see if you rotate the cube in the light so that one face is darker than the others and there is no half-shadow cast across part of a face.

5.3 Tangrams

Most of us have at some time played with tangrams, a puzzle of Chinese origin in which a collection of seven geometric shapes can be rearranged from a square to create thousands of designs. Here are a few suggestions for tangram designs which may be used for marketing purposes.

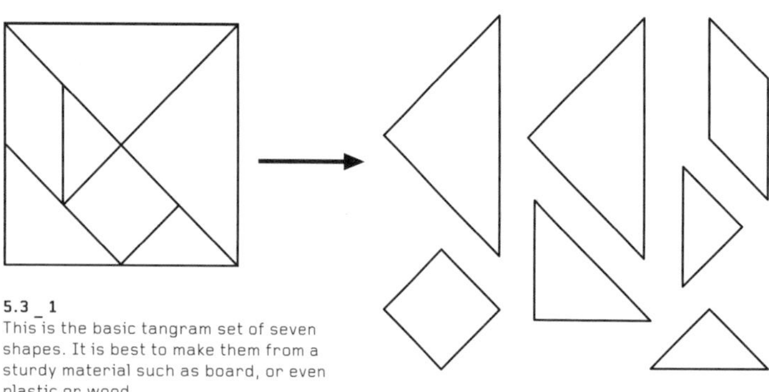

5.3 _ 1
This is the basic tangram set of seven shapes. It is best to make them from a sturdy material such as board, or even plastic or wood.

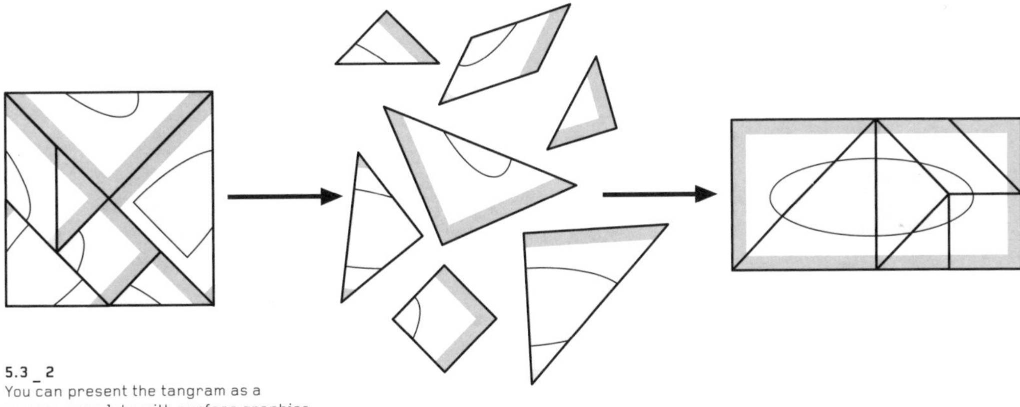

5.3 _ 2
You can present the tangram as a square, complete with surface graphics. Arranged as a square, the graphics make no sense, so the receiver has to rearrange the pieces to create another shape, in this case, a 2 x 1 rectangle. The graphics may be anything, such as an illustration, message or logo.

5.3 _ 3
However, not all tangram designs are appropriate for carrying surface graphics. Here's a particularly appealing design of someone with an umbrella. The umbrella, head and both feet are disconnected from the body, which means there is no continuity of the surface and thus, no continuity of the graphics. Someone trying to put the pieces together would not know where to put the five pieces disconnected from the body. So, a successful design must have all the pieces connecting edge to edge to create one continuous surface.

Tangram Designs

Here are some suggestions for designs to use. Of course, there are many others. If you're feeling adventurous, you could even try to create your own.

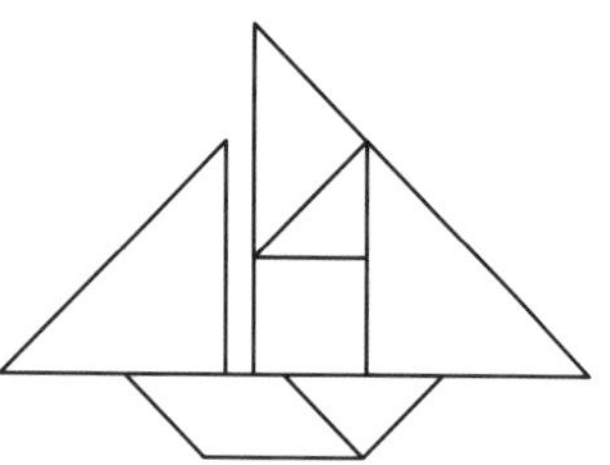

5.3 _ 4
Yacht
Suitable for sailing clubs, cruises ...

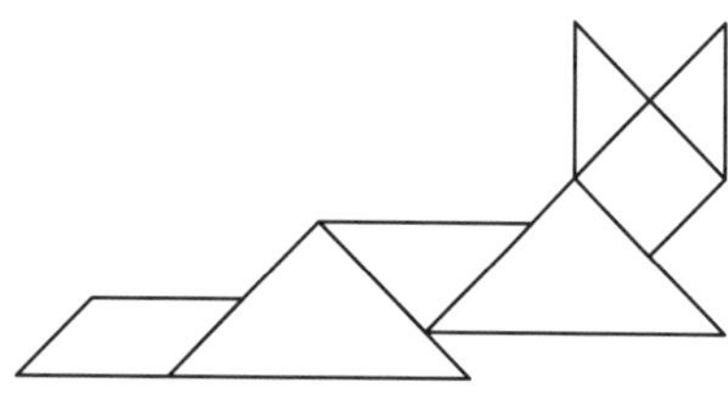
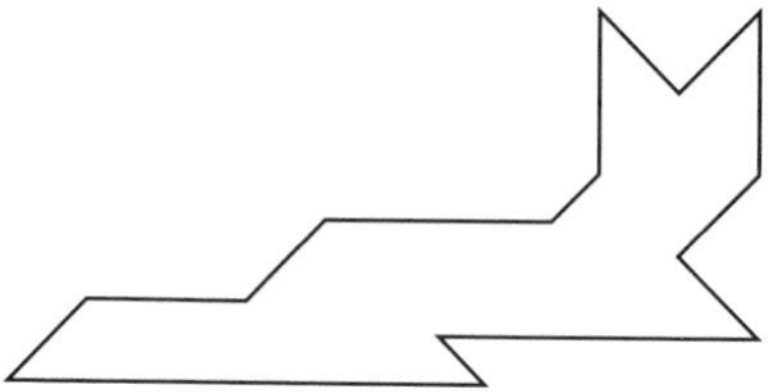

5.3 _ 5
Cat
Suitable for animal services, veterinarians, catteries ...

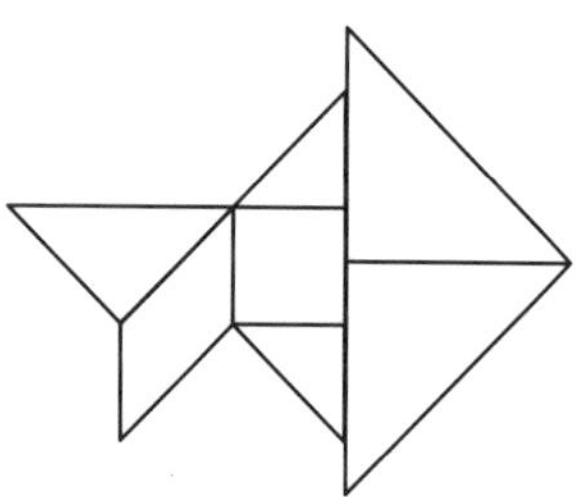
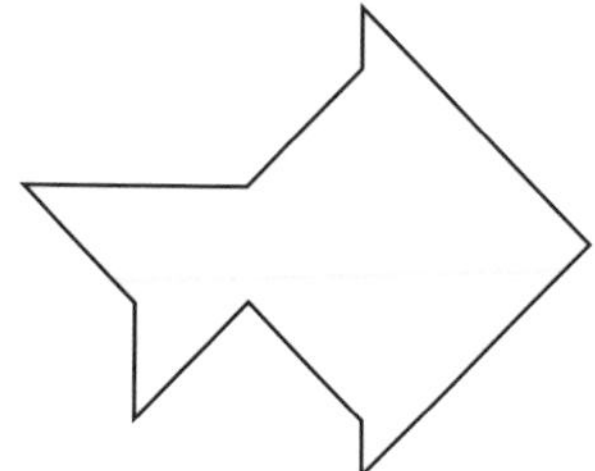

5.3 _ 6
Fish
Suitable for rod fishing, bait, aquarium services, fishmongers ...

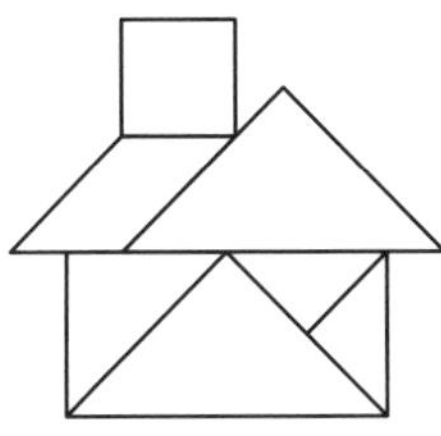

5.3 _ 7
House
Suitable for estate agents, valuers, builders, tradesmen, decorators ...

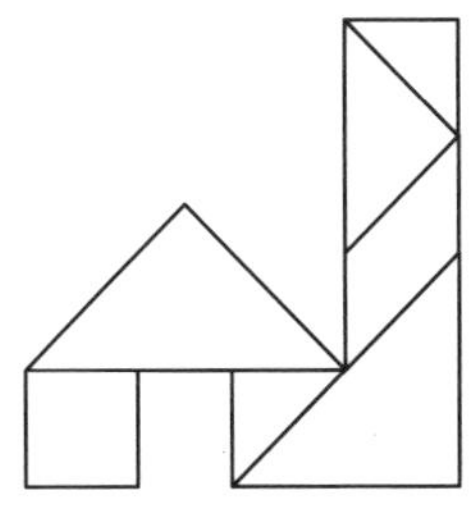

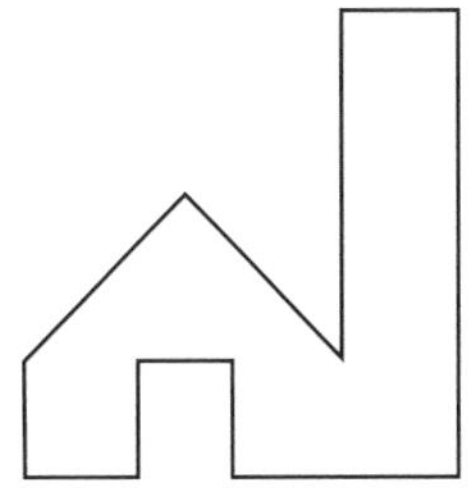

5.3 _ 8
Factory
Suitable for manufacturers, estate agents ...

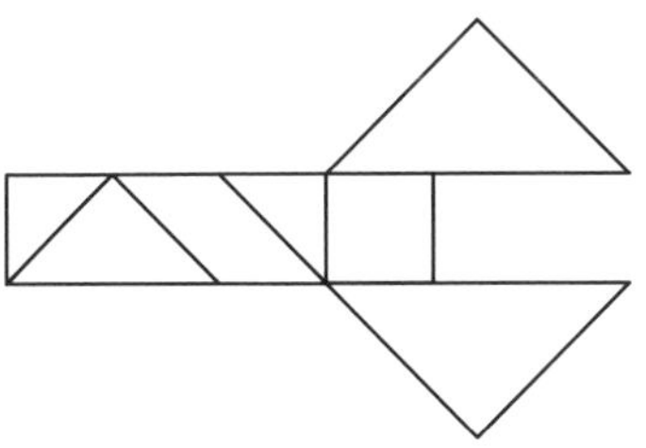

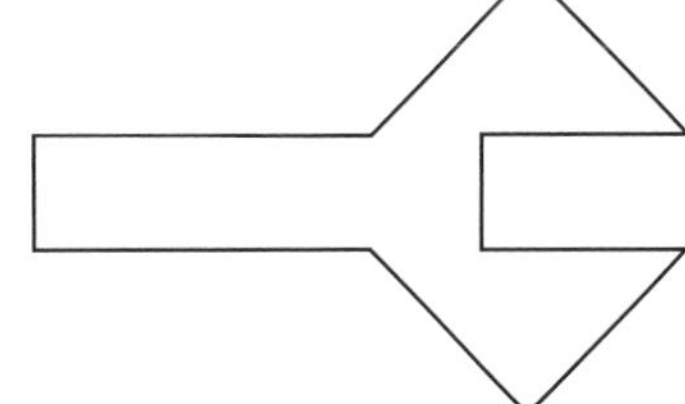

5.3 _ 9
Spanner
Suitable for mechanics, DIY ...

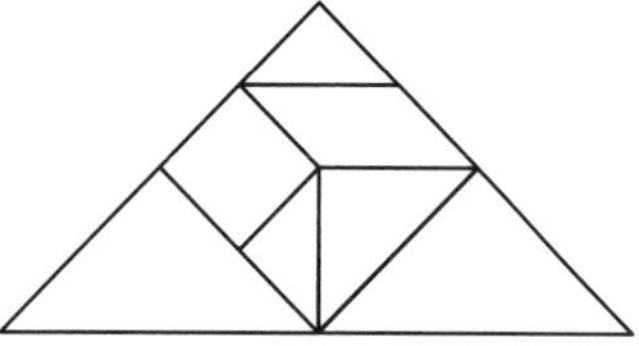
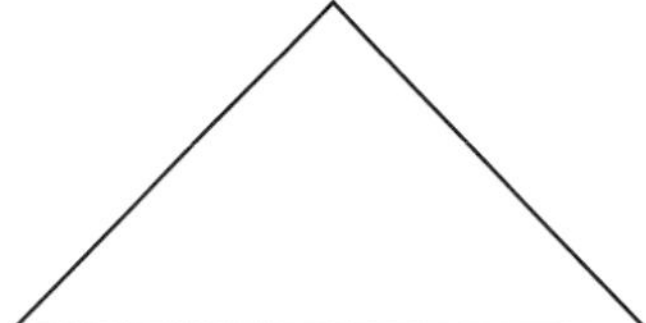

5.3 _ 10
Triangle
Suitable for mountaineering, sandwich making ...

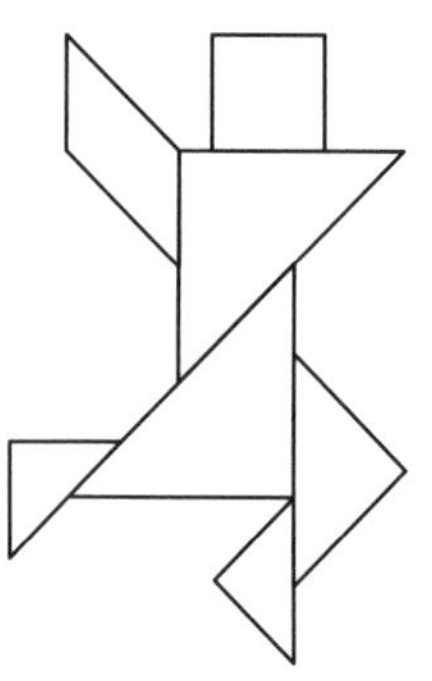
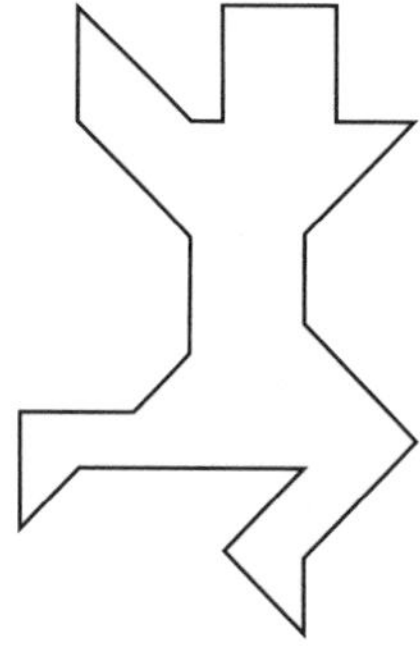

5.3 _ 11
Figure
Suitable for sports centres, keep fit, well-being ...

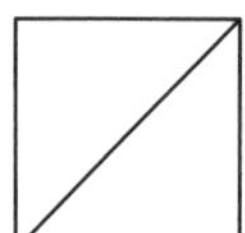
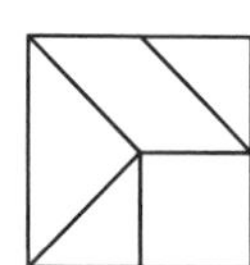
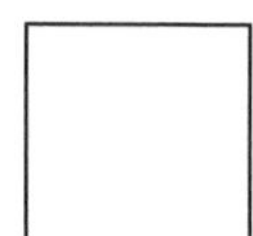
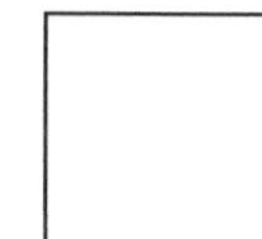

5.3 _ 12
Two Squares
Suitable for any activity involving separation or multiplying ...

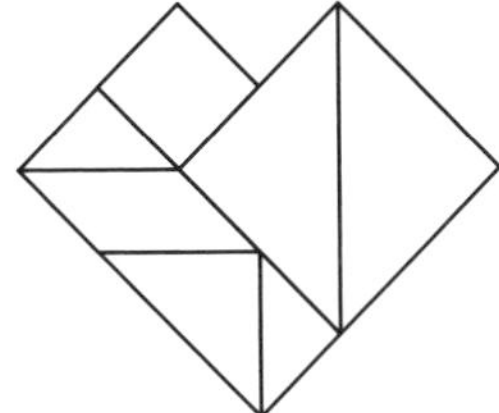
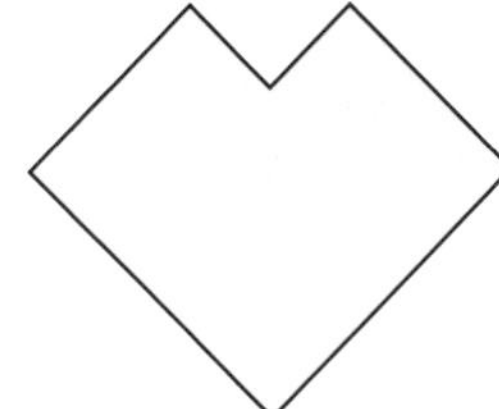

5.3 _ 13
Heart
Suitable for a singles club, romance, healthy heart activities...

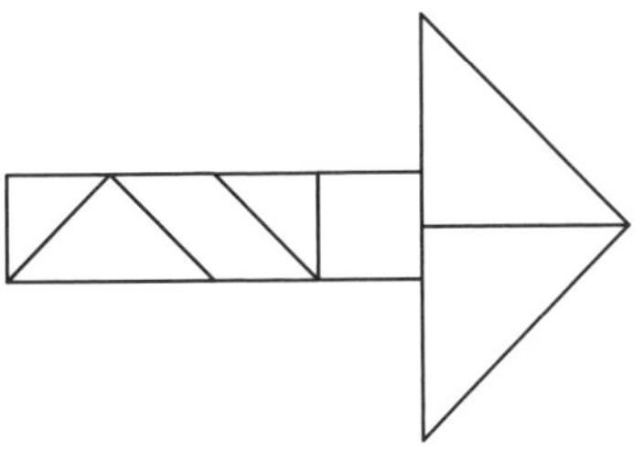
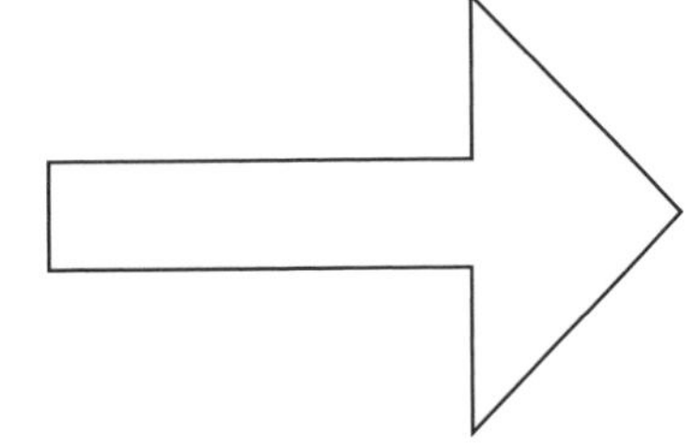

5.3 _ 14
Arrow
Suitable for travel, motivation ...

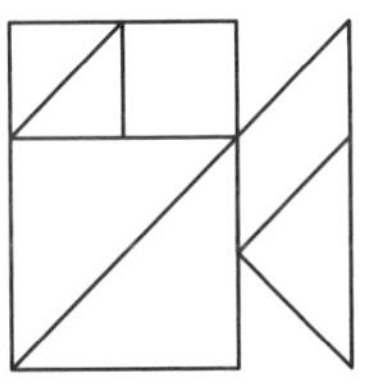
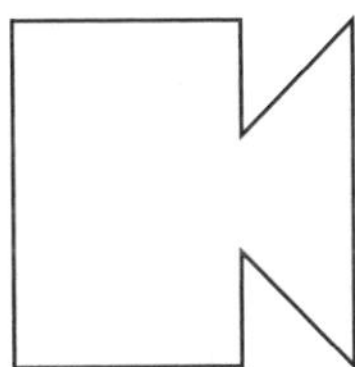

5.3 _ 15
Camera
Suitable for a movie club, photographic services ...

5.4 Inside-out Cube Puzzle

Some puzzles are simple to solve, others fiendishly difficult. This one – turning a cube inside-out – is poised nicely between the two, offering a small but not frustrating challenge. The key to easy flexing is to make the faces strong and the hinges weak.

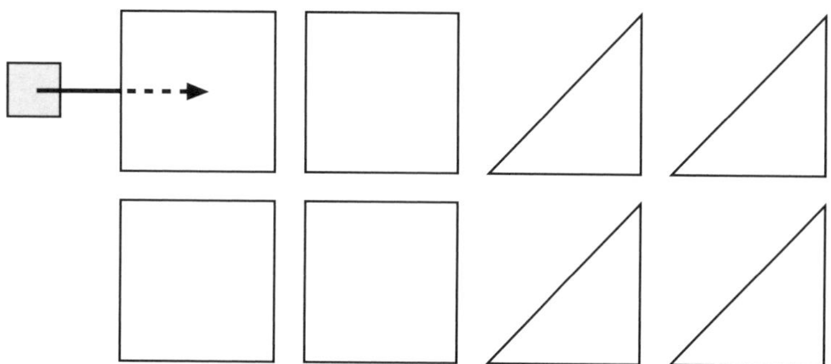

5.4 _ 1
Cut four squares and four triangles, as shown. The backs of the pieces should be a different colour to the front. A good size for the pieces is about 8–10cm. Make them from stiff card or board, not from thin card.

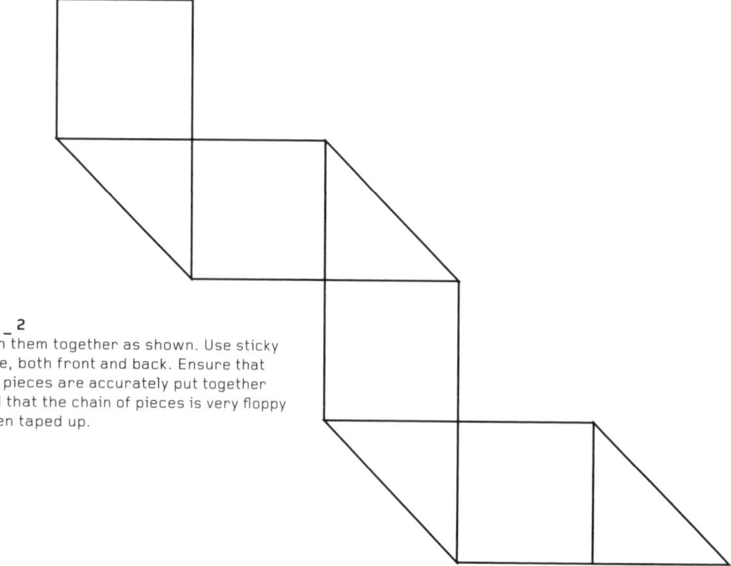

5.4 _ 2
Join them together as shown. Use sticky tape, both front and back. Ensure that the pieces are accurately put together and that the chain of pieces is very floppy when taped up.

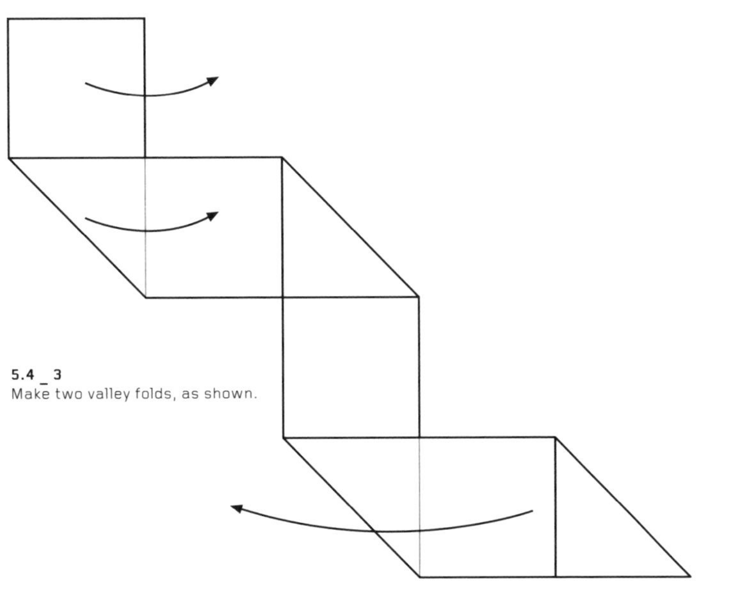

5.4 _ 3
Make two valley folds, as shown.

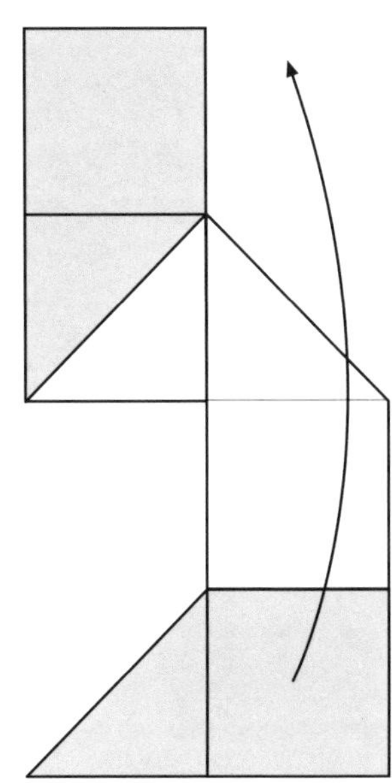

5.4 _ 4
Make a valley fold, as shown.

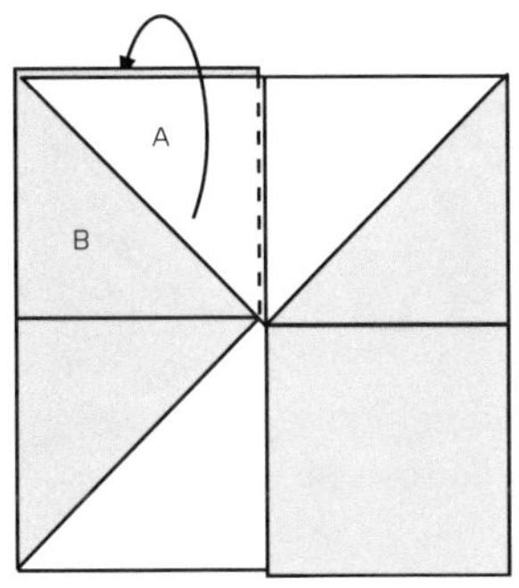

5.4 _ 5
Note that the white triangle A is in front of the coloured square B. Flip A to lie behind B ...

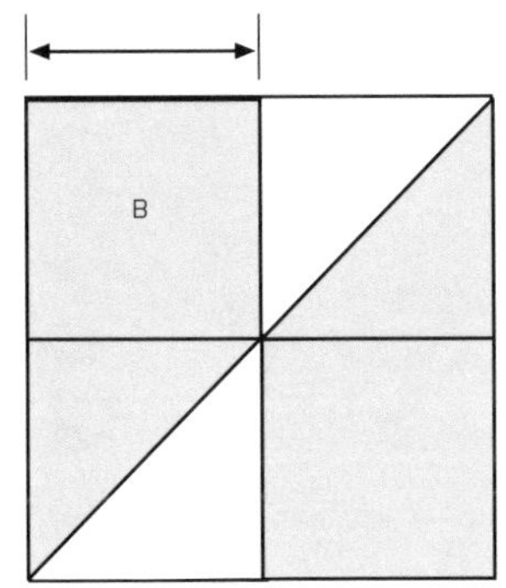

5.4 _ 6
... like this. Tape A and B together, where shown. This will make a continuous band of squares and triangles.

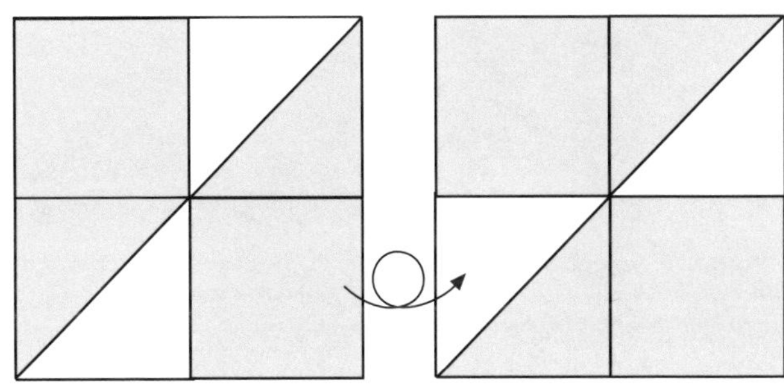

5.4 _ 7
Check that this is how the construction looks, front and back.

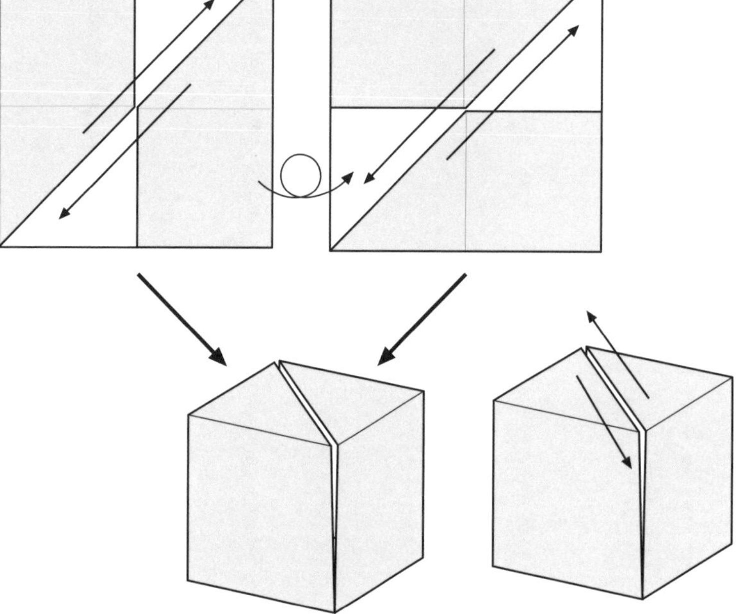

5.4 _ 8
On the front layer, make two horizontal mountain folds. Simultaneously on the back, make two vertical mountain folds. The construction will suddenly acquire an interior volume between the front and back layers and change from being two-dimensional to being a three-dimensional cube!

5.4 _ 9
This is the cube, here seen coloured. To turn it inside out, first flatten it again.

5.4 _ 10
Valley fold the top edge down to the bottom edge.

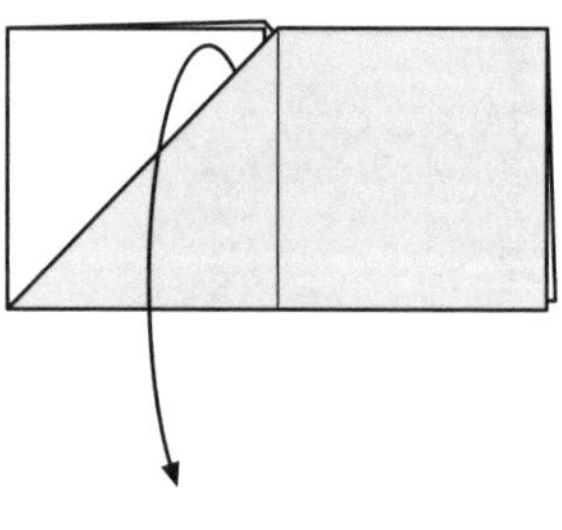

5.4 _ 11
Pull down the coloured triangle and the coloured square.

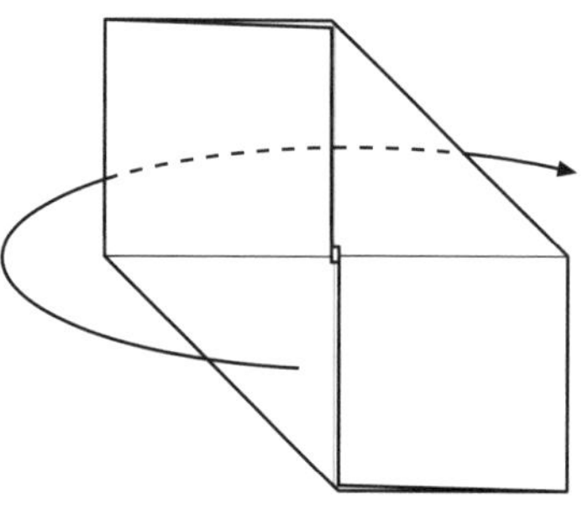

5.4 _ 12
Mountain fold the triangle, the square on the left behind the triangle and the square on the right.

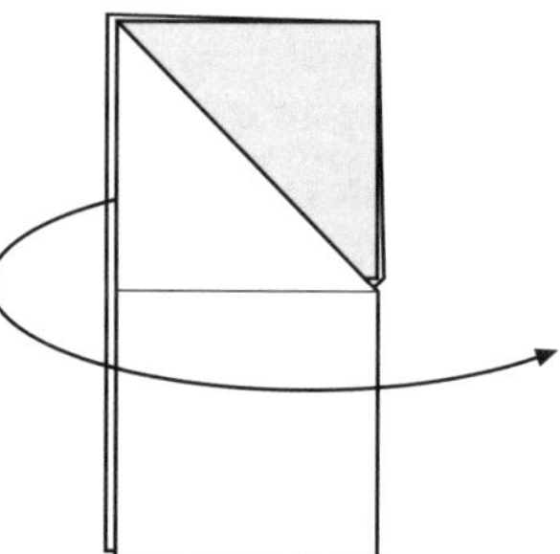

5.4 _ 13
Unfold to a square, separating the edges at the left.

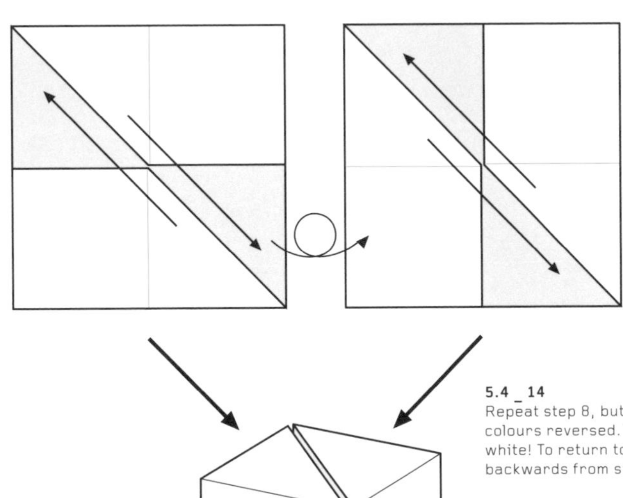

5.4 _ 14
Repeat step 8, but this time with the colours reversed. The cube will now be white! To return to a coloured cube, work backwards from step 13 to step 8.

5.5 Left-to-right Transformation Illusion

Some puzzles are charming for their simplicity, being almost naive. This is one of the best, still baffling if you are not watching closely. It is not a puzzle to give to someone to solve, but something you must perform yourself. In that sense, it's a kind of 'bar room' trick.

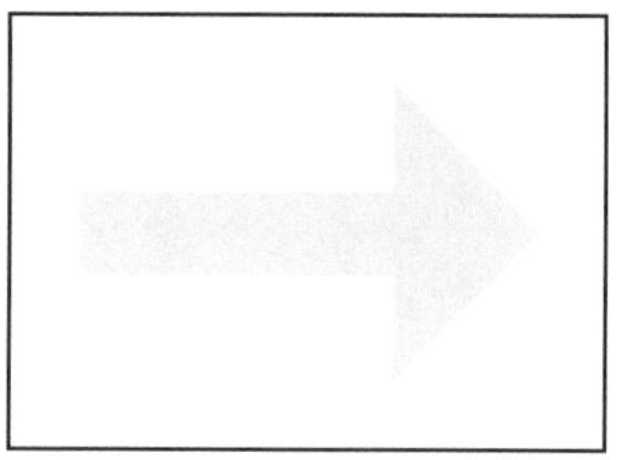

5.5 _ 1
Decide what you want to turn from right to left. Here, it's an arrow, but it could also be an illustration, slogan, bank note ... anything.

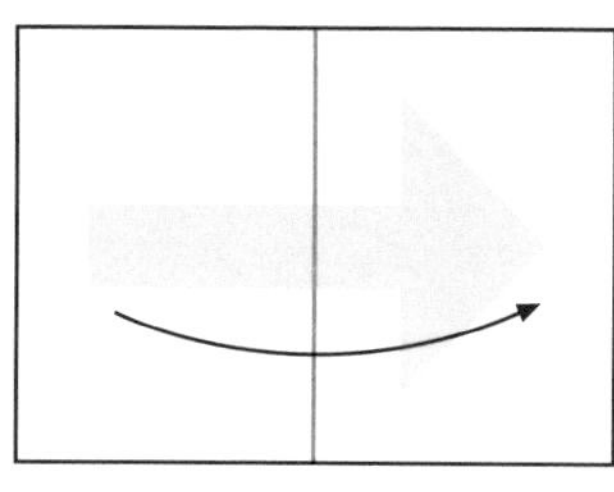

5.5 _ 2
Fold the left edge across to the right.

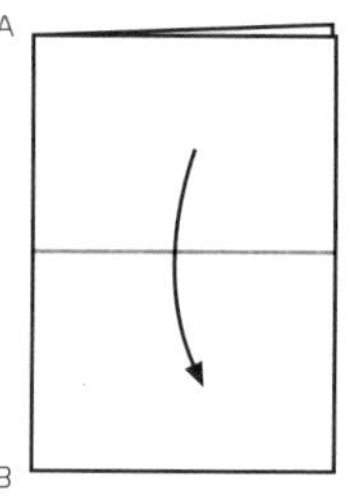

5.5 _ 3
Fold the top edge down to the bottom, laying A on top of B.

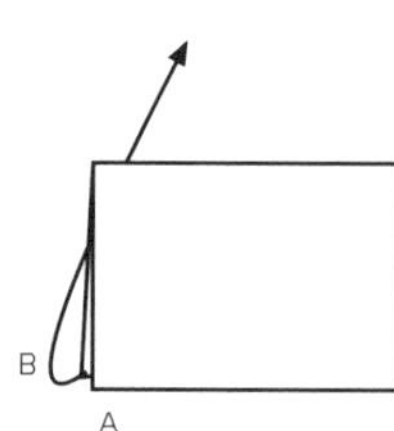

5.5 _ 4
This is the crucial part of the trick. Unfold B behind and upwards, leaving A at the bottom ...

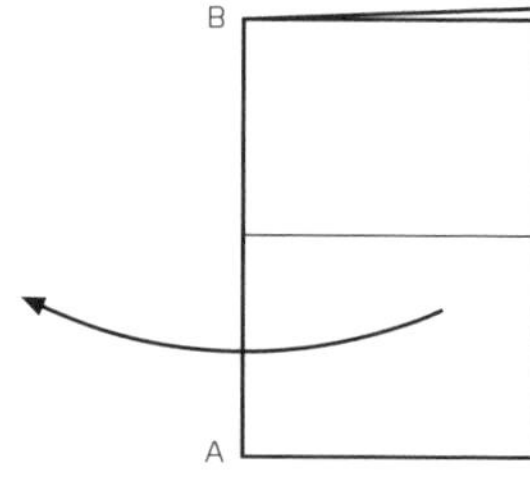

5.5 _ 5
... like this. Open the paper, folding the top edge across to the left.

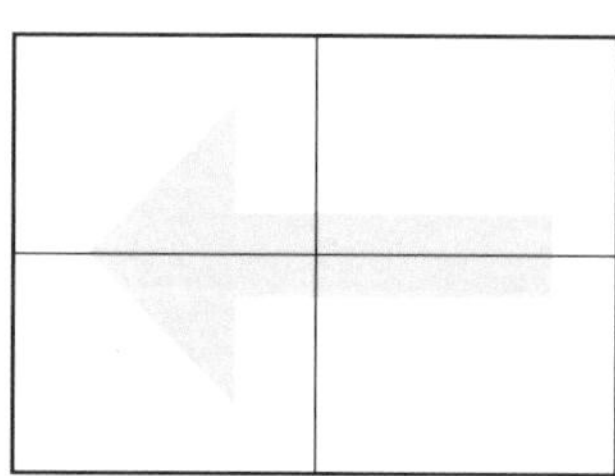

5.5 _ 6
The arrow has turned from right to left!

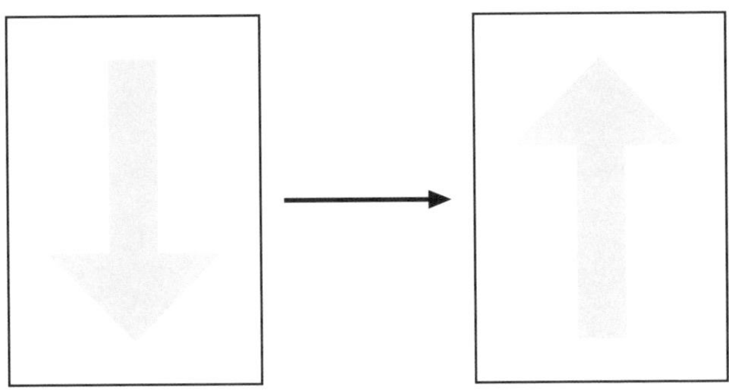

5.5 _ 7
The same reversal can be performed making an arrow point down and then up (or vice versa).

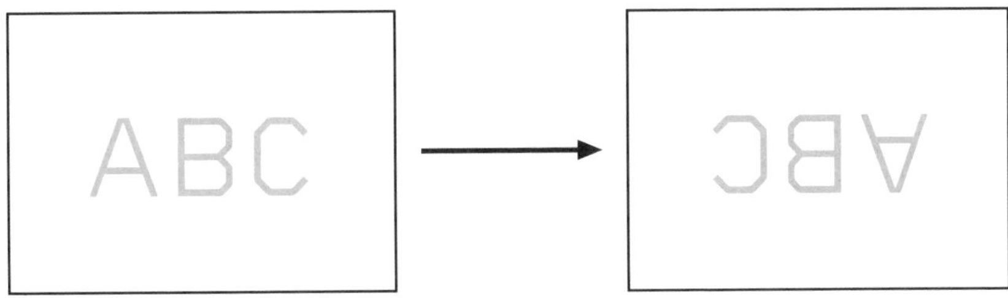

5.5 _ 8
With symmetrical shapes such as the arrow, it isn't immediately apparent that it doesn't flip, but actually rotates upside down. If you are using non-symmetrical imagery – such as letterforms – then it is apparent that the letters have been rotated, not flipped. This may reduce the impact of the trick, though with the right pattern, it will still be an amusing effect.

5.6 Chain-to-square Puzzle

Most paper and card manipulation puzzles – including those in this chapter – have a clear line of manipulation. However, this extraordinary puzzle offers many different possibilities for making the basic square shape and also for making other shapes.

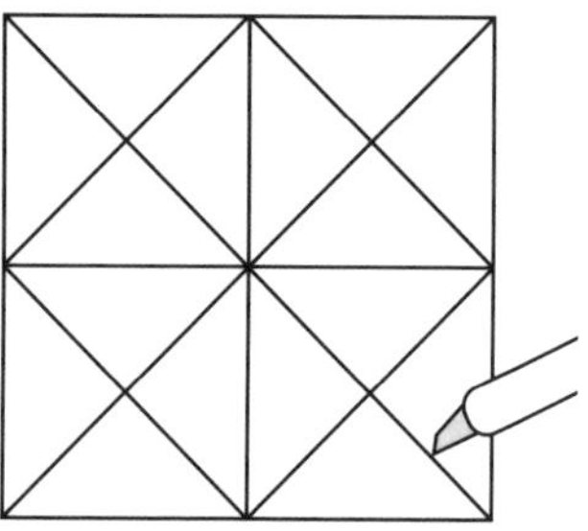

5.6 _ 1
Use stiff board or even plastic or wood to make sixteen triangles. Before making them, check step 2.

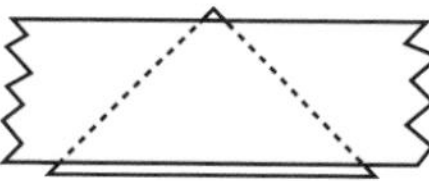

5.6 _ 2
The triangles will be taped together. It is much easier to tape them together accurately if the height of the triangles is just a little more than the width of the tape you wish to use.

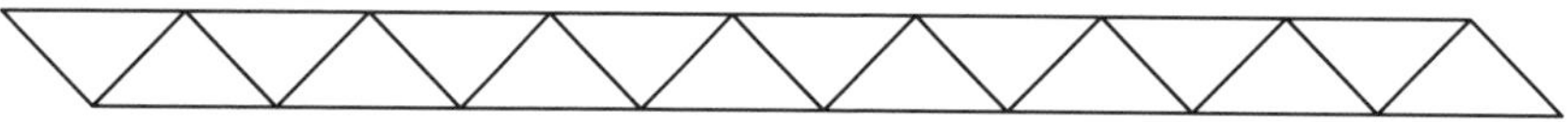

5.6 _ 3
Arrange the triangles in a line. It is important they are accurately in line, so sandwich them between two lengths of thick card (or something similar), ensuring the line is accurate.

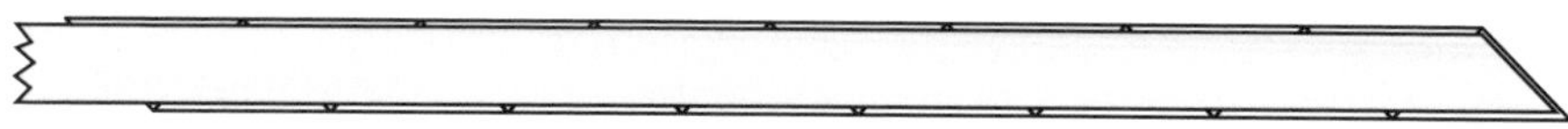

5.6 _ 4
Run tape carefully along the line of triangles. Cut it flush at the right, but allow extra tape at the left.

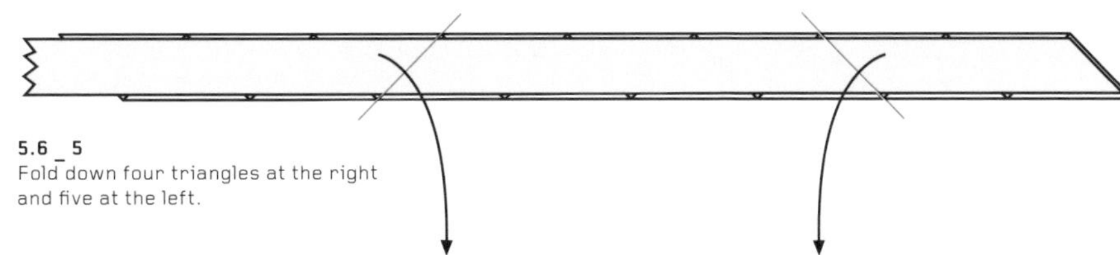

5.6 _ 5
Fold down four triangles at the right and five at the left.

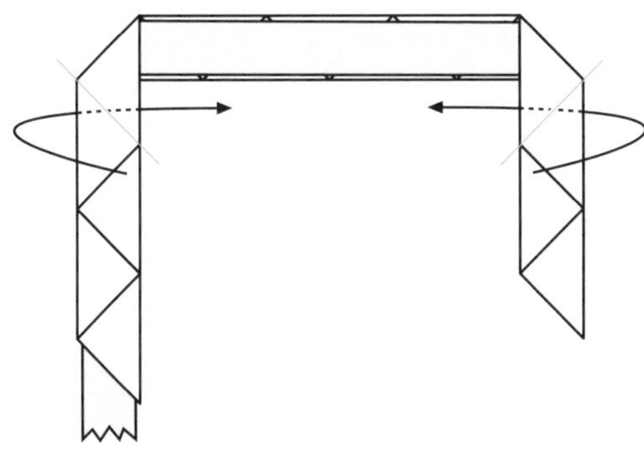

5.6 _ 6
Make two mountain folds, as shown.

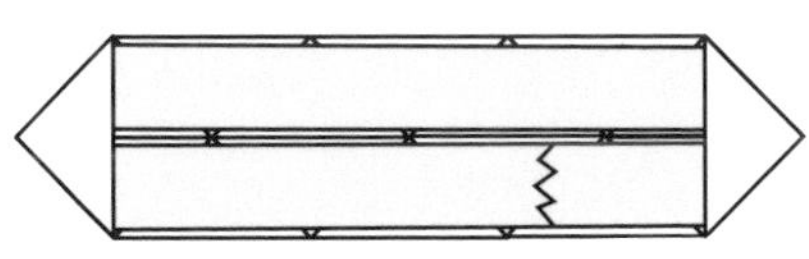

5.6 _ 7
The two ends of the line of triangles should fit snugly together. Hold them together with the extra length of tape, creating an endless chain-loop of triangles.

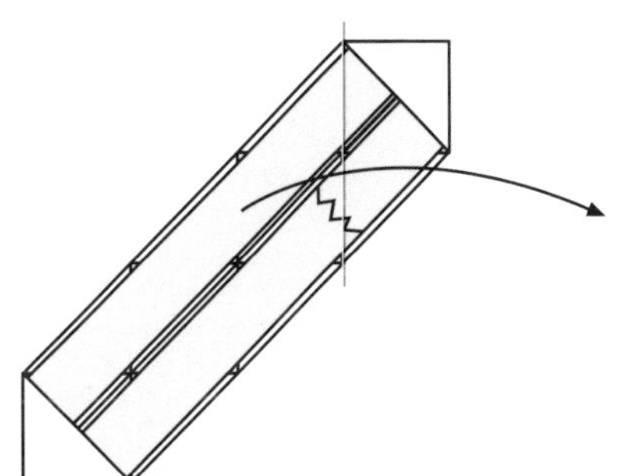

5.6 _ 8
Rotate the chain as shown, then make a valley fold.

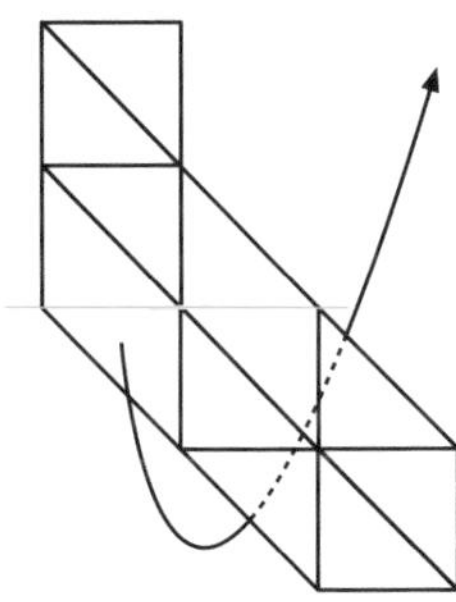

5.6 _ 9
Mountain fold seven triangles behind and upwards.

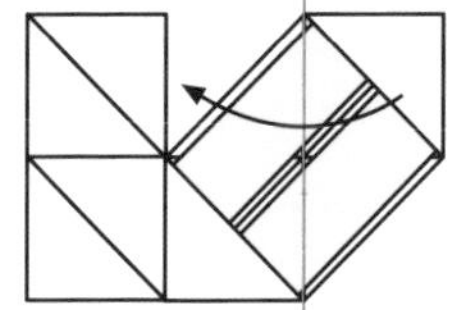

5.6 _ 10
Valley fold as shown.

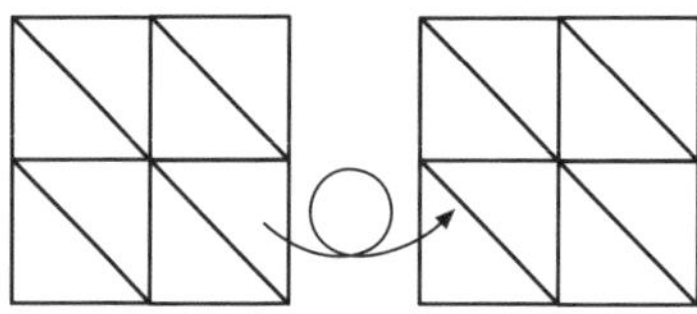

5.6 _ 11
This is the collapsed square, a double thickness of triangles. Turned over, the triangles slope in the same direction as the other side.

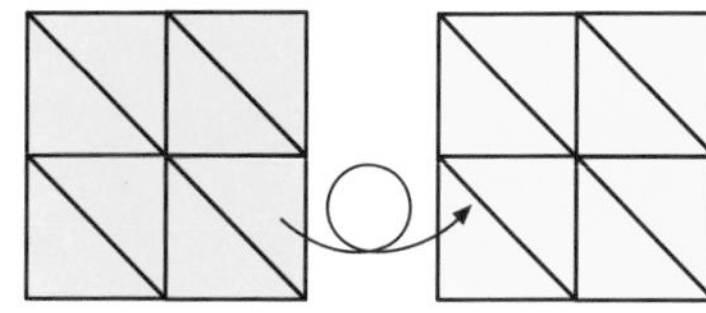

5.6 _ 12
For clarity, the two sides have been given different colours.

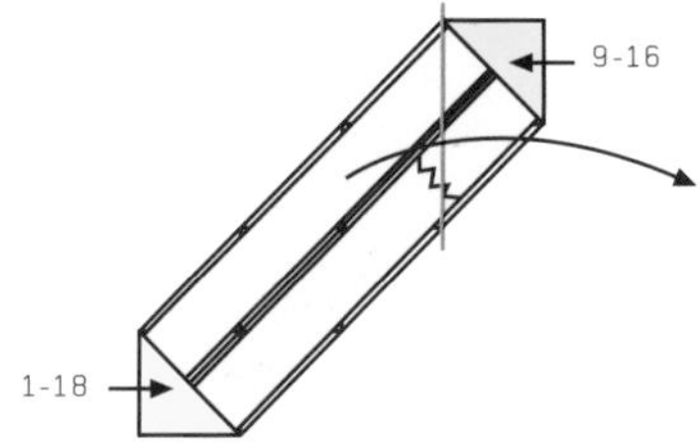

5.6 _ 13
Depending on which two triangles are at the ends of the chain, the chain can be collapsed in one of eight different ways following the method in steps 8 to 11, to create eight different surfaces. Only one of those eight possibilities is entirely one colour on one side and the second colour on the other side. The other seven possibilities are mixtures of colours. Thus, if the bottom orange triangle is numbered between 1 and 8, the top green triangle will have a number greater than the bottom number, between 9 and 16.

To understand this, it is well-worth numbering the triangles 1 to 16 and placing different pairs of triangles at the end of the chain.

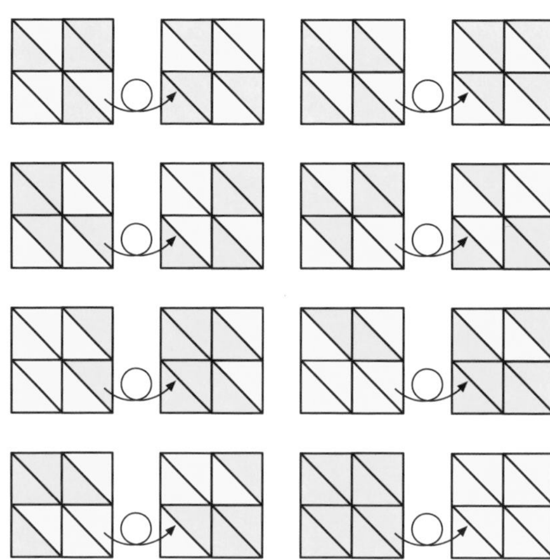

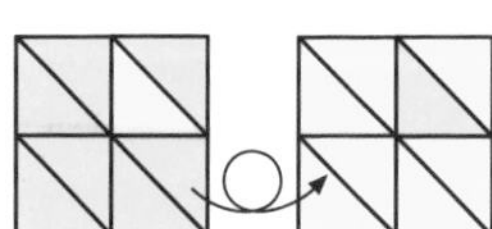

5.6 _ 14
Most confusingly, it is also possible to fold the chain so that just one rogue triangle is on the wrong side. To achieve this, the folding must be different to the sequence described in steps 8 to 11. Can you find this new way to fold the chain? It makes a nice puzzle to be given the square with a rogue triangle and to find a way to eliminate it.

5.6 _ 15
The chain can be manipulated to create many shapes other than squares. Here are some of them, though there are others. Any shape with eight visible triangles must also have eight on the reverse side, so the puzzle is two-sided. A shape with more than eight will have the tape exposed on the reverse, so the puzzle is only one-sided.

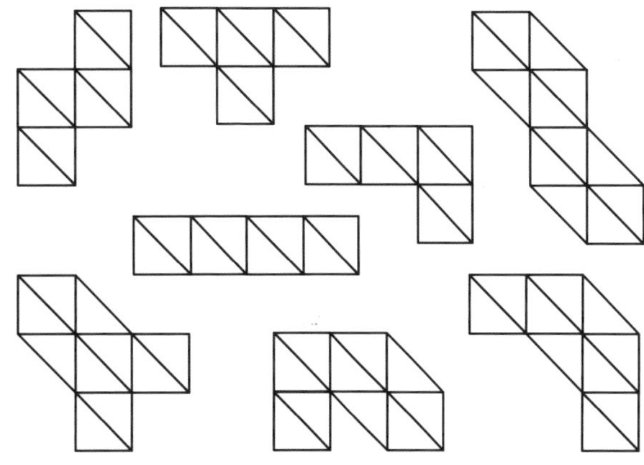

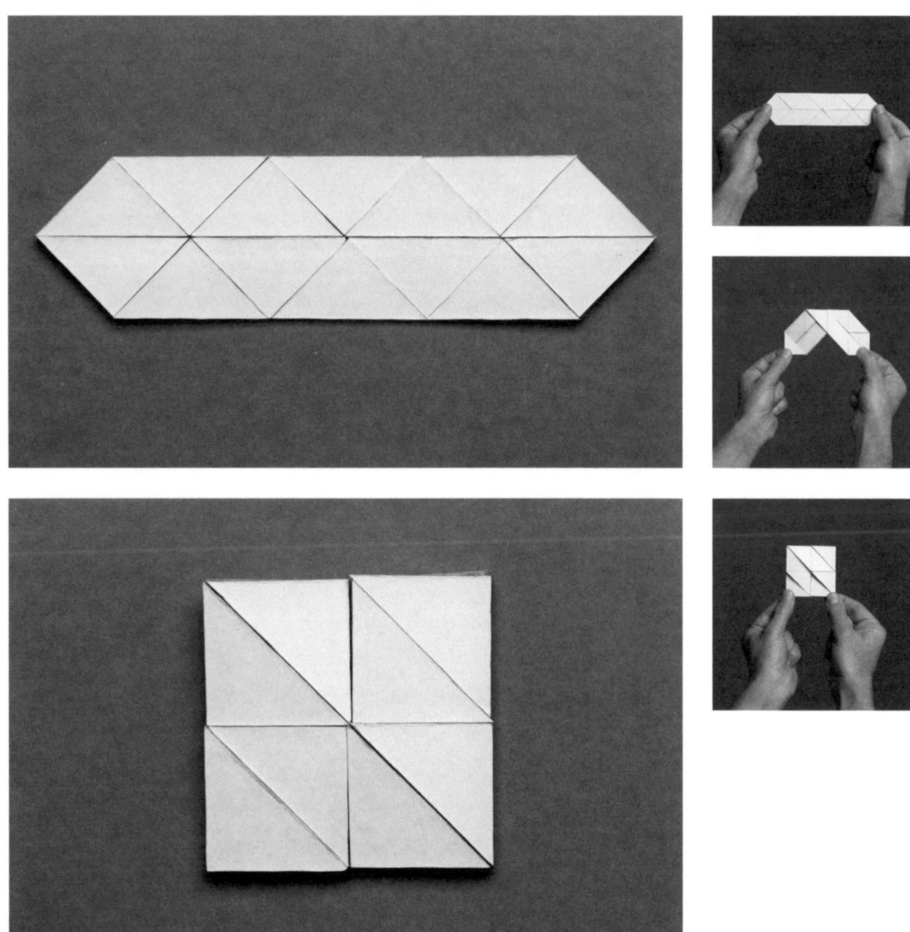

06:

FOLDED BOOKLETS

Introduction

A book is a book is a book. Right? Well ... not really. The dominance of the machine-made book, booklet or brochure over the handmade has created a limited number of book forms for reasons of cost, reliability of production and the technical constraints of the printing and book production processes. But outside the world of mass-produced books is a world of handmade books, where pretty much anything goes.

The booklets in this chapter represent generic concepts that can be machine printed, but hand-assembled. In each case, the number of pages and the proportions of the page/booklet can be changed.

Imagine presenting information with one of the creative booklet ideas shown in this chapter, instead of with a traditional 'z-fold', 'gatefold' or 'concertina fold' ways of folding a booklet. Think how much more interesting the presentation of that information would become! That's the point of creating a booklet made in an unusual way – to present something in a familiar form (a booklet with pages) but with a sizeable twist of creativity. Done well, it can make a good job great.

In recent years there has been a great upsurge of interest in handmade books. If you want to know more, there are some excellent 'how to' books. There are also many fairs, exhibitions and markets in museums, galleries and arts centres of 'artists' books'. The content of these books may not be relevant but the cut and folded forms of the books will be inspiring. If there is such an event near you, try to visit.

6.1 Eight-page Booklet

Here is an elegant idea from East Asia for making an eight-page booklet. All eight pages are on the same side of the sheet, so if you are printing on the paper, it needs to be printed only on one side. The instructions shown here create rectangular pages, but by using paper of a different proportion, you can create pages of another proportion, even square.

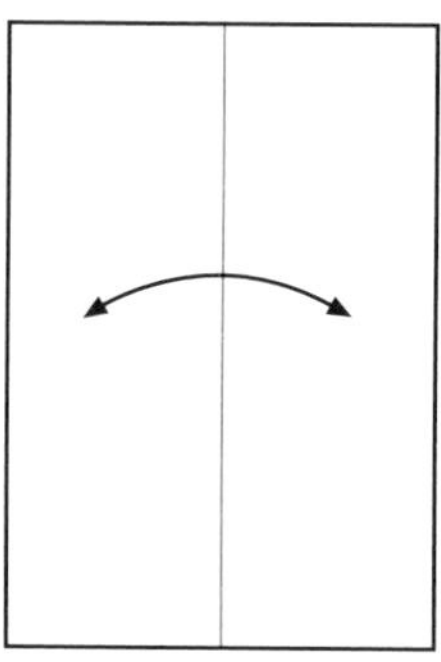

6.1 _ 1
Begin with an 'A'-proportioned sheet. A3 paper will create A6 pages. Fold in half down the middle. Unfold.

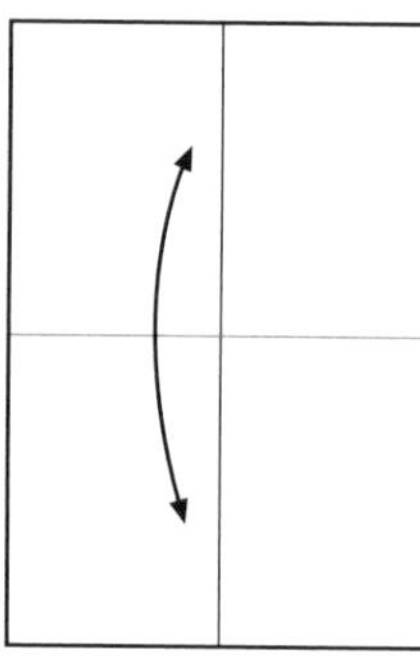

6.1 _ 2
Fold in half across the middle. Unfold.

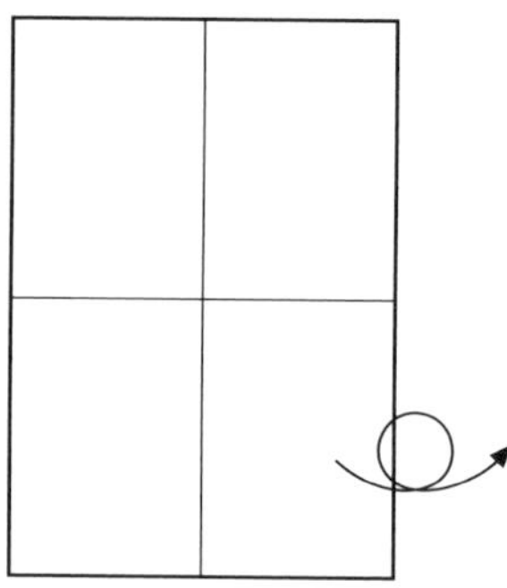

6.1 _ 3
Turn the paper over.

6.1 _ 4
The existing folds are both mountain folds.

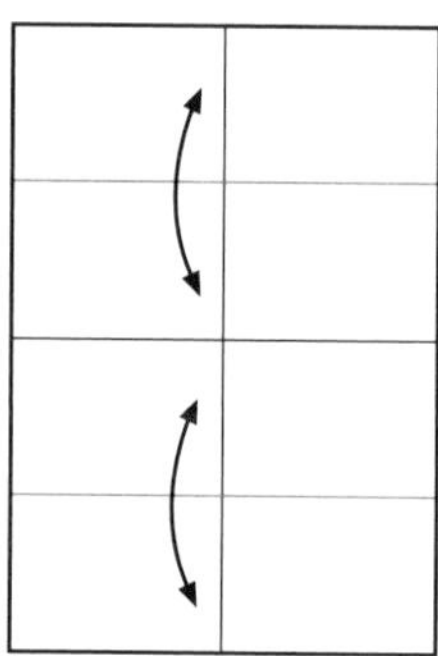

6.1 _ 5
Fold the short edges to the centre line. Unfold.

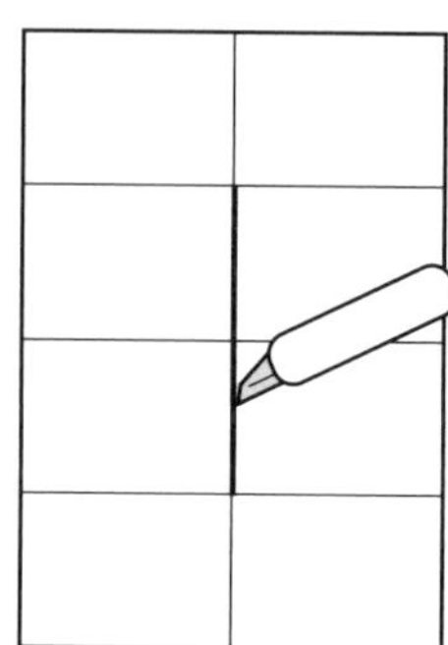

6.1 _ 6
Make a cut down the centre line, connecting the top and bottom quarter folds.

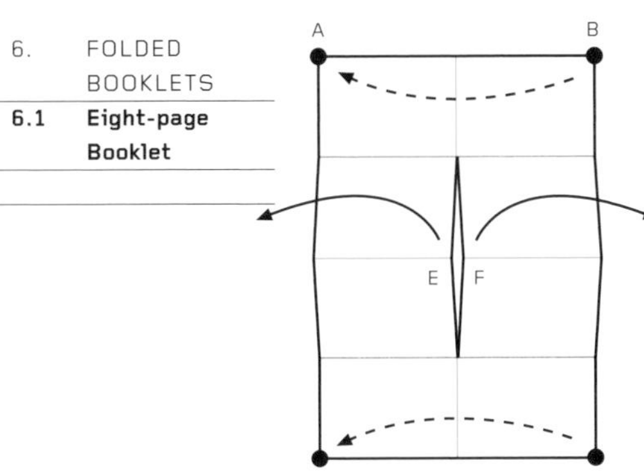

6.1 _ 7
Every mountain and valley cease will now form. Open the cut, separating E from F. At the same time, fold B behind to touch A, and fold D behind to touch C ...

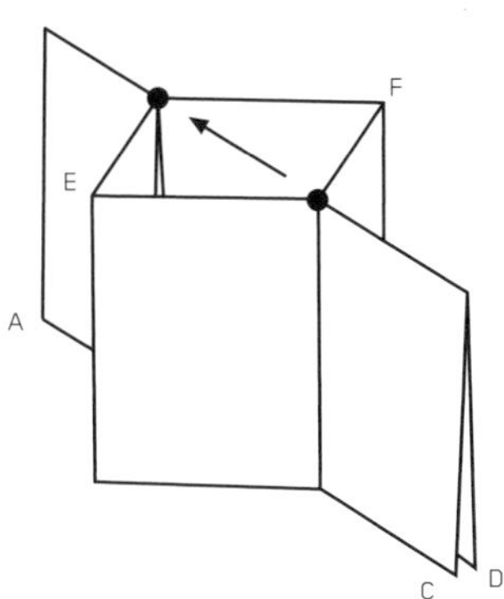

6.1 _ 8
... like this. Note the square tube down through the centre of the paper. Close the tube by folding dot to dot.

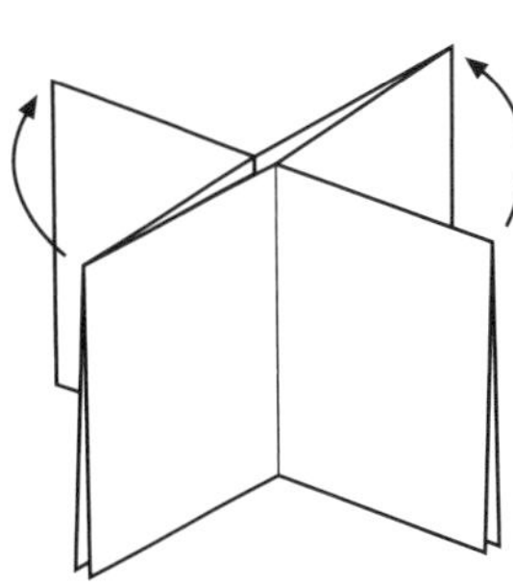

6.1 _ 9
The paper is now an 'X' shape. Flatten it further.

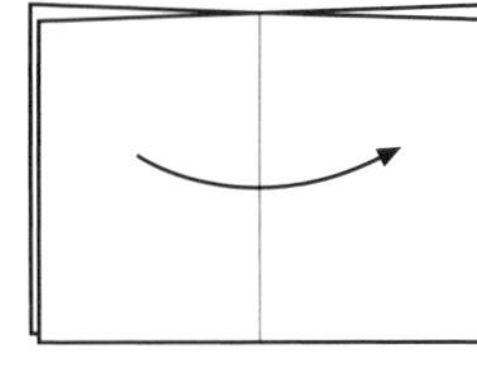

6.1 _ 10
Fold in half.

6.1 _ 11
The booklet is complete. Booklets with more pages can be made if the basic folding pattern of 4 x 2 rectangles is increased to 6 x 2 or 8 x 2. The centre cut separates all the rectangles except those at the top and bottom of the sheet.

6.2 Back-and-forth Book

Here's an idea that can expand and expand to include a very large number of pages, even in excess of a hundred. As with the eight-page booklet above, the shape of the pages can change, depending on the proportions of the rectangles folded in step 1.

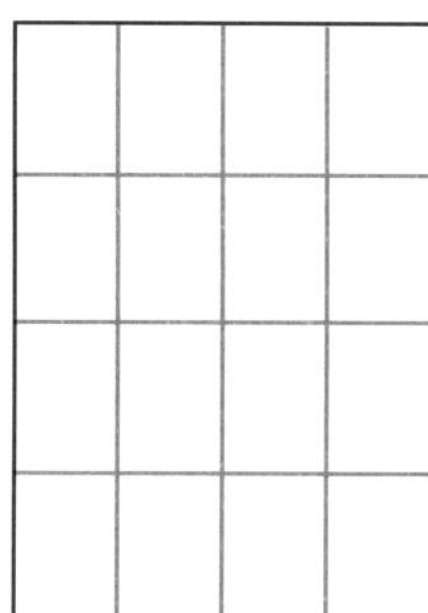

6.2 _ 1
Fold an A4, A3 or even A2 sheet into quarters, horizontally and vertically.

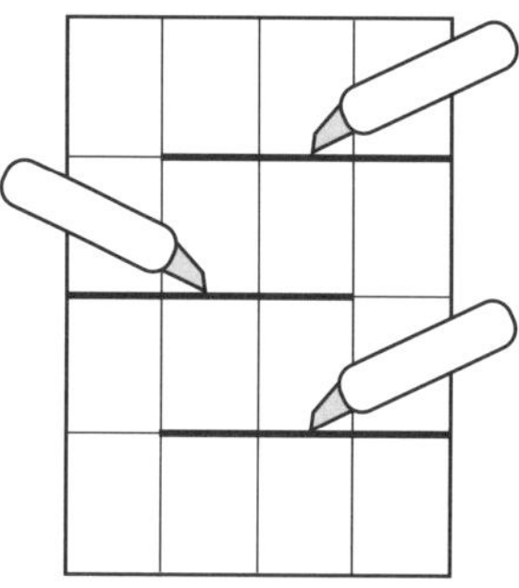

6.2 _ 2
Make three cuts as shown, alternating the edge from which they start.

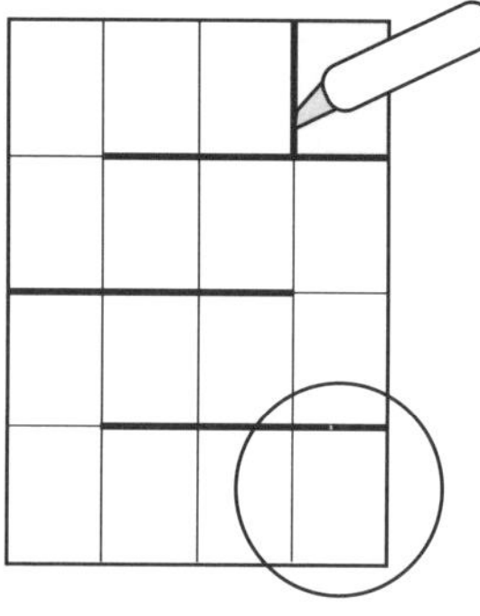

6.2 _ 3
Cut off the rectangle at the top right. The next step enlarges the circled rectangle.

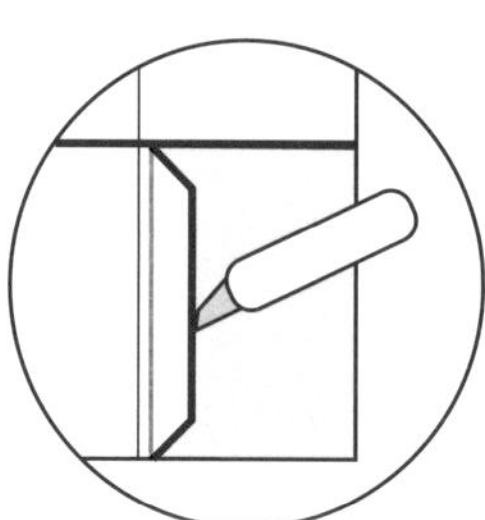

6.2 _ 4
Cut off most of the rectangle, but leave a roof-shaped tab at the left. Add a second crease, close to the crease at the edge of the rectangle. The distance between the two creases is the width of the spine of the booklet, so place the second crease with care.

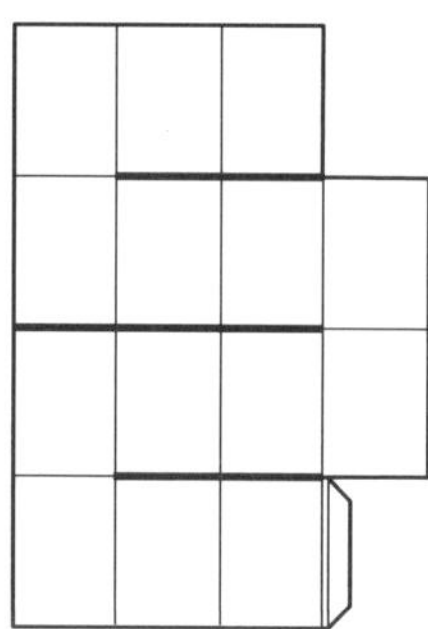

6.2 _ 5
The cutting and folding is now complete. The booklet can be assembled.

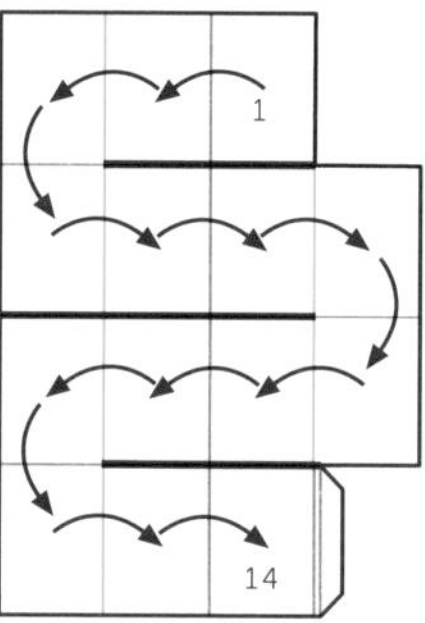

6.2 _ 6
Beginning at rectangle 1 make alternate valley and mountain folds all the way down the chain of connected rectangles, eventually finishing at rectangle 14.

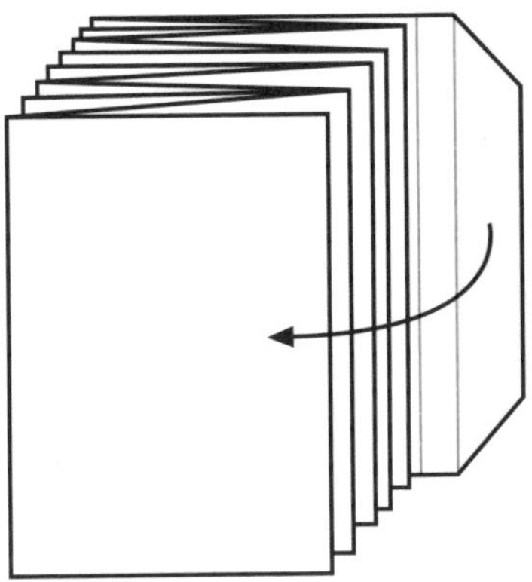

6.2 _ 7
This is the result. Apply glue to the roof-shaped tab and stick it to the front rectangle, thus creating the spine and holding the booklet together.

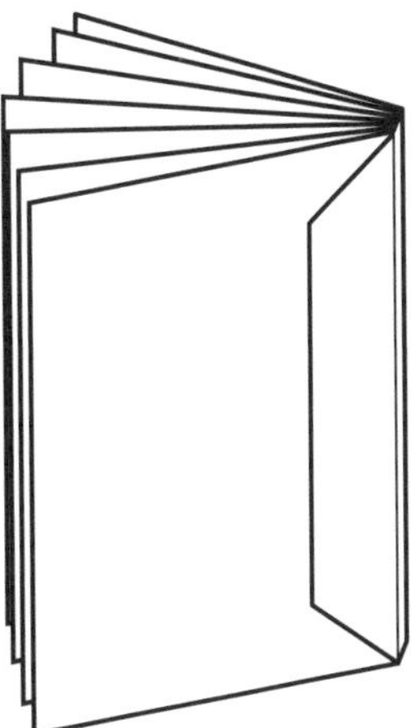

6.2 _ 8
The booklet may be considered complete at this point.

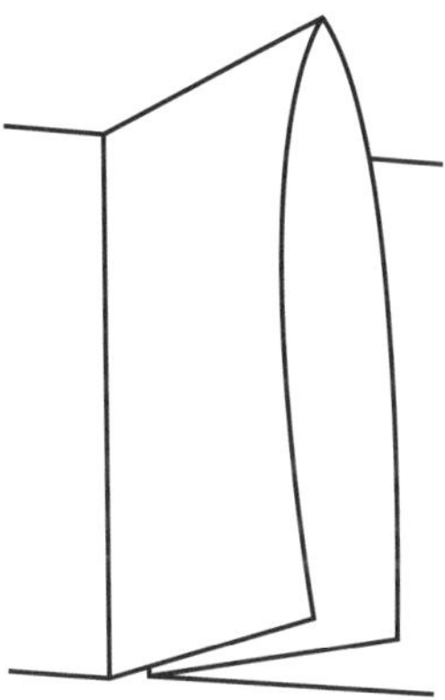

6.2 _ 9
However, a few of the double-thickness pages have an open corner, which might be considered unsightly.

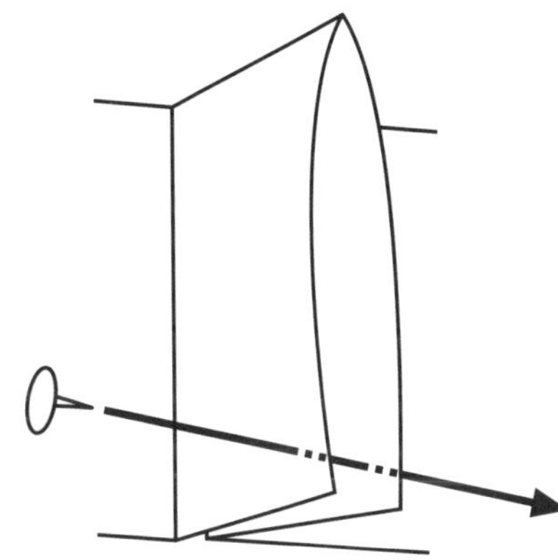

6.2 _ 10
To close an open corner, begin by pushing a pin through the two layers, near the corner ...

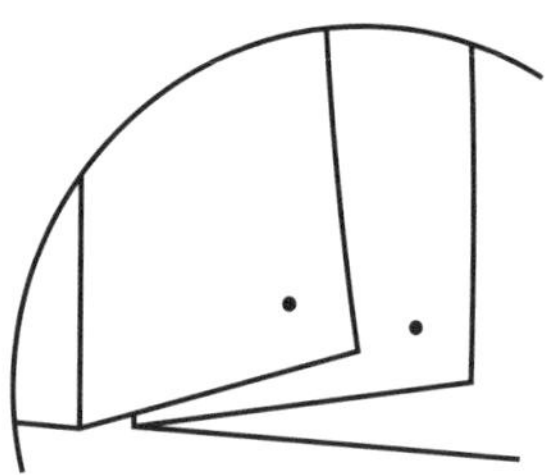

6.2 _ 11
... like this, to create two holes.

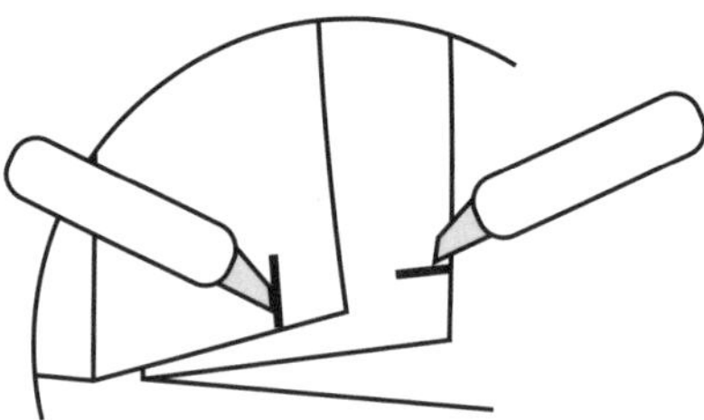

6.2 _ 12
Starting at the holes, make one horizontal cut and one vertical cut.

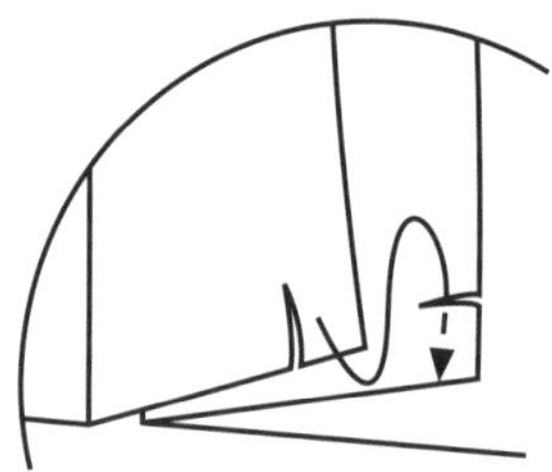

6.2 _ 13
Interlock the two cuts ...

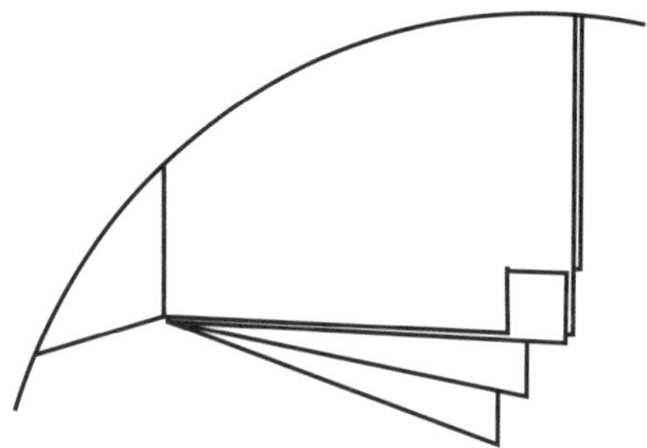

6.2 _ 14
... like this, holding the loose corners tight shut.

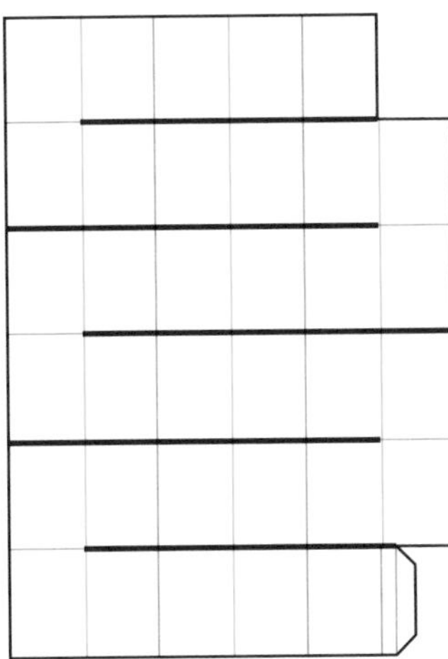

6.2 _ 15
Booklets with many more pages can be made, such as this one. Note how the two creases in the bottom left rectangle are further apart than described above. This is because the extra pages create a thicker spine and hence, the two creases need to be further apart.

6.3 Origami Book

There are many one-piece origami books, made by folding a square of paper. However, they are generally complex and difficult for the inexperienced folder to make. This two-piece version is much simpler and can contain as many pages as you wish.

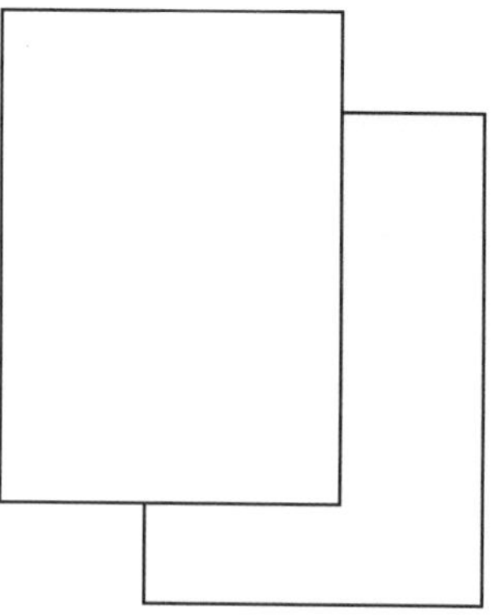

6.3 _ 1
Begin with two sheets of A4 copier paper, preferably of different colours. A3 or even A2 may also be used, though heavier weights of paper may be needed to compensate for the increase in scale.

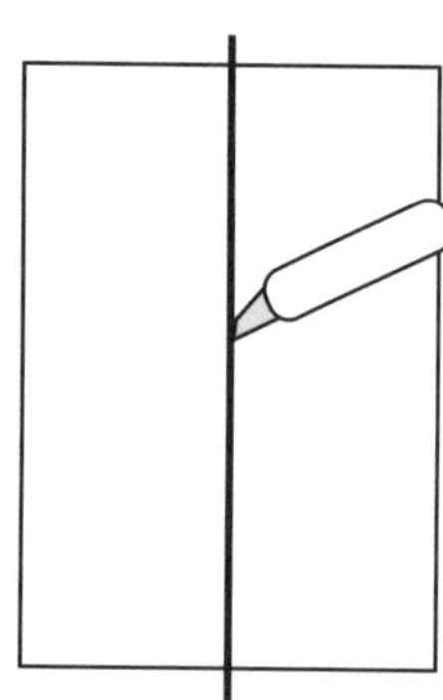

6.3 _ 2
Cut the white sheet in half (this is the sheet from which the pages will be made).

6.3 _ 3
This is half an A4.

6.3 _ 4
Fold the paper into zigzag eighths (alternate valley and mountain folds. Also fold a mountain down the middle.

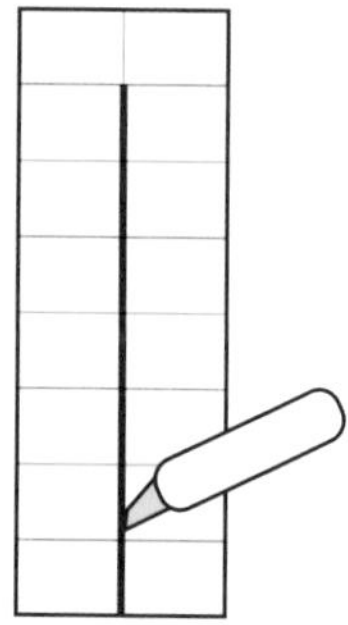

6.3 _ 5
Cut along the centre fold, leaving only the top eighth uncut.

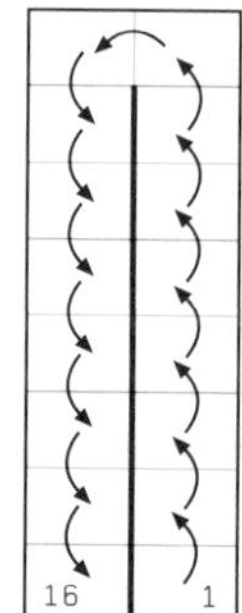

6.3 _ 6
Concertina all the folds, staring at 1 and finishing at 16.

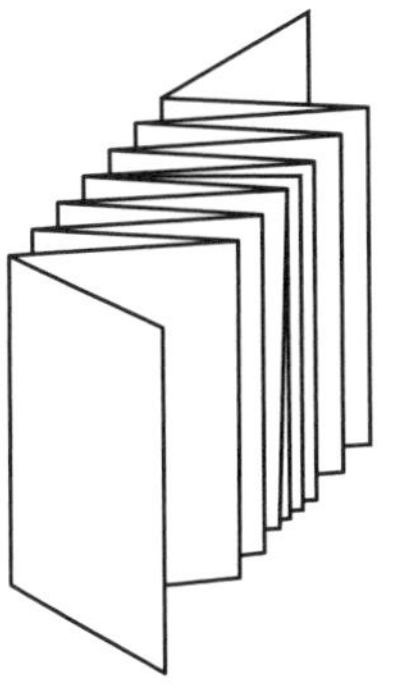

6.3 _ 7
This is the result.

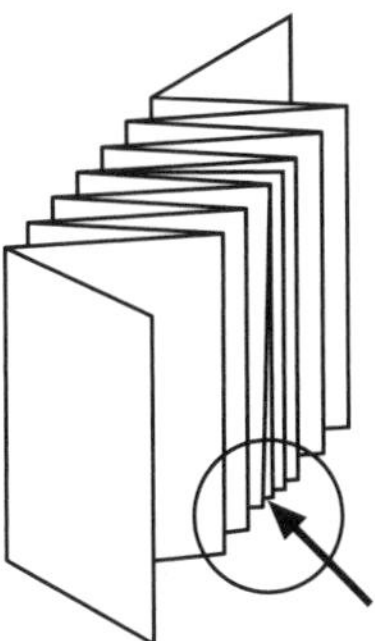

6.3 _ 8
The double corner in the middle of the zigzag is loose ...

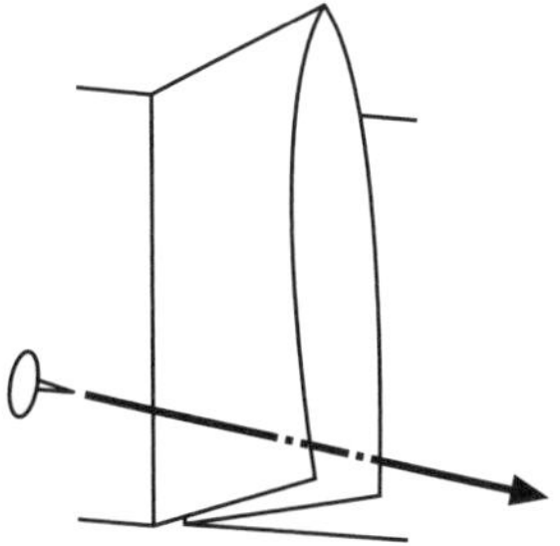

6.3 _ 9
... so it may be closed tight shut using the method described above in steps 9–14 of the back-and-forth book, page 96.

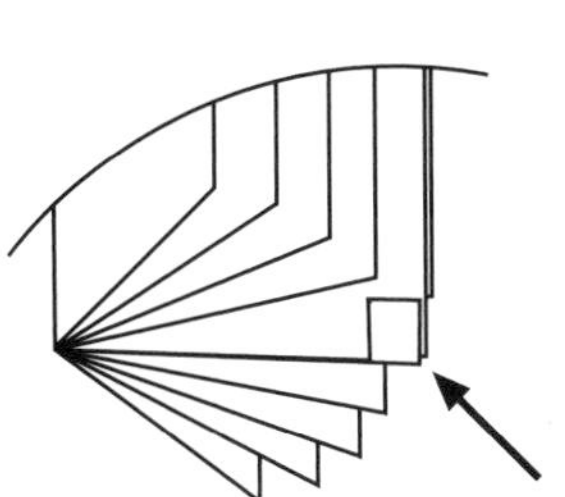

6.3 _ 10
This is the result.

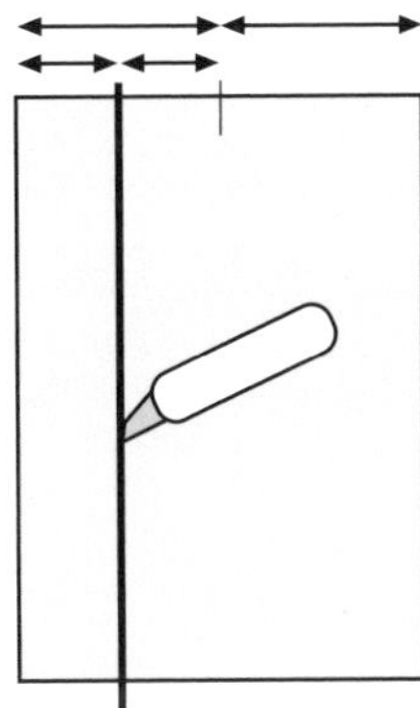

6.3 _ 11
On the coloured A4, cut off one quarter of the long side.

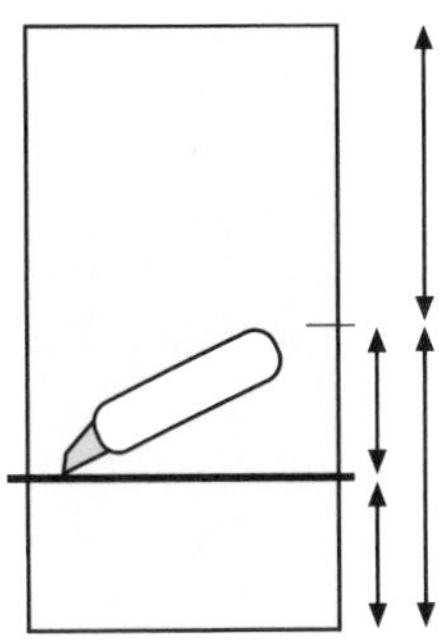

6.3 _ 12
Then cut off one quarter of the short bottom edge (the remaining three quarters could be used to make three more book covers).

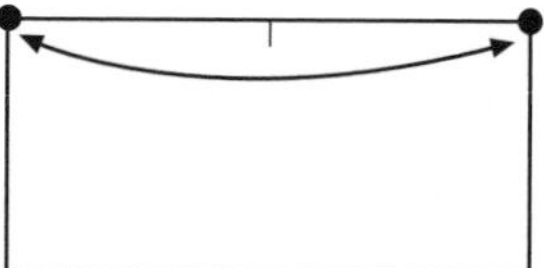

6.3 _ 13
Fold dot to dot and pinch the top edge.

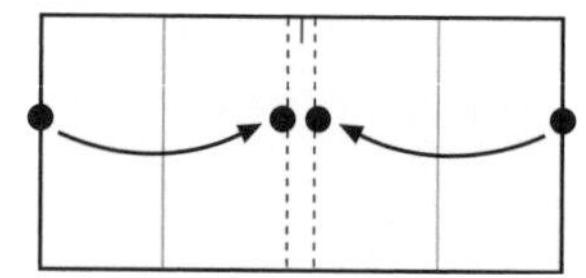

6.3 _ 14
Fold the two short edges almost to the pinch, leaving a gap between them. This gap will be a little greater than the width of the spine.

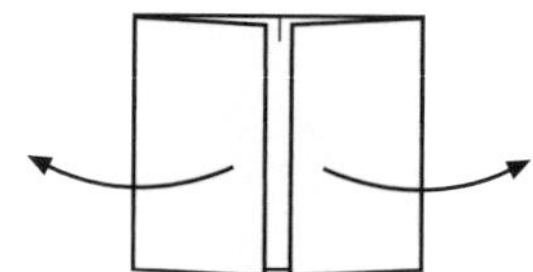

6.3 _ 15
Unfold the previous step.

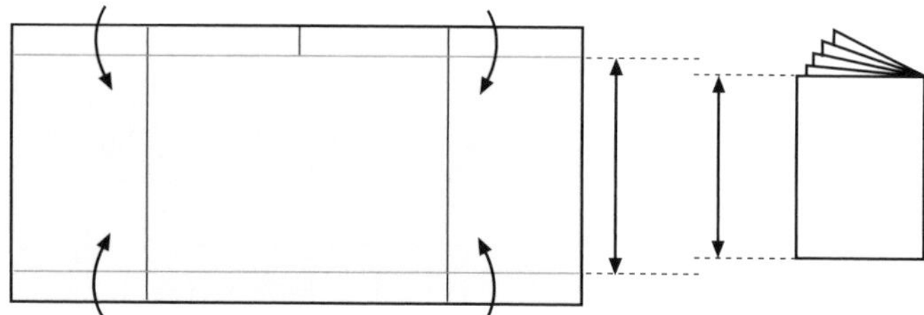

6.3 _ 16
Make two long valley folds close to the top and bottom edges. The placement of these two folds is crucial. The distance between them is a little greater than the height of the book's pages. If the placement of this fold is incorrect, it can be changed later.

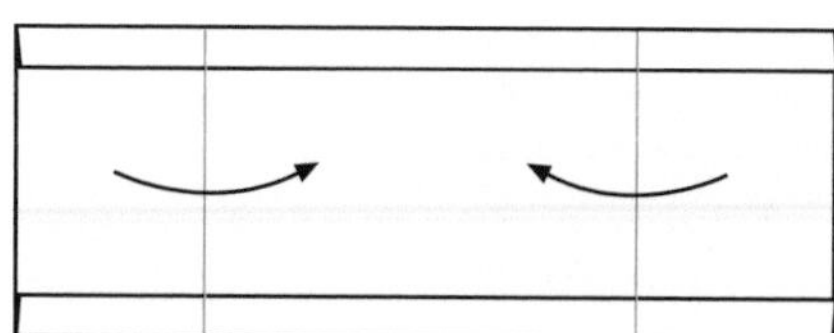

6.3 _ 17
Refold step 14.

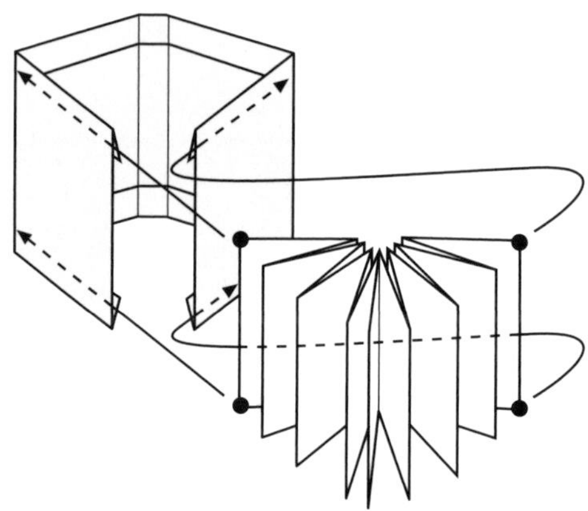

6.3 _ 18
Fan open the pages of the book. Slide the single layer front and back pages of the book under the narrow hems created in step 16. This will lock the pages into the cover.

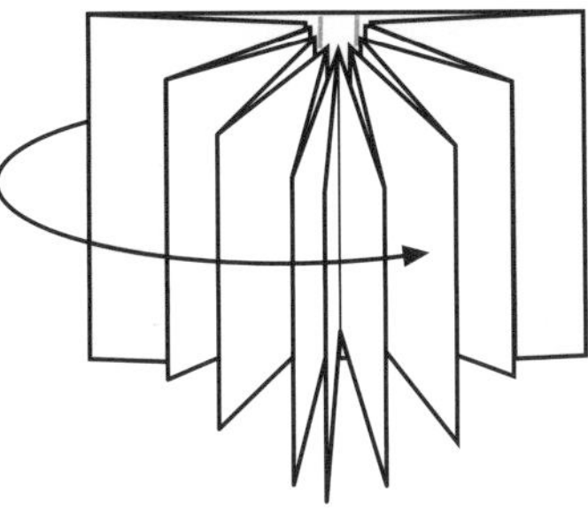

6.3 _ 19
Make two folds in the cover to create the spine. If you are making multiple copies, you will probably be able to make these folds earlier, already knowing what the spine width will be. Even if they are made now, it may be easier to make them with the pages removed from the cover.

6.3 _ 20
This is the completed origami book. Two white A4 sheets and two coloured A4 sheets will make four books.

6.4 Expanding Booklet

Booklets need not have conventional rectangular pages, so to conclude the chapter, here's a lovely example of a fold-out book which expands from a small space to create a large surface area. Made large, it can even hang on the wall. The example shown here has five pages, but it can have more pages or fewer, as you choose.

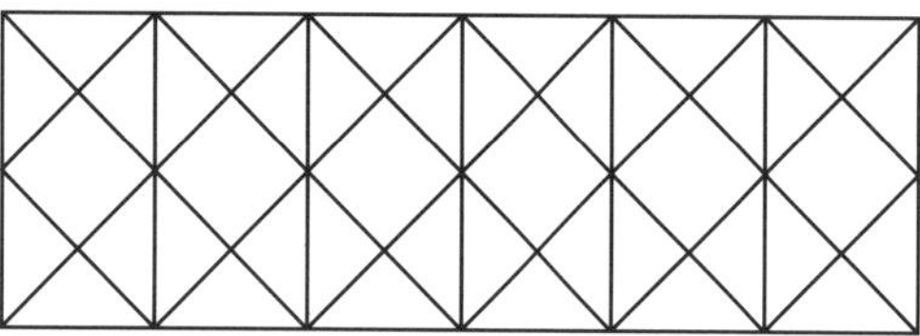

6.4 _ 1
Using 200–250gsm card, create a 3 x 1 rectangle and divide it accurately, as shown.

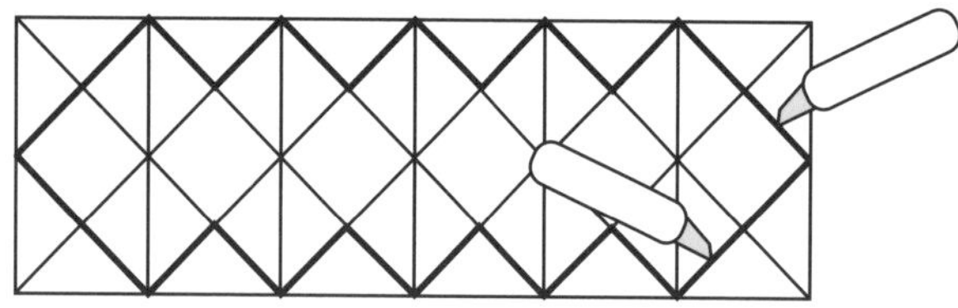

6.4 _ 2
Cut off triangles around the edge, to create a sawtooth silhouette …

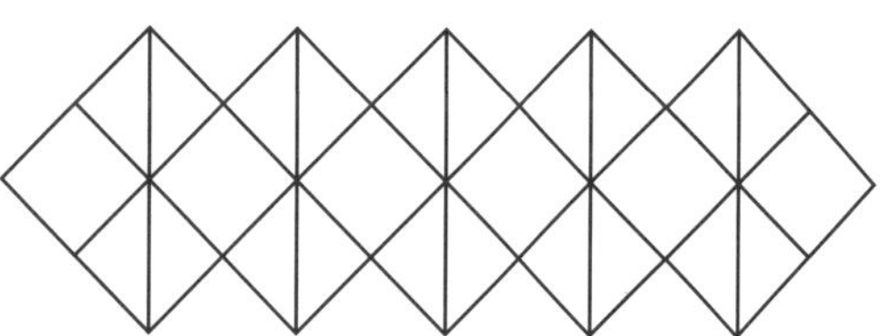

6.4 _ 3
… like this.

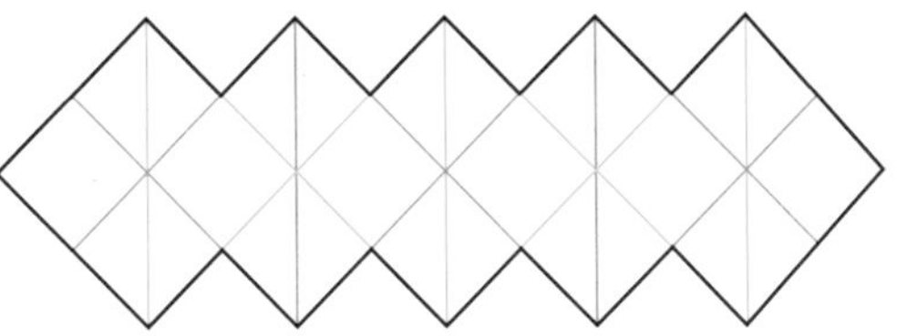

6.4 _ 4
Make the specific pattern of mountains and valleys shown here.

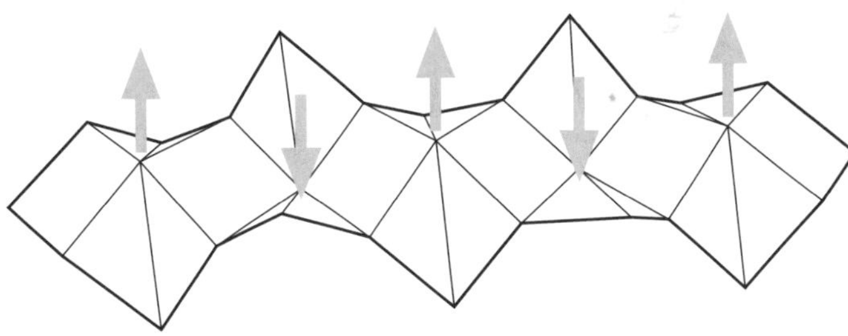

6.4 _ 5
The folds can now be collapsed. The nodes where two mountain folds and a valley meet will pop upwards; the nodes where two valleys and a mountain meet will pop downwards. When this has been done accurately, the booklet – amazingly – will concertina up to the size of a small square.

07:

NOVELTIES

Introduction

This final chapter presents promotional ideas that cannot easily be shoe-horned into other chapters. In that sense, it is both the most uncoordinated, but also the most creative and open-ended chapter in the book.

Its diversity asks the question about what may – or may not – be considered a good idea to help you promote a message, service or product. There is no simple answer to that, except to make the comment that whatever it is, it should be ingenious, memorable, interactive, easy to print on, easy to assemble and apparently so 'obvious' that it leaves someone wondering why they hadn't thought of it first (such a reaction is always the test of a great design, in any form).

Its diversity also asks you, the designer, to think creatively; to keep your eyes open for tricks, conundrums, illusions, craft ideas, toys, games, puzzles, party decorations and more, which can be adapted for use as promotional devices. In truth, there are many great ideas out there that can be used, but which remain unused because their usefulness remains unrecognized. If this book – and in particular this chapter – has increased your awareness of how paper and card can be cut and folded to create memorable promotions, then it has done its job.

7.1 Spinning Spiral

Few folded structures are as elegant as this spiral. Carefully made and positioned in gently moving air, it will spin vigorously. Its single, one-layer surface means that it is easy and inexpensive to apply effective surface graphics.

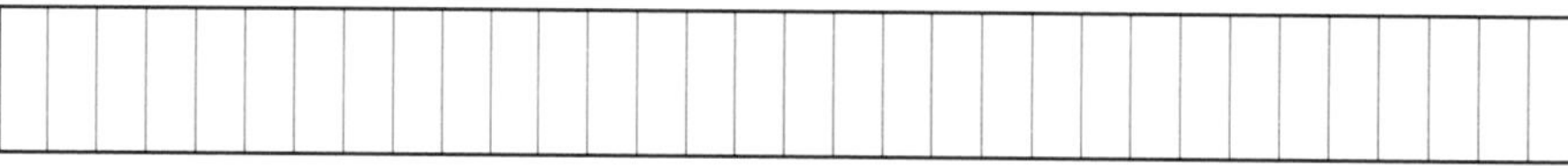

7.1 _ 1
Cut 100gsm paper to a rectangle somewhere between 11 x 1 and 12 x 1. A good depth is about 8cm. Divide it into 32 equal sections with valley folds. These divisions can be measured with a ruler, or if you want to do it purely by folding, refer to the author's previous book *Folding Techniques for Designers*, where a folding method for dividing into 32 is given.

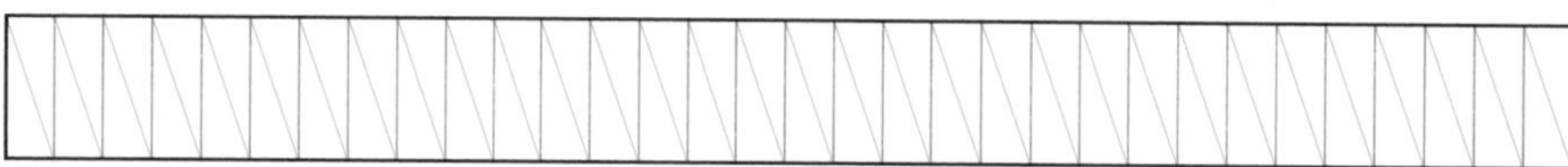

7.1 _ 2
Add mountain folds across the diagonal of each of the 32 panels. Make sure they are folded very accurately.

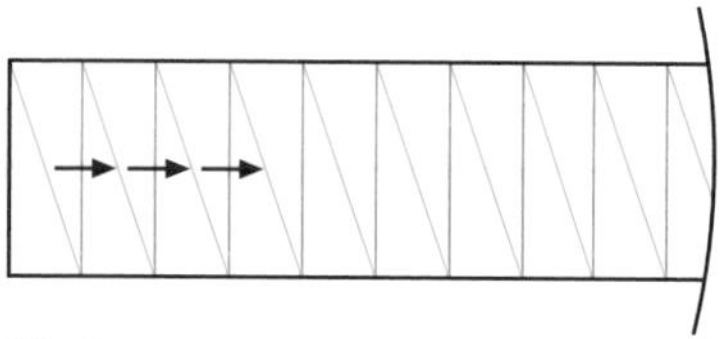

7.1 _ 3
Begin to fold each mountain and each valley in turn, being careful not to omit any of the folds ...

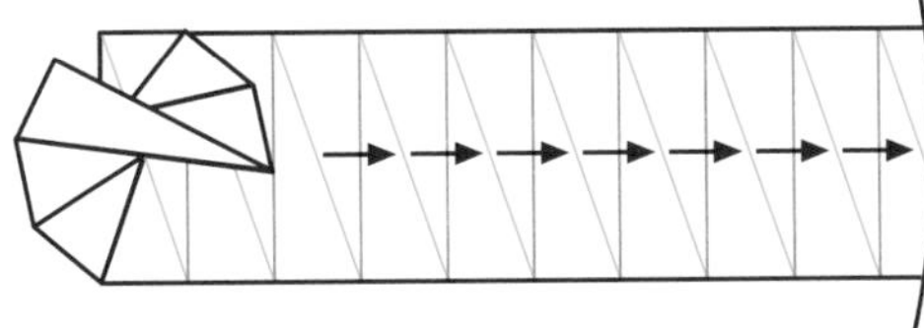

7.1 _ 4
... like this. The strip will begin to create a circle. Continue to make all the folds, right across the strip.

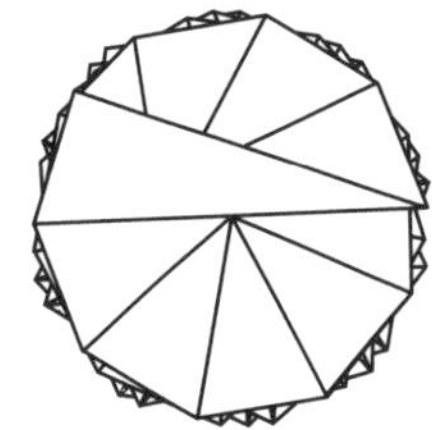

7.1 _ 5
This is the final result. The paper is flat. To make the spiral, separate your first finger and thumb by about 2cm and with your other hand, pull the strip up through the gap between them. This will open the pleats to create a spiralling strip.

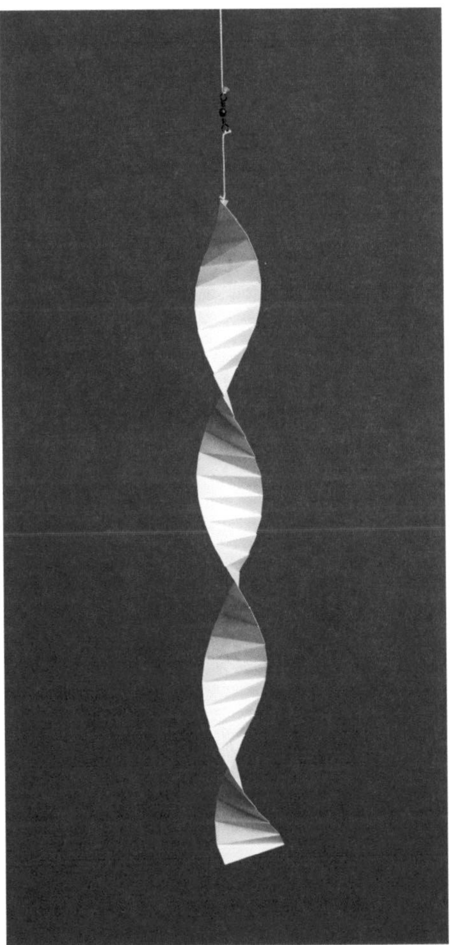

7.1 _ 6
The spiral is complete. Note that to spin effectively and also to look its most beautiful, the spiral should twist through no more than three complete rotations from top to bottom. If it is twisting more, pull it again between your first thumb and forefinger, but this time with a smaller gap between them. Make a hole in the middle of one end and hang it from a cotton thread.

A very useful addition is a small fishing swivel, seen in the photograph. Cut the cotton a little above the spiral and then tie the swivel between the loose ends. It will allow the spiral to spin perpetually in one direction, without twisting and breaking the thread. Fishing swivels can be bought where fishing rods are sold. They are very inexpensive and come in packets of a dozen or so.

7.2 Hanging Letters

Just once in a while an idea comes along that is extraordinary for its speed, simplicity, versatility and apparent obviousness. The hanging letters is one of those ideas. Once you have tried it, you'll be looking for opportunities everywhere ... and everyone will want to join in.

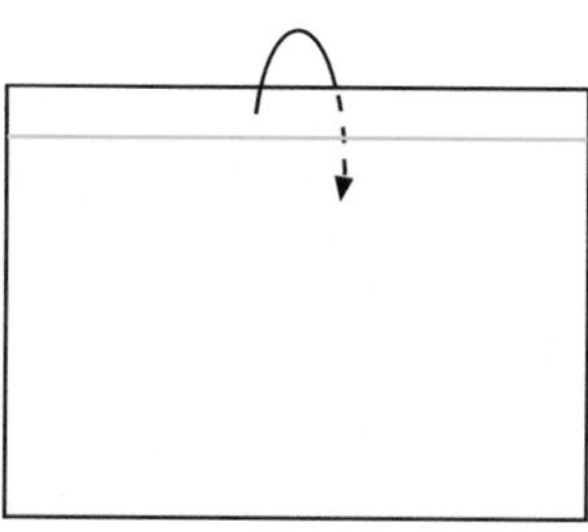

7.2 _ 1
Take a sheet of A4 paper and fold the top edge behind by about 3–4cm.

7.2 _ 2
Draw a letterform that is the full height of the folded paper.

7.2 _ 3
Cut out the letter, also cutting through the double layer at the top.

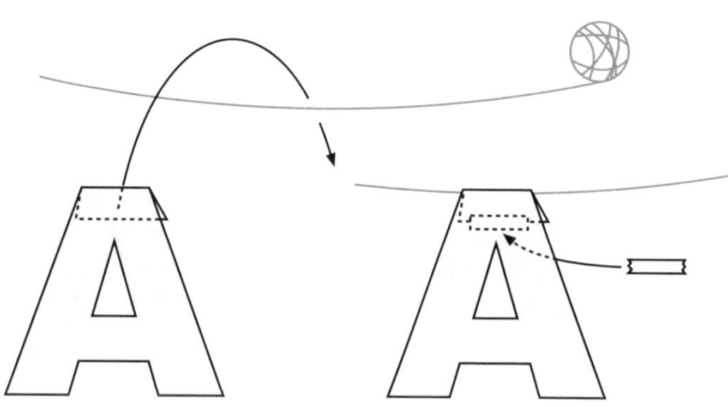

7.2 _ 4
Fasten a line of cotton thread, string or fishing line where you want the letter to hang. Pull it reasonably tight. Hang the letter on the line.

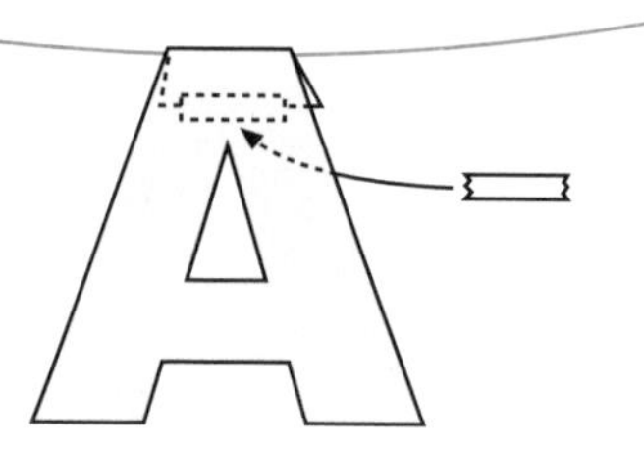

7.2 _ 5
To prevent the letter from falling off the line, add a small piece of sticky tape to the back, securing the folded layer flat.

7.2 _ 6
This is the completed hanging letter.

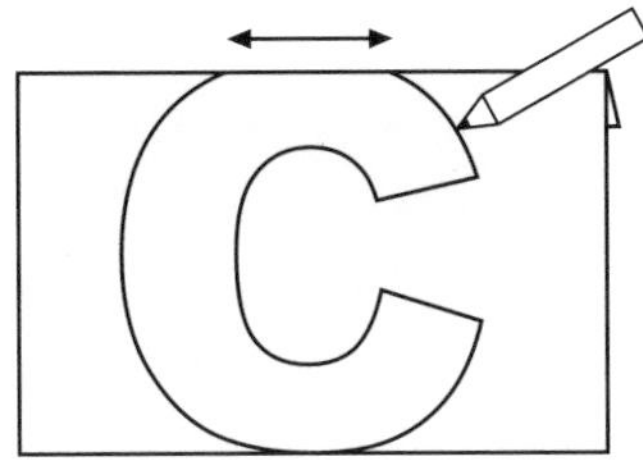

7.2 _ 7
Some letters are curved at the top – the C shown here is an example, also G, O and a few others. In order to make the fold at the top, it is necessary to cut off the top of the letter, as shown, thus creating a folded edge. Be aware of this when designing your letters.

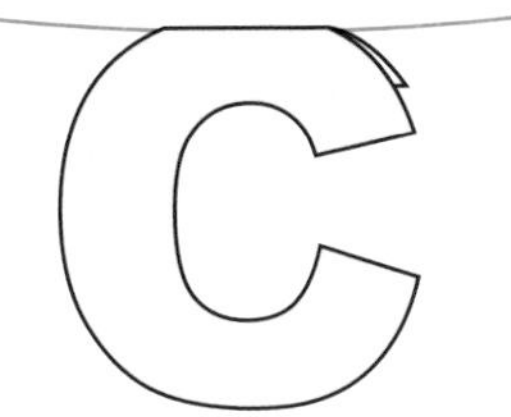

7.2 _ 8
The C is shown here, hanging.

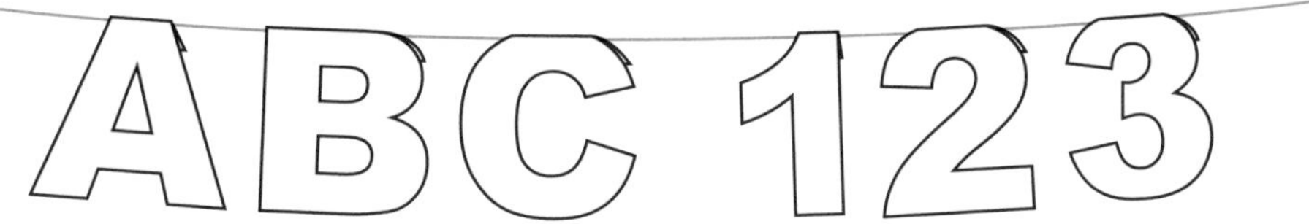

7.2 _ 9
Any letter can be cut, though it is advisable to cut only upper-case letters, as they are all the same height – the ascenders and descenders on lower-case letters can be problematical. Numerals may also be cut. In fact, anything can be cut, including images. For extra effect, add colour to the cut-outs.

7.3 Chain of Cubes

The construction of this chain of cubes is purely geometric, yet despite the rigour of its assembly, the result is fun and very festive, ideal to send for any celebratory occasion or festival. The version shown here has four links (cubes), but the idea can be extended infinitely.

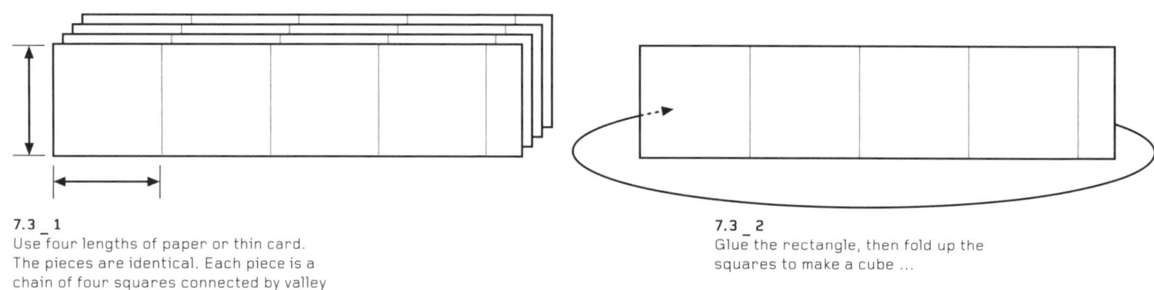

7.3 _ 1
Use four lengths of paper or thin card. The pieces are identical. Each piece is a chain of four squares connected by valley folds, plus a small rectangle at one end.

7.3 _ 2
Glue the rectangle, then fold up the squares to make a cube ...

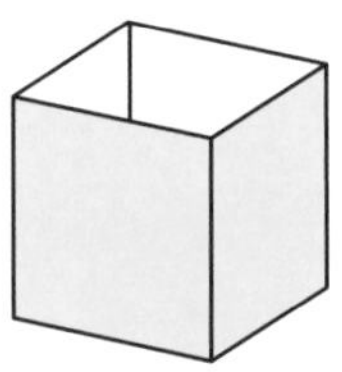

7.3 _ 3
... like this.

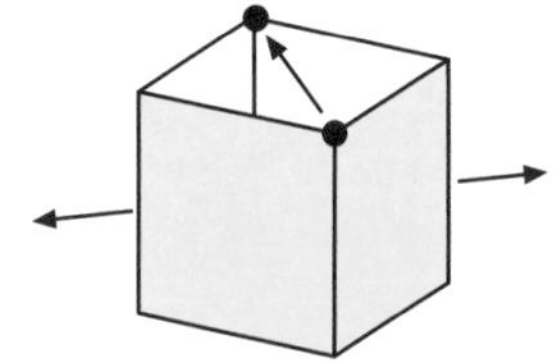

7.3 _ 4
Check that the cube will flatten, dot to dot ...

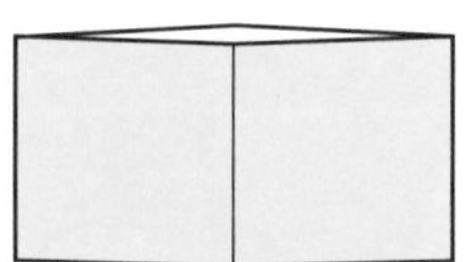

7.3 _ 5
... like this. Open it back to a cube.

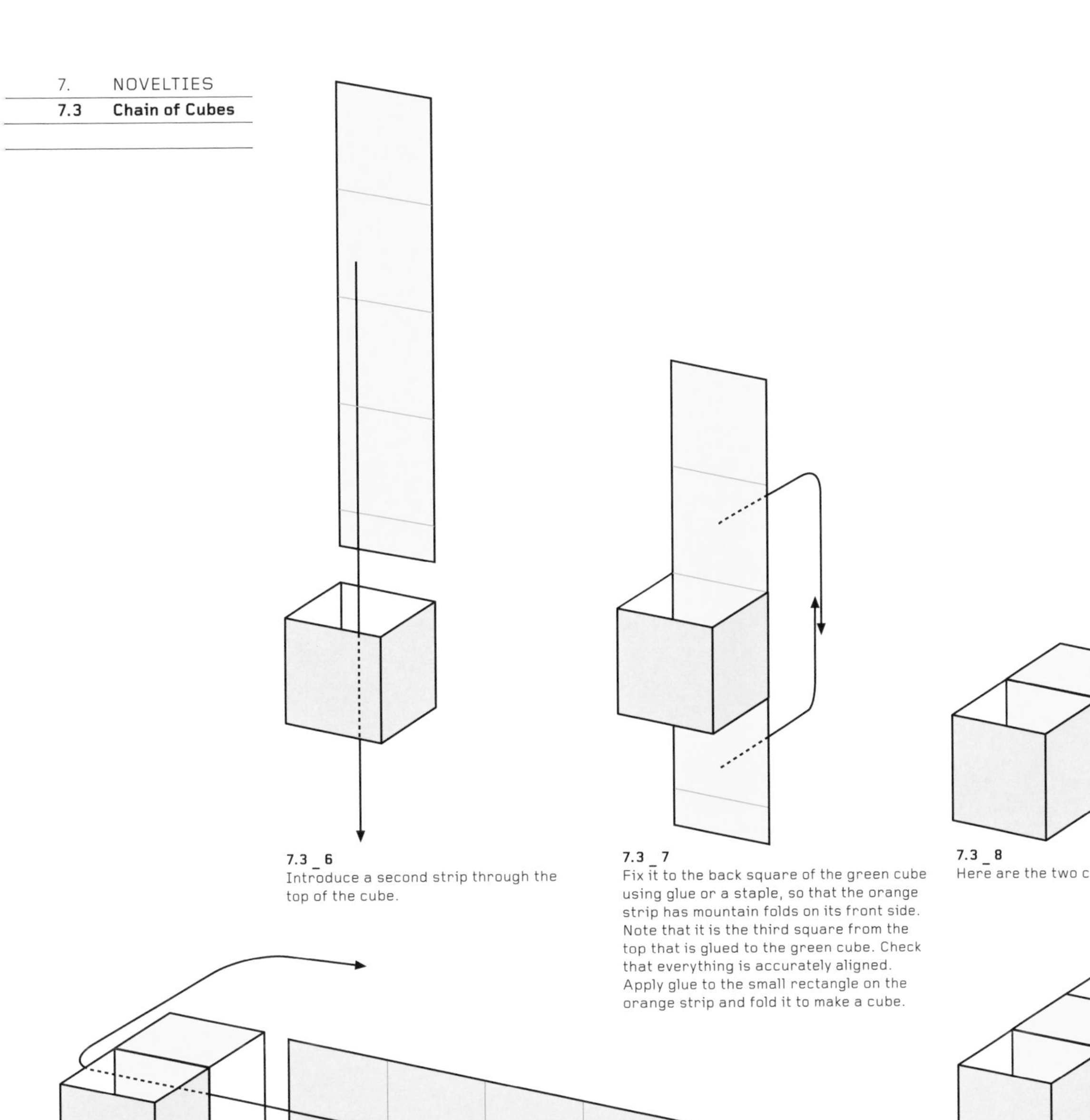

7.3 _ 6
Introduce a second strip through the top of the cube.

7.3 _ 7
Fix it to the back square of the green cube using glue or a staple, so that the orange strip has mountain folds on its front side. Note that it is the third square from the top that is glued to the green cube. Check that everything is accurately aligned. Apply glue to the small rectangle on the orange strip and fold it to make a cube.

7.3 _ 8
Here are the two cubes.

7.3 _ 9
Similarly, introduce another green strip through the side of the orange cube. Fix it in place with glue or a staple. Apply glue to the small rectangle and glue the ends of the strip together to create a third cube ...

7.3 _ 10
... like this.

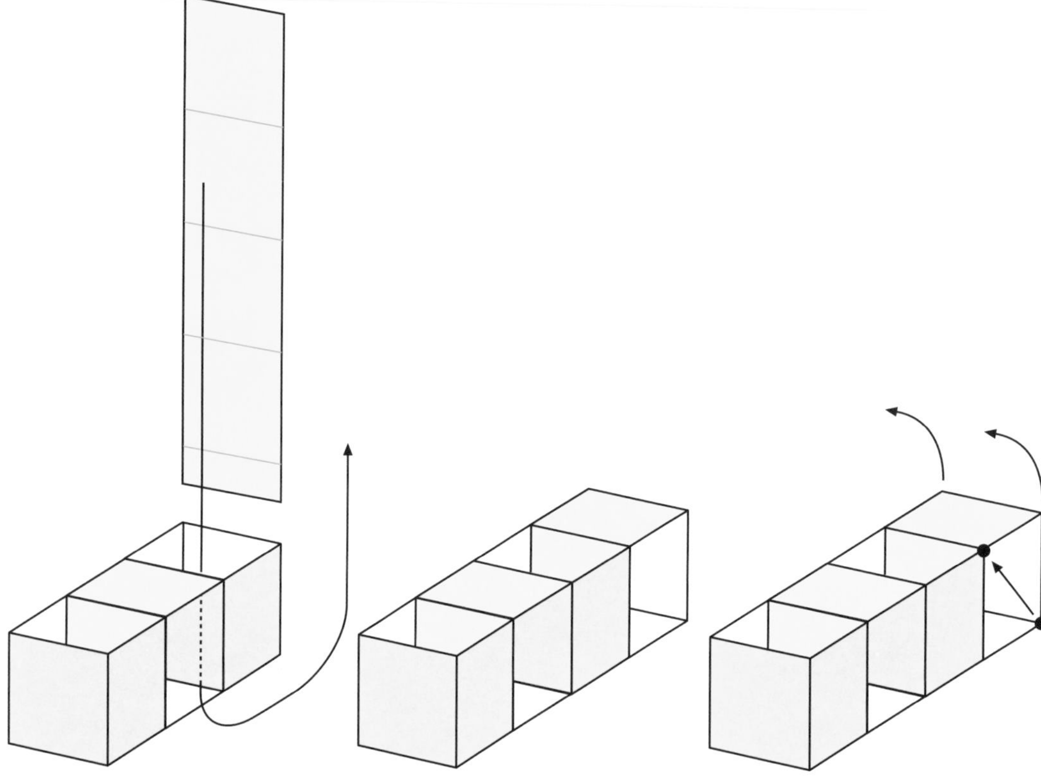

7.3 _ 11
Repeat one more time to create a fourth cube. Remember to keep everything accurately aligned.

7.3 _ 12
This is the chain of cubes, looking very festive. It now needs to be flattened.

7.3 _ 13
Fold dot to dot, so that the orange cube flattens ...

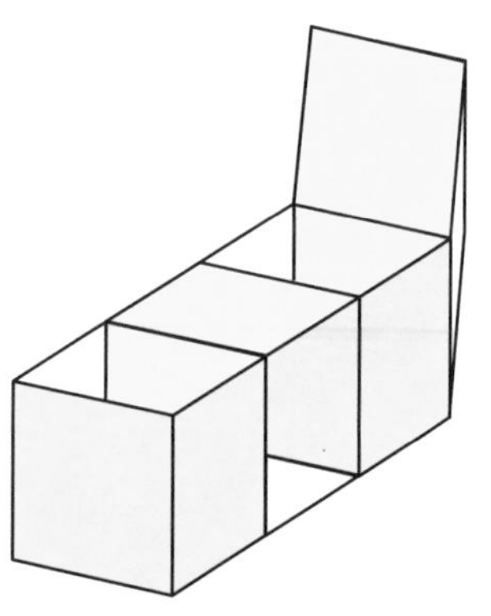

7.3 _ 14
... like this.

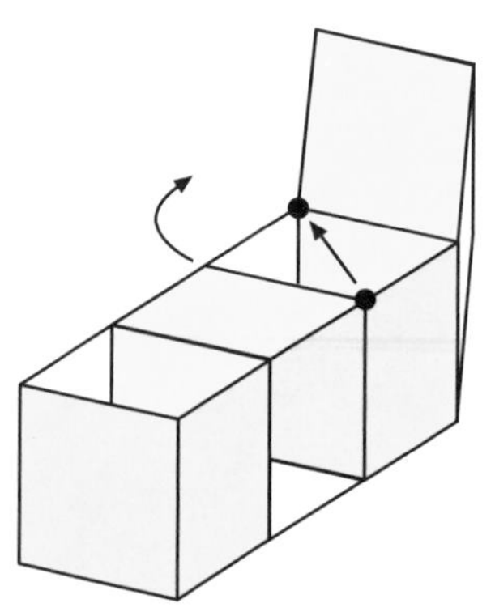

7.3 _ 15
Similarly, flatten the green cube in front of the flattened orange cube ...

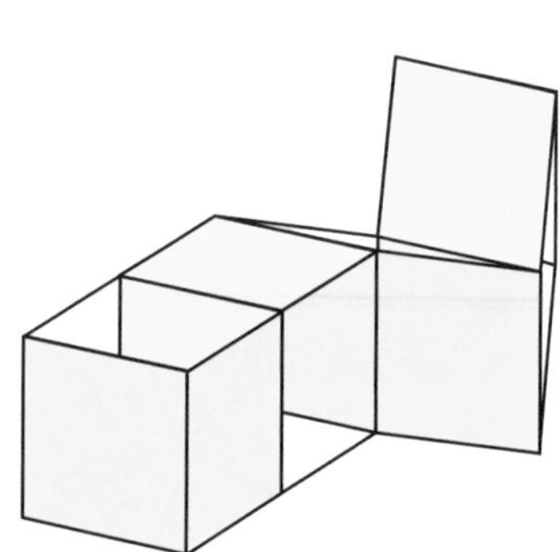

7.3 _ 16
... like this.

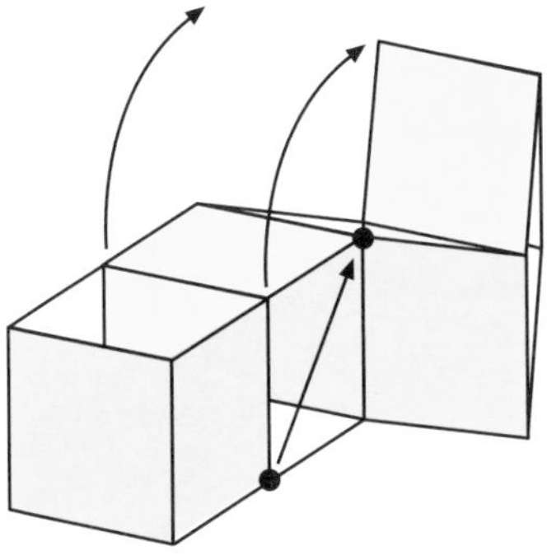

7.3 _ 17
Flatten the orange cube, dot to dot ...

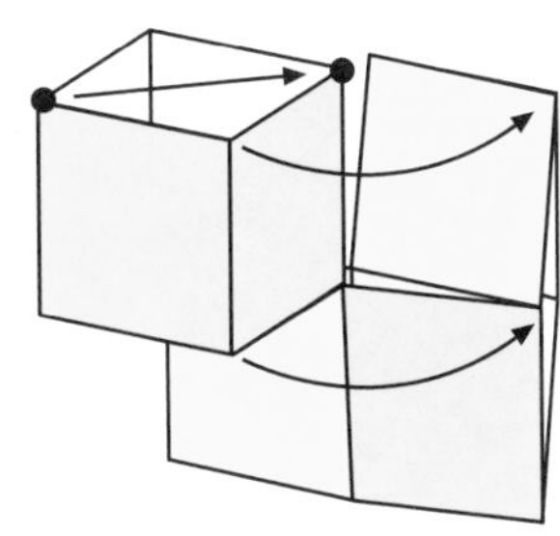

7.3 _ 18
... like this. Finally, flatten the front cube to the right. Steps 13–18 may seem slow, but they can be done in two or three seconds or less.

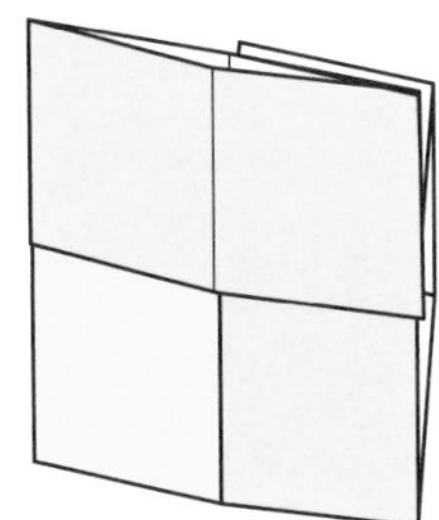

7.3 _ 19
This is the chain of cubes in its flattened state. There are other ways to flatten the cubes, but none are as compact as this square shape.

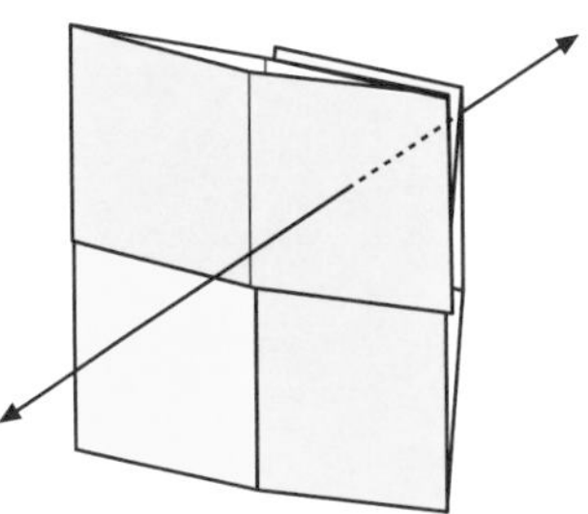

7.3 _ 20
To create the chain instantly, pull apart the front and back cubes! The effect is very dramatic.

7.4 Desktop Trophy

Here's another of those versatile ideas with a hundred uses, both fun and serious. The cube and the triangular base offer many large, uninterrupted surfaces on which to print surface graphics. So … who do you know who deserves an award?! Go on, make their day.

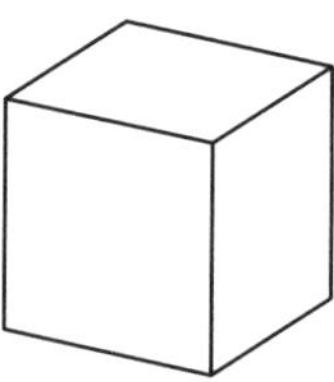

7.4 _ 1
The cube is the Jackson Cube from page 36. However, you could make a cube by another means.

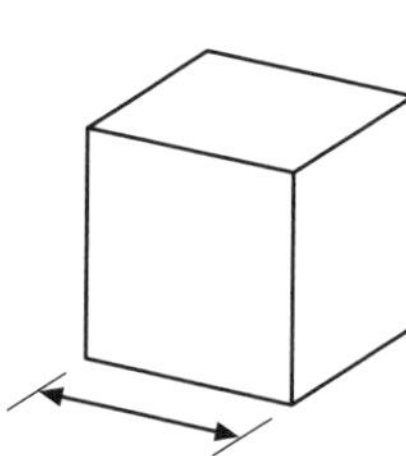

7.4 _ 2
Measure the side length of the cube.

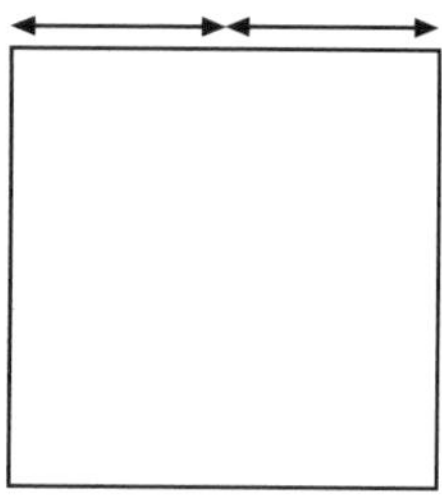

7.4 _ 3
Cut a square from 250gsm card that is twice as long as the side length of the cube.

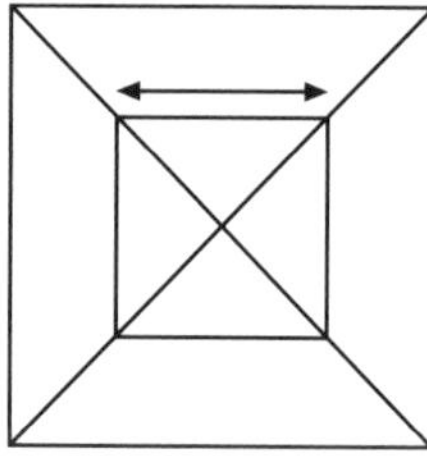

7.4 _ 4
Draw a square in the middle that has the side length of the cube.

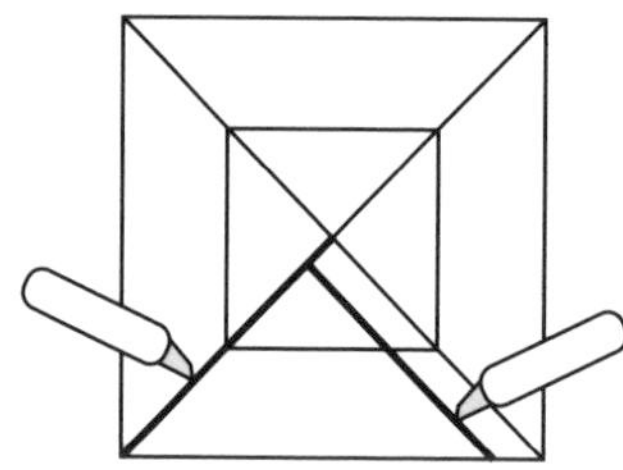

7.4 _ 5
Make two cuts as shown. The cut on the left runs from the corner of the square to the middle; the cut on the right runs a little to the left of the other diagonal …

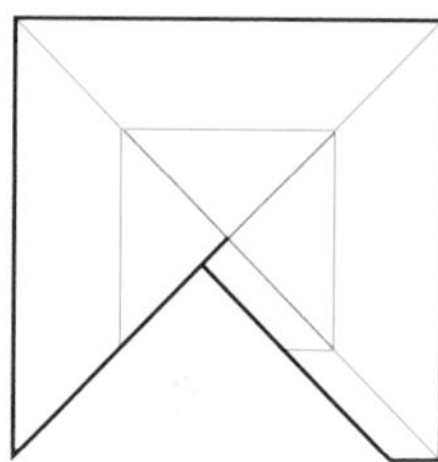

7.4 _ 6
… like this. Create mountain and valley folds, where shown.

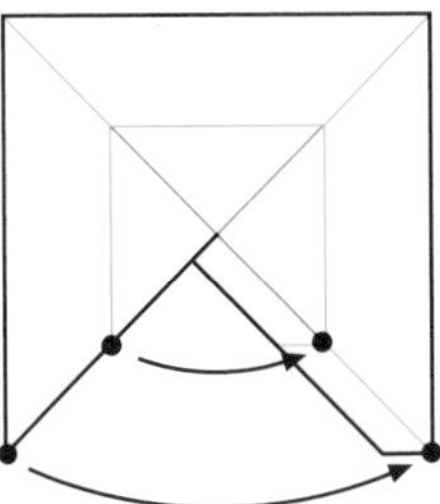

7.4 _ 7
Apply glue to the narrow rectangle, then bring the two pairs of dots together. However, the pyramid that forms needs its apex inverting down into the pyramid ...

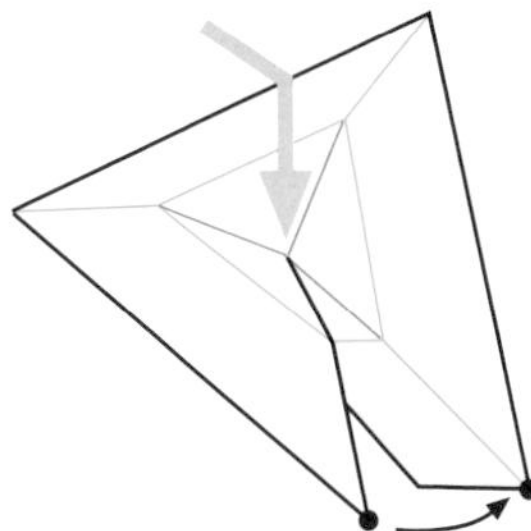

7.4 _ 8
... like this. Close the pyramid, ensuring that the apex is inverted (note the valley folds in the middle).

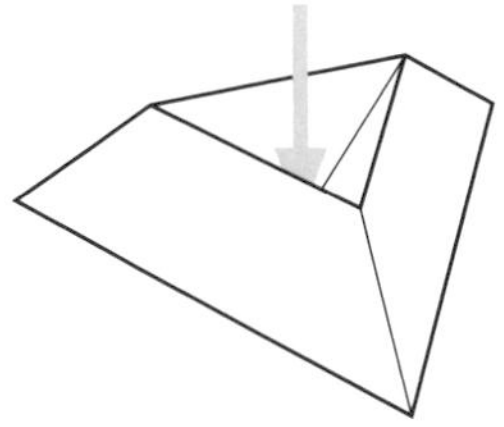

7.4 _ 9
This is the result, a concave corner, ready to receive a convex corner from the cube.

7.4 _ 10
Place the cube into the inverted top of the pyramid. Secure it with glue. If the cube and its base are made from gold or silver card, the trophy will look like it has been made from precious metals!

7.5 Masu Box

The Masu box is a classic origami box from Japan. The version presented here is an engineered variation, whose advantage over the origami box is that it is less bulky (the excess layers are cut away) and can therefore be made from sturdy card, which the origami box cannot be made from. So, this version is stronger than the traditional Masu.

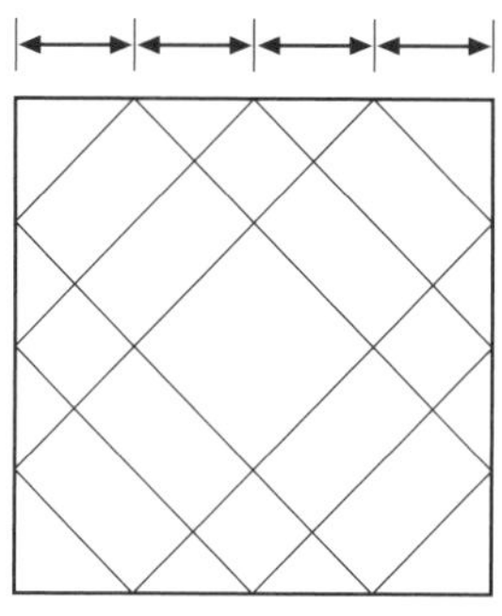

7.5 _ 1
Use 200–250gsm card, about 20–25cm square. Carefully draw the lines as shown, using halves and quarters as guides.

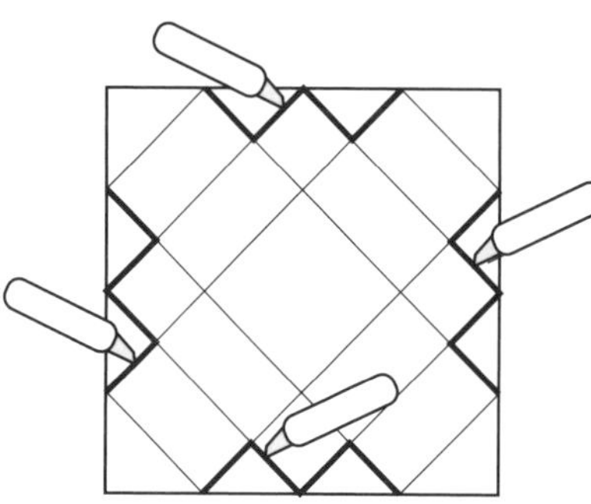

7.5 _ 2
Make four 'M'-(or 'W'-)shaped cuts around the edge of the card, removing eight triangles.

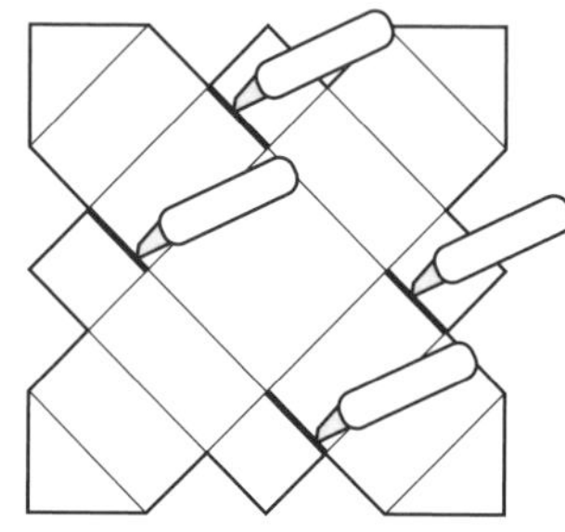

7.5 _ 3
Make four cuts, as shown.

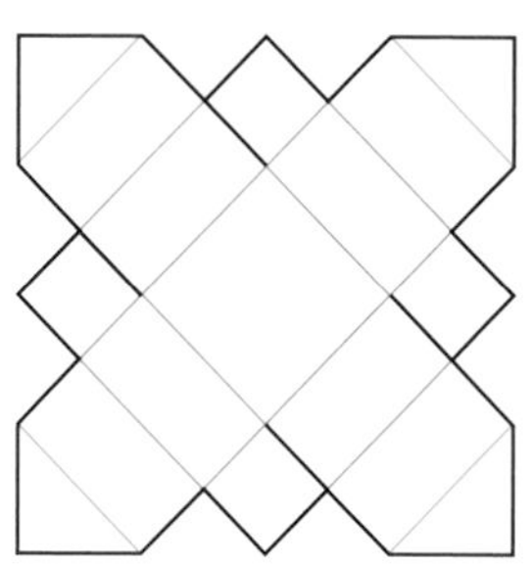

7.5 _ 4
Make mountains and valleys as shown.

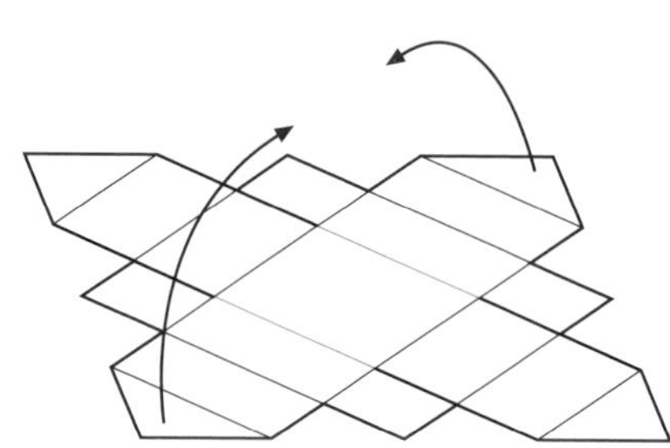

7.5 _ 5
Make two short valley folds as shown, lifting up two opposite corners to the vertical ...

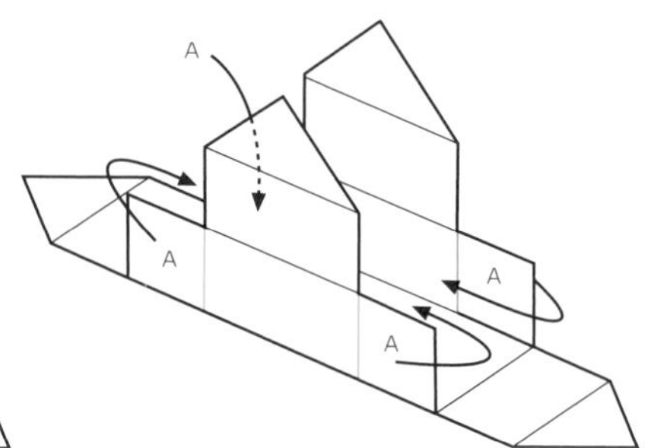

7.5 _ 6
... like this. Fold the four flaps marked A in at 90 degrees (one of the flaps is hidden).

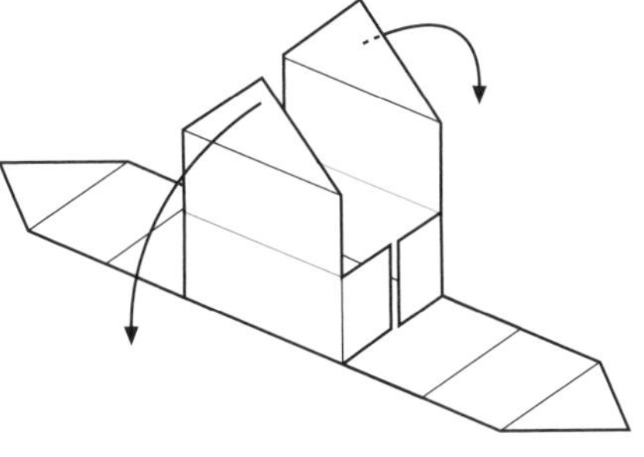

7.5 _ 7
Make a valley and a mountain fold where shown, folding the two 'roof' sections outwards (this has no structural effect, it just makes the next step easier).

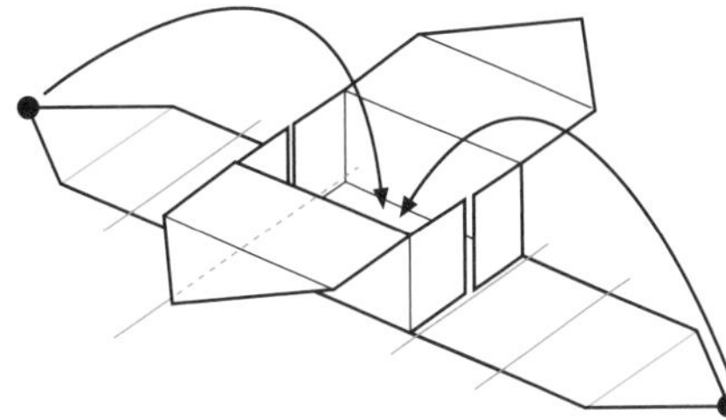

7.5 _ 8
Wrap the two dotted corners up and over the small square flaps made in step 6, then fold them into the middle of the box. The two dots will touch each other on the floor of the box.

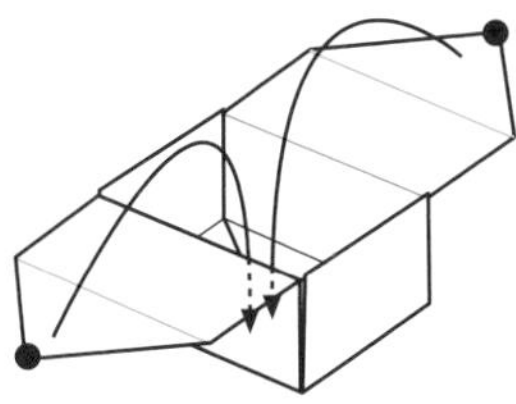

7.5 _ 9
Similarly, fold in the remaining two corners, again allowing the two dots to touch each other in the middle of the floor of the box.

7.5 _ 10
This is the completed Masu box. Note how the four corners meet each other in the middle of the base of the box. By changing the proportions of the drawing in step 1, boxes that are shallower or taller may be made by the same method.

7.6 Tower of Collapsing Cubes

Finally, a real piece of folding magic. The tower of cubes will stand very stably and then twist flat in an instant. Pulling it back into three-dimensions is just as dramatic. The floors and the twisting sides are both based upon the unit for the Jackson Cube (see page 36).

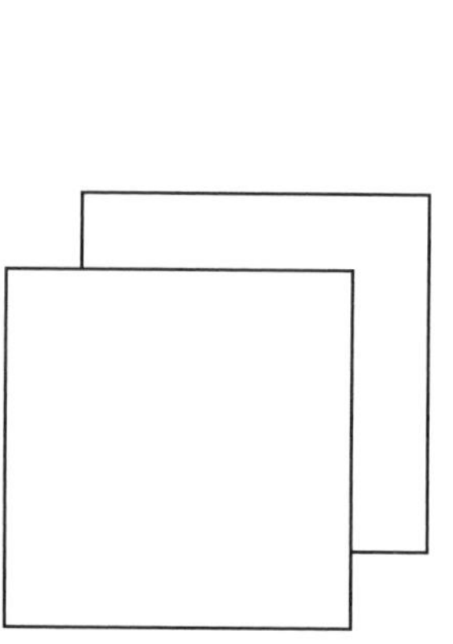

7.6 _ 1
Begin with two squares of 80–100gsm paper, about 20cm square.

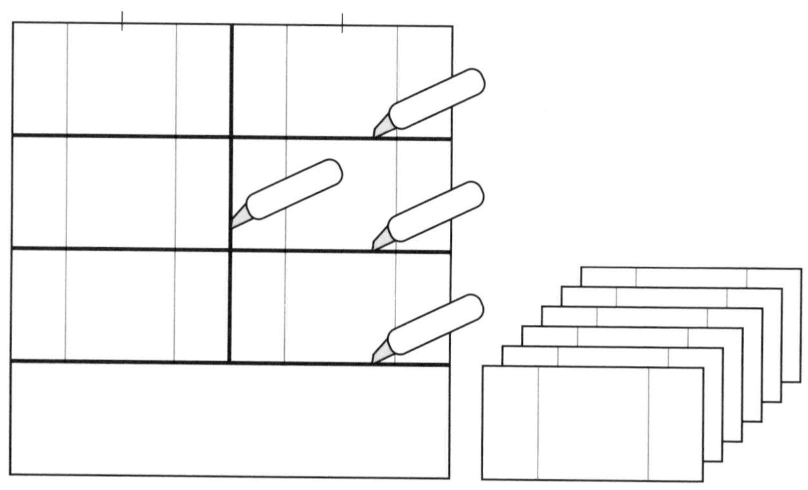

7.6 _ 2
Divide one square into horizontal quarters, discarding the lowest quarter. Cut the remaining three quarters in half, to create six pieces, each 2 x 1. Add valley folds where shown. These units are identical to the Jackson Cube units, but made of paper, not card.

7.6 _ 3
Here are the six completed units.

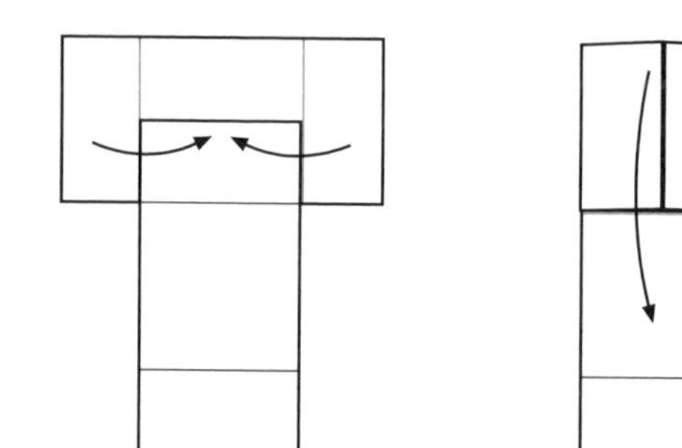

7.5 _ 4
Take two units. Overlap one over the other in the shape of a 'T'.

7.6 _ 5
Fold in the sides over the upper unit.

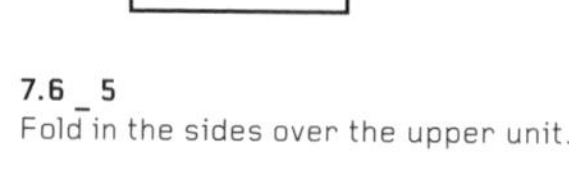

7.6 _ 6
Fold down the top section, as shown.

7.6 _ 7
Tuck the bottom flap into the pocket.

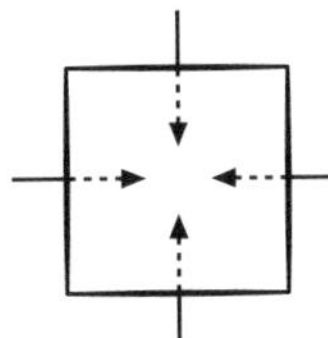

7.6 _ 8
This is a completed 'floor' unit. Note that each side has a pocket. If it is a little puffy, press it flat. Make two more floor units with the remaining four rectangles.

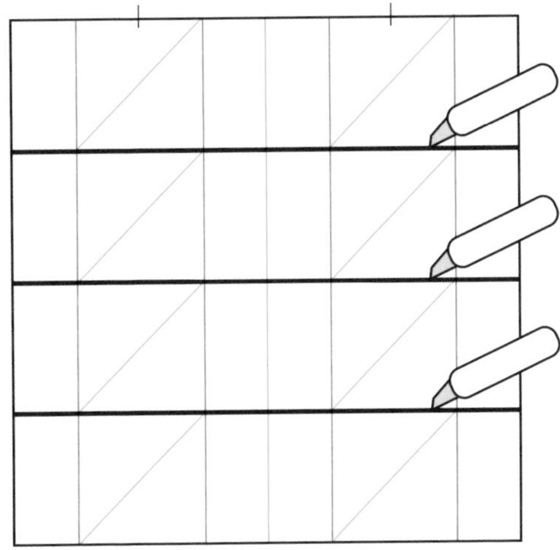

7.6 _ 9
Divide the second square of paper similarly to how the first square of paper was divided. However, this time, add diagonals as shown and cut the paper only into four horizontal strips. Note how the mountains and valleys are placed.

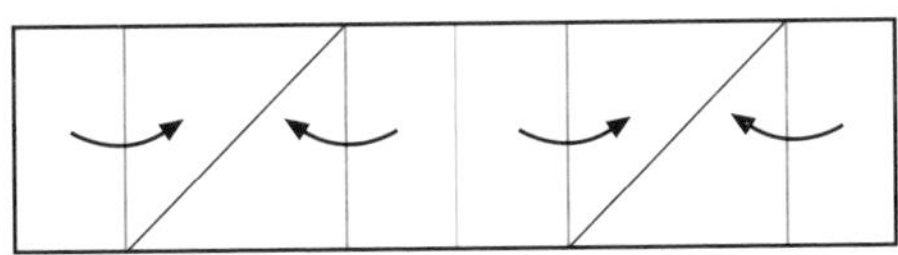

7.6 _ 10
Fold up the five vertical folds ...

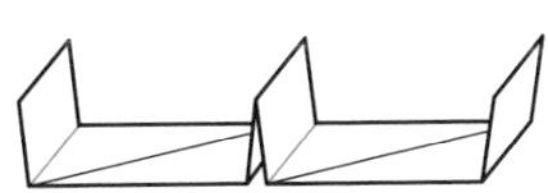

7.6 _ 11
... like this. Repeat with the other three strips.

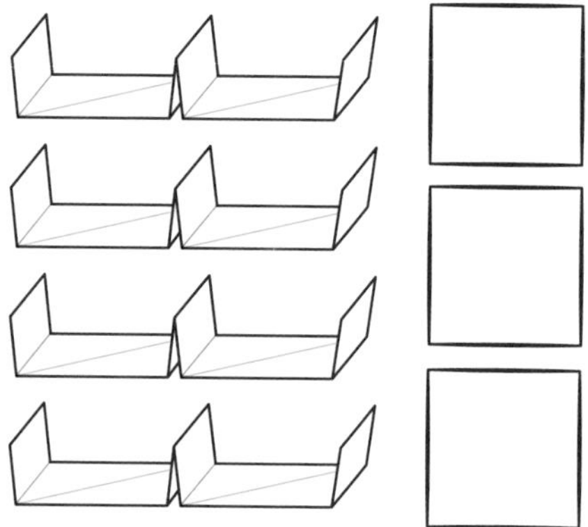

7.6 _ 12
This is the complete set of units: four double-side panels and three square floor units.

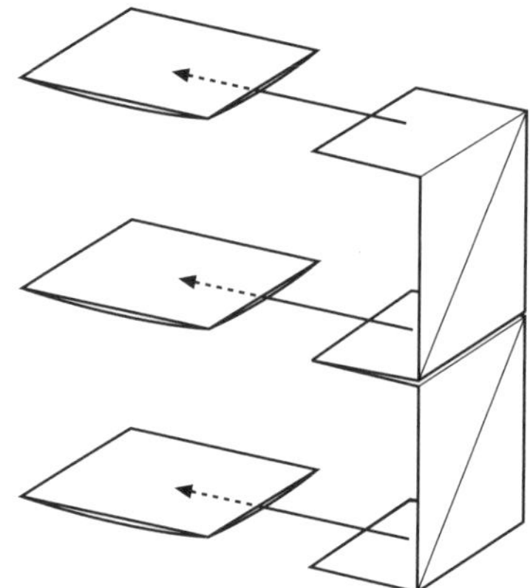

7.6 _ 13
Insert the three horizontal tabs on a vertical panel into pockets in each of the floor units. Make sure that each tab goes completely into the pocket ...

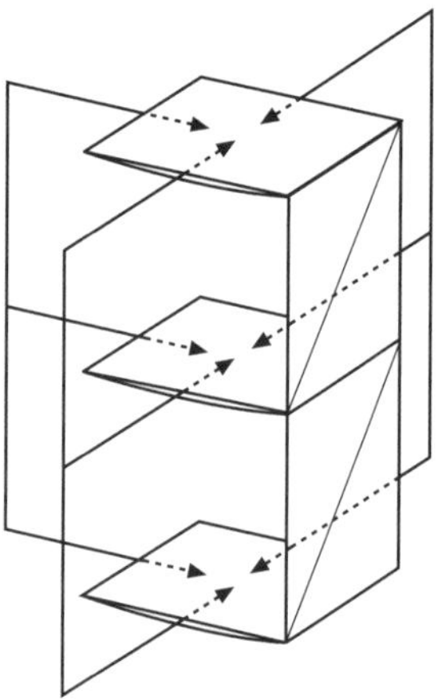

7.6 _ 14
... like this. Now, in a similar way, insert the tabs on the other panels into the three floor units (for clarity, the panels are not drawn. The arrows show the tabs will go into the pockets).

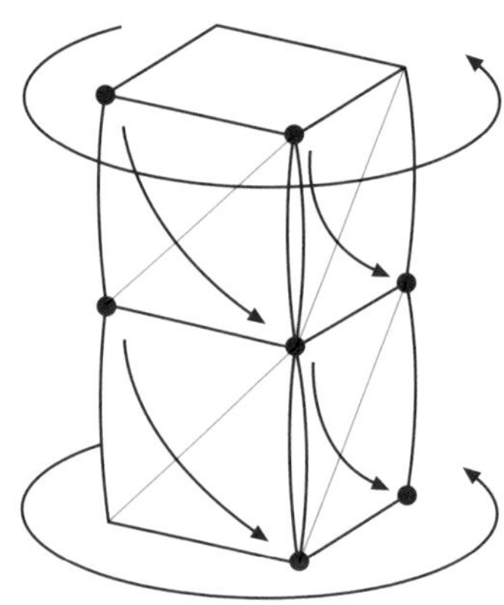

7.6 _ 15
This is the completed structure. Now for the fun! Hold the top and bottom squares in your two hands and twist both cubes anticlockwise, collapsing the four pairs of dots onto each other. The tower will quickly collapse flat ...

7.6 _ 16
... like this. The reverse procedure will quickly erect the cubes again. For a really spectacular effect, more cubes can be added to the tower.

How to Use What You Make

You want to make something from the book. But how do you choose which design best suits your needs?

It can be a difficult decision. To help you narrow the choice, here are a few questions you should ask yourself. Depending on your answers, some of the designs in the book will be more appropriate than others. Try not to automatically choose a personal favourite. For any number of reasons, it may be unsuitable.

So, ask yourself:

Why are you making it?
(as a promotion, as a toy, to educate, to inform ...?)

What information is it conveying?
(about a new product or service, the location of a party ...?)

Who is it for?
(the general public, friends, children, business people...?)

How will you give it?
(send it by mail, give it in person ...?)

How many will you make?
(just one, a dozen, hundreds, thousands ...?)

What is your budget?
(none at all, I'm a billionaire ...?)

What is the tone?
(serious, funny, informative, cryptic...?)

What is your deadline?
(tomorrow, next week, next millennium ...?)

What do you want the recipient to do with it?
(call you, come to your store, display it ...?)

Will there be a follow-up?
(is it a one-off or part of an ongoing campaign?)

How Should I Make my Chosen Design?

The answers you give above will be very specific to the job in hand and the decision of what to make will be personal to you. However, there is one matter on which specific advice can be given here, namely, how to make your chosen design. There are two basic ways to make it – by hand, or by manufacturing it.

By Hand

This is the recommended way if you are making something in relatively low numbers, though production runs of several hundred or even several thousand are possible by hand if you have the time or perhaps a team of willing helpers, happy to do a repetitive task.

But before anything can be cut or folded, the surface graphics (that is, the text, images and illustrations) need to be designed and printed. Here are some suggestions for how to create them:

1. Use graphics or CAD software to create the surface graphics and then print them using a standard computer printer.
2. Create a collage using scissors and glue. Print copies with a black/white or colour copying machine.
3. Screen-print the surface graphics, or make them by some other hand-printing method.
4. Make accurate copies of the cut–fold pattern on a copier machine, to create a template. Then draw the surface graphics by hand onto the copied template.

Once the surface graphics are printed or otherwise created by hand, the design can be cut and folded along existing printed lines. Depending on your method of production, those lines could have been drawn in a computer or drawn by hand.

Alternatively, a template of the cut–fold pattern can be cut from card and drawn around each time a copy is made. If you are creating the surface graphics by hand, it may be better to use the template to cut and fold the design before the graphics are made, rather than afterwards.

To Manufacture

If you want to make a large production run or to have your design look as slick and professional as possible, then it is better – and also more economic – to manufacture it, rather than to make it by hand. The process will generally be in three parts: printing, die-cutting and assembly.

1 Printing. The surface graphics are printed, usually by the offset process.

2. Die-cutting. The printed surface is cut to shape and the folds stamped in.

3. Assembly. The flat die-cut design is folded up (and perhaps also glued) to create the finished design.

The technology of die-cutting is relatively low-tech and very well understood by the companies who offer such a service. If you are unfamiliar with the process, it is recommended that you discuss your project in some detail with them. They will be pleased to offer advice about paper or card weights, printing and assembly.

The most important part of preparing your design to be die-cut is to be totally confident that the registration between the printing and the die-cutting is accurate, so that when the printed surface is die-cut, no mistakes are made. For this, you may need the assistance of a professional graphic designer to prepare the files in the correct manner. Sometimes, an offset printing company will have close links with a die-cutter and together they will offer a complete service of design, preparation, printing, die-cutting and assembly, though of course, the more work they do and the less work you do yourself, the more it will cost.

For relatively simple or small-scale die-cutting projects, the cost per unit may be considered relatively inexpensive and cheaper even than preparing hundreds or thousands of examples by hand. The results can look very impressive – well printed, accurately cut and folded and precisely assembled. If you die-cut once, you will surely soon return to do it again.

Provenance

With the increasingly frequent exchange of ideas and information made possible by the internet, it is becoming very difficult to establish with absolute certainty the provenance (that is: the origin and ownership) of every one of thousands of cut-and-fold paper constructions, including those in this book.

I have been careful to include in the book only those constructions that I believe beyond reasonable doubt to be in the public domain, or that to the best of my knowledge are my original creation, or that have been adapted by me from sources that I have credited where known. If you know with certainty any provenances different to those given opposite, I will correct mistakes in future editions.

Here is a list of my sources.

Tri-hexaflexagon
A classic design, documented in many basic texts about flexagons. It was created by a graduate student of mathematics, Arthur H Stone, at Princeton University, in 1939.

Square Flexagon
Uncertain provenance. Shown to the author in the 1970s at a meeting of origami enthusiasts.

Windmill Base Manipulations
A classic traditional Japanese origami 'action model'. The gluing flat of the faces is – to the author's knowledge – his own idea.

Shapeshifter
Uncertain provenance. First seen by the author as a giveaway in a packet of potato crisps in the late 1980s, minus any ©, ® or patent number. It was published in his 1998 book for children, *Paper Tricks* (Michael O'Mara Books).

Pivoting Cubes
The design is developed from an idea of flat, pivoting squares, published by the origami master Kunihiko Kasahara. His 2-D idea was later developed as a 3-D array of pivoting cubes made from a continuous strip of ticker-tape by the originator of 'Knotology', Heinz Ströbl. This version is a further development by the author.

Flexicube
A marketing gimmick of uncertain provenance, known in the 1960s, but probably created well before.

Six-piece Cube
A creation of the author's from the early 1980s. It is so simple that he feels sure someone, somewhere must have designed it before him, but he has yet to find an earlier reference.

Three-piece Cubes
Developed by the author from the six-piece cube.

Two-piece Cubes
As above.

Jigsaw Cubes
As above.

Tetrahedron
This is a system sometimes taught in schools to construct polyhedra, probably of nineteenth-century origin.

A4 Pyramids
These designs are adaptations by the author from origami structures developed by various origami creators. They use the natural (and beautiful) $1{:}\sqrt{2}$ proportions of A-sized papers.

A4 Random Envelope
Traditional origami, based on the Japanese 'Tato' wraps.

A4 Angled Envelope
As above, but a modern variant of uncertain provenance.

A4 Wrap
Nominated by the author as a separate design, after learning the Japanese envelope (below).

Japanese Envelope
This is a design of uncertain provenance, but Japanese in origin.

French Envelope
A traditional design from France.

Square CD Envelope
Designed by the author for the book.

Engineered Envelope
Designed by the author in 2005, as a commission.

Impossible Illusion
A traditional 'bar room' trick.

Negative/Positive Cube Illusion
Developed by the author from a traditional illusion. The origami artist Jeremy Schafer has a very different origami version of the same illusion.

Tangrams
Traditional.

Inside-out Cube Puzzle
Recreated by the author (correctly or otherwise) from a sequence of thumbnail photographs seen in a Japanese graphic design magazine, published in the early 1970s.

Left-to-right Transformation Illusion
A traditional illusion, introduced to the author by the origami master, Eric Kenneway.

Chain-to-square Puzzle
A design of uncertain provenance. It is from the author's collection, manufactured in the Far East and minus any ©, ® or patent numbers.

Eight-page Booklet
A traditional Japanese method of making a booklet.

Back-and-forth Book
A design of uncertain provenance known to book binders.

Origami Booklet
A redesign by the author of a two-piece origami book by an unknown designer.

Expanding Booklet
Seen by the author in a bookshop in the 1980s, as a wall-mounted novelty counting book/poster for young children. Unknown provenance.

Spinning Spiral
Traditional.

Hanging Letters
Seen by the author in a 1960s children's craft book, published in the USA.

Chain of Cubes
Sent to the author in the mid-1980s by students of graphic design as an invitation to their end-of-year show.

Desktop Trophy
Adapted by the author from two known designs.

Masu Box
A traditional engineered version of a traditional Japanese origami design.

Tower of Collapsing Cubes
A reworking by the author of a collapsible cube of his design, originally made with the same two-fold module that creates his six-piece cube. Origami artists including Heinz Ströbl, Kunihiko Kasahara and Larry Hart have created different versions of the same twisting mechanism to create square-sectioned towers that similarly instantly collapse and erect.

Acknowledgements

My interest in cut-and-fold paper constructions was aroused by a wonderful book given to me as a teenager – Joseph S Madachy's *Mathematics on Vacation* – which I still possess. It contains excellent chapters on flexagons and dissection puzzles. Without that book, this book could not have been imagined and I thank Mr Madachy for his inspiration.

Several decades in the recurring company of people interested in origami has introduced me to many excellent paper puzzles, tricks and curiosities. I must thank Eric Kenneway, Mick Guy, John S Smith, Ray Bolt, Robert E Neale and Seiryo Takekawa among many others, for sharing their work and enthusiasm. My thanks also to Tim Rowett, John Sharp, Gary Woodley, Max Eastley and others, for revealing to me the riches to be found in the odd, the overlooked and the apparently trivial, in paper as in many other things in life. Through them, I hope I learnt to separate the intelligent from the clever and the Big Idea from the Big Show.